Mediation, Conciliation, and Emotions

Revised Edition

Mediation, Conciliation, and Emotions:

The Role of Emotional Climate in Understanding Violence and Mental Illness

Revised Edition

By Peter D. Ladd and Kyle E. Blanchfield

LEXINGTON BOOKS
Lanham • Boulder • New York • London

Published by Lexington Books
An imprint of The Rowman & Littlefield Publishing Group, Inc.
4501 Forbes Boulevard, Suite 200, Lanham, Maryland 20706
www.rowman.com

Unit A, Whitacre Mews, 26-34 Stannary Street, London SE11 4AB

British Library Cataloguing in Publication Information Available

Library of Congress Cataloging-in-Publication Data

Names: Ladd, Peter D., author. | Blanchfield, Kyle E., author.
Title: Mediation, conciliation, and emotions : the role of emotional climate
    in understanding violence and mental illness / by Peter D. Ladd and Kyle E.
    Blanchfield.
Description: Revised Edition. | Lanham : Lexington Books, 2016. | Revised
    edition of Mediation, conciliation, and emotions, 2005. | Includes
    bibliographical references and index.
Identifiers: LCCN 2016007530 (print) | LCCN 2016013802 (ebook) | ISBN
    9781498532754 (cloth : alk. paper) | ISBN 9781498532761 (Electronic)
Subjects: LCSH: Mediation--United States--Psychological aspects. | Conflict
    management--United States--Psychological aspects | Dispute resolution
    (Law)--United States--Psychological aspects. | Emotions. | MESH:
    Negotiating. | Dissent and Disputes. | Emotions.
Classification: LCC HM1126 .L33 2016 (print) | LCC HM1126 (ebook) | DDC
    303.6/9--dc23
LC record available at http://lccn.loc.gov/2016007530

♾™ The paper used in this publication meets the minimum requirements of American
National Standard for Information Sciences—Permanence of Paper for Printed Library
Materials, ANSI/NISO Z39.48-1992.

Printed in the United States of America

Dedicated to peace lovers everywhere

Contents

Part III: Emotions and Mediation

Figures and Text Boxes

Figures

Text Boxes

Preface

Emotions have received mixed reviews through the ages, especially in comparison with rational thinking and cognitive decision making. In the seventeenth century, the philosopher, René Descartes made the mind/body thesis favoring rational thought over bodily emotions in his famous decree, "I think therefore I am." For many years after, emotions became the unstable relative of natural science and logical reasoning. In the field of rational decision making, emotions were viewed as distractions or in more serious cases, obstacles—emotional imperfections to structured rules of nature.

At the turn of the twentieth century, emotions shifted again, and were more deeply scrutinized through the classic figure of Sigmund Freud. Freud hypothesized that emotions were profoundly embedded in the unconscious "Id." He questioned Descartes's conscious split between emotions and logic, by placing them in the inner workings of the unconscious mind. Emotions became a part of the underlying forces that affect our decisions, and help to pre-determine our lives. Now emotions could occasionally interfere with the conscious decisions found in one's "Ego." According to Freud the "Id" was the self-centered, irrational part of us where basic needs were met. In this light, emotions became irrational and threatened to disrupt our higher levels of rational thinking and decision making.

As the twentieth century hit its midpoint, psychologists such as B. F. Skinner, changed the focus away from rational thought to observable behavior. This again gave emotions a secondary role in the decisions we make, and in the disputes we resolve. Skinner believed that feelings interfere with a proper understanding of human behavior. For example, conflict resolution originates from a learned response, and feelings become a part of one's learned behavior. This rather singular thinking made emotions a byproduct of measurable behavior whether in regard to problem solving or conflict resolution.

In the same era as Skinner, humanistic psychology began recognizing emotions as crucial when dealing with personal decision making, and with decisions regarding others. The psychologist Carl Rogers openly discussed emotions as a key ingredient in people recovering from numerous forms of psychological pain. By creating a therapeutic climate based on positive regard, empathy and authenticity, people could make better decisions in their lives. With Rogers, positive emotions took on a new significance. They were elevated to the same level as rational thinking and measurable behavior. The three schools of psychology, Freud, Skinner, and Rogers, had delivered their conclusions on the importance or unimportance of emotions in human decision making and problem solving. The field of psychology now had choices regarding emotions that continued through the twentieth century, by influencing such areas as, research and clinical practice.

In the twenty-first century, emotions are now a priority of neuroscientists who are exploring the pivotal role of emotional and social intelligences in decision-making, negotiation and conflict resolution. Through neuroscientific research emotions have joined thoughts, and behavior in directly shaping how we and others handle conflicts, and the ultimate outcome of these conflicts. Research in this area shows that emotions, thoughts and behavior cannot be neatly separated from each other. They occur in concert within the neuropathways of our brains and affect our ability to solve problems. However, neuroscience is not only making connections between emotions, thoughts and behavior taking place within our brains. It also is showing how emotions respond to our environment, where one or more people can be influenced by an overriding emotion affecting an entire group such as, anger being the overriding emotion of a mob. In many ways, human experience and our brains are tied by an indissoluble bond, where emotions found in disputes are directly influenced by the neuropathways of our brains reacting directly to human experience.

The topic of emotions found in present day conflict resolution has evolved from a long history where emotions were, separated from thought by Descartes, to becoming the irrational complication of the unconscious mind by Freud. Skinner reduced emotions to a secondary role through learned behavior, while Rogers elevated them as the basis for creating a healthy therapeutic climate in psychotherapy. The twenty-first century shows neuroscience embracing emotions both within the brain but also through the influence of human experience.

We start the revised edition of *Mediation, Conciliation, and Emotions* at a point in research where emotions found in conflicts are not only understood by advances in neuroscience, but also through an understanding of human experience. We believe that neurological research is limited to the laboratory setting without some form of phenomenological thinking. Neuroscience has stirred up a renewed interest in phenomenology or the study of human experience. Specifically, human experience causes neurological changes, and neurological changes are better understood through the study of human experience. The revised edition accepts the contributions of neuroscience regarding emotions, but focuses more on human experience—specifically research into the emotions and emotional climate found in conflict situations. We explore emotions by using case studies to point out how emotions and the emotional climate of a conflict can alter its outcome.

In our work as mediators and conciliators (peacemakers) over the past twenty-five years, we have discovered the power and influence held within each person's emotions, but also in the emotional climate of a conflict. In mediation, success in isolating issues and negotiating agreements may only come after the emotions of people in dispute, along with the emotional climate in the mediation have been stabilized by the mediator. In conciliation (peacemaking), beyond each person's emotions, it may be the emotional climate that needs to change through the skills of a conciliator before any mediation, negotiation, or any other form of conflict resolution can take place.

Through books and articles, the fields of mediation and conciliation have considered emotions research and are beginning to recognize their role in any given conflict. However, since the original edition of *Mediation, Conciliation, and Emotions* the world of human experience has made some dramatic changes, both from a personal perspective, but also from a cultural one. We have learned that long standing emotional climates, over time, can become a part of different cultures. Therefore, we also would like to add a cultural perspective concerning emotions in conflict resolution, where human experience may be affected just as much by culture as by neuroscience.

Also, we want to continue our perspective on emotions by aligning the concept of emotional climates in conflicts into two categories. The first category deals with those emotional climates that may lead to violence. The emotions of anger, resentment, revenge, jealousy and hatred all have the potential for violence, and we give examples of how these emotional climates can be the breeding grounds for violence in our schools, workplaces, communities, and in our society. The other emotional climates found in the revised edition focus on their connection to mental illness. Beyond any personal emotions, there are emotional climates that can generate dysfunctional behavior in people who interact within them. We have included anxiety, fear, resentment, apathy, greed, guilt and egotism into this category, and show how they can contribute to certain mental health disorders.

The revised edition presents these emotional climates through story telling. The emotional climate of any conflict is an invisible phenomenon that cannot be completely understood through the use of natural scientific methods. However, when presented through stories they reveal themselves, and can be appreciated for their impact on any given conflict. We take a phenomenological research approach to capture each story's human experience. Again, though such an approach is not a statistical, natural scientific approach, it demonstrates and maps out an invisible phenomenon in a more holistic and understandable manner. Emotions affect the climate of any conflict, and reveal themselves when viewed more holistically in human experience.

Taking all of these matters into consideration, we believe the climate is right for another look at emotions in conflict resolution through a revised edition of this book. Understanding mediation and conciliation may be considered a small part of the wisdom needed to face our emotions, but for practitioners of conflict resolution, emotions are unavoidable. They are at the center of every conflict.

Acknowledgments

We want to acknowledge all those people who shared their actual stories of emotional conflict over the years, and allowed us to use them as everyday examples throughout the book. We have changed the names, and places found in the stories in order to protect the privacy of those who have generously helped us. Real-life stories add validity to the importance of human experience in more humanistic research.

We would like to thank those who generously participated in the formation of the book, especially Yasmeen Razi Zaidi who took responsibility for making sure we included a cultural perspective in the book, and contributed to the research found in the cultural sections in each chapter. Yasmeen was instrumental in giving the book a greater world view. Her roots from the country of Pakistan can also be viewed as a contribution to the holistic perspective we tried to emphasize throughout the book's formation. Also, acknowledgment goes out to Elizabeth (Dawn) Taylor who helped in the editing of the final manuscript. It becomes hard to see the picture when inside the frame. Dawn gave clear eyes to the final project.

Acknowledgment goes out to our friends on the Akwesasne Mohawk Reservation who understand a more holistic and spiritual side of resolving conflict, and who influenced the experiential story telling approach taken in the book. We believe that story telling creates a world of rich possibilities that cannot be found using only factual research. Our many years working with Native people has guided us to a different view of how to approach conflict resolution research.

We want to thank the graduate students from the Graduate Mental Health Counseling Program and the Graduate Educational Leadership Program, at St. Lawrence University, who over the years asked that conflict resolution be described in recognizable terms—taking our knowledge far beyond the established academic literature.

Acknowledgment, also, goes out to our mentors. First, to Victor Frankl who deeply influenced my (Peter) thinking and who made my graduate studies forty years ago still relevant and meaningful. Also, to Carl Rogers who we both had the privilege to meet and got to know by contributing to his book, *Freedom to Learn for the Eighties.* These wise professionals understood true scholarship from a human perspective, and showed the humility found in true wisdom. We thank them for their guidance, and hopefully have continued their belief in humanity through our writings.

Front Cover Image

We would like to thank the artist Huong who graciously allowed us to use her painting, *Youth, War, and Peace* as the image found on the front cover of this book. It has been said that great art comes from great sorrow. Huong endured enough sorrows for a lifetime as an artist, a former journalist, a mother, a Vietnamese boat refugee, and at last a fervent Peace Activist. At the age of twenty-

five, she fled Vietnam at the end of the war and escaped to America with courage and spirit to launch an art career that has since caught the imagination of art
audiences and critics alike. Self-taught, dedication, and determination encouraged Huong to work nonstop for the past forty years with more than 200 solo
exhibits throughout America and Canada. During the last decade the artist has
been working on two monumental projects called "The War Pieces" and "The
Peace Mural" which is dedicated to all the war victims and sends out a message
of Peace to the World. Over nearly four decades, she has addressed human
rights, justice, war, and ultimately, peace.

November 30, 2015

Peter D. Ladd
Kyle. E. Blanchfield
St. Lawrence University

Introduction

"The emotional climate of a conflict is easier to change than the people in it"

Behavior and Feelings

What are the characteristics of a conflict? Answering this question requires an understanding of two related phenomena that interact when people are in dispute with each other. When people experience a conflict, a disruption takes place that is behaviorally and emotionally different from what people were experiencing before the conflict began, and will change again when the conflict has finally ended (Bennet, 2012; Shapiro, 2002; Gulliver, 1979). If you ask people what they experienced during a conflict, most likely they will describe the dramatic series of events that took place, and how these events affected them. They will describe specific behavior and feelings, and these two elements are at the heart of understanding any given conflict.

Usually people describe their behavior, and many conflicts are resolved by discussing the issues associated with this behavior. Sometimes we solve our conflicts independently and other times outsiders such as judges, lawyers, parents or teachers help us work through the issues connected to our conflicts. But, as human beings, invariably more than issues affect us. Beyond the issues or the behavior, we are vulnerable to the feelings associated with conflicts—especially those generating high emotion (Hubbard et al., 2013; Aberill, 1980). For example, a small, non-dramatic disagreement between two friends over who is the best tennis player suddenly goes too far and becomes a highly emotional event, keeping them apart for weeks. What outwardly appeared to be harmless behavior, inwardly was filled with hurt and embarrassment.

Feelings are the ingredients frequently overlooked when settling conflicts. Inward emotions may be intrinsically connected to peoples' outward behavior, and solving one may require a resolution of the other. Adding to this phenomenon is the difficulty many of us experience during attempts at conflict resolution

1

when behavior and feelings are woven tightly together, such as found in divorce proceedings, where solving only half the problem seems unsatisfactory.

Fifty years ago this was not as prevalent. We were in the middle of an Industrial Age, where recognized professionals solved conflicts by separating issues based on behavior from the personal feelings experienced by conflicting parties (Raines, 2013; Goldberg, Green & Sander, 1989). Many conflicts that focused on behavior were resolved by professionals making judgments such as judges or administrators who came from many fields of endeavor. While psychiatrists, psychologists and counselors usually dealt with people's feelings. In many respects, these professionals continue to practice their separate roles into twenty-first century. However, our contemporary Information Age has changed our society, and has made significant changes in the way people perceive everyday conflicts. Through the internet and other media devices we have become increasingly aware of new alternatives in the conflict resolution process. The experience of outward behavior and inward feelings have discovered effective styles of conflict resolution, where both issues and emotions found in problems are not being separated by professionals. In our contemporary world, people in conflict want to share important issues and are looking for ways to share their feelings. Having a better understanding of the connection between behavior and feelings, and their impact on the conflict resolution process, can make our experience with conflicts more meaningful.

Issues and Emotions in Conflict Resolution

Are there differences in everyday conflicts, and if conflicts are different, are there different methods for resolving them? It is accurate to assume that conflicts are different and different conflicts require different methods of conflict resolution (Ladd, 2007; Ladd, 1989). Assuming one method of conflict resolution will be successful in all cases can be a misleading unchecked assumption. For example, if two teenage boys are suspended from school for fighting over a female friend, it should come as no surprise that the problem may continue beyond the use of suspension to resolve the conflict. Suspension may solve the issue portion of the problem by focusing on violations of school policy for fighting, but emotions of anger, jealousy and revenge may remain buried in the feelings of both boys—causing the school lingering future problems. Countless problems go unresolved because the methods used do not match the true nature of the conflicts in question. Understanding different types of conflict resolution helps in deciding the most accurate methods for resolving different types of conflicts. Resolving conflicts can be divided into *three general categories* according to how most of us experience them in everyday living.

Issue-Oriented Conflict Resolution

Judges, arbitrators, bosses, principals and others in a position of authority are familiar with issue-oriented conflicts. They have the difficult task of upholding a previously established set of laws, guidelines or rules. Their training requires an expertise where judgments are made about others in conflict, and their understanding of relevant issues surrounding these conflicts is regarded as a mandatory prerequisite for a successful resolution. They are the fact finders who determine the degree that others are in violation of the rules, and ultimately conflicts are resolved through their final judgments. They are trained to focus on issues, especially issues where rules are broken. They must remain objective or others will perceive them as unfair (Menkel-Meadow, 2009; Simkin, 1971). Emotions enter into their conflict resolution but are not a priority. Issues are connected to rules, not personal beliefs or peoples' feelings. They are our parents, our teachers, and local town officials who guard the social fabric of our communities and mend it when violated. People in these positions have feelings like the rest of us, but put them aside while upholding the laws or rules connected to their positions of responsibility. They are from all walks of life and they function at many levels of society. What they have in common is their commitment to resolving conflicts, where order is disrupted and rules are broken. Their decisions are effective when rules are upheld, and guidelines remain intact, and people continue everyday living in a structured and orderly environment (figure I.1).

Blending Issues and Emotions in Conflict Resolution

The second general category of conflict resolution found in everyday experience is not about issues or emotions, but a mixture of the two. Mediators, facilitators, negotiators and other similar professionals are society's neutral third parties who bring people together to resolve opposing points of view. These are the referees, in the conflict resolution world, and as referees they do not pass judgment on issues, nor do they have the task of upholding previously established rules. Their task is in bringing opposing parties together to talk to each other (Cheng, 2015; Brown, 1982; Folberg, 1982). This is accomplished by allowing issues and emotions to flow freely while someone facilitates a fair and balanced discussion. At times, issues may be the center of the discussion, as found in a conflict over services rendered by a contractor on repairs to a house. Other times, emotions may dominate the discussion, as in the example of two roommates in conflict over strained relations after a wild party in their apartment. And, sometimes conflict resolution focuses on both, as in two brothers having to divide the estate of their late parents, where their emotional attachment to artifacts is as crucial as a fair and equitable distribution of their possessions.

In this category of conflict resolution, the word equality remains a major concern. People in conflict need equal opportunity to discuss their perception of the conflict. They need equal input into arriving at options that are mutually agreeable, and they need a balanced agreement that reflects their position regarding each persons' point of view. Final agreements are usually some blend of discussed issues and/or strongly held emotions. Blending issues and emotions in conflict resolution can be highly democratic. The process views both issues and emotions with equal importance. Words such as dialogue, discussion and interaction are synonymous with this approach. It relies on people talking to each other about their issues and their feelings and continues to gain popularity in our Information Age (figure I.2).

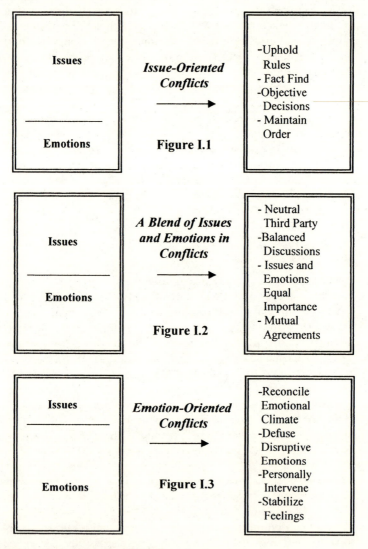

Emotion-Oriented Conflict Resolution

The ubiquitous nature of emotion-oriented conflicts makes all of us potential practitioners in conflict resolution. Professionally, conciliators, peacemakers, counselors, psychologists, psychiatrists, social workers, ministers and other helping professionals are society's designees charged with defusing conflicts that emotionally cause trauma in everyday living. Their concern is with emotional climate surrounding one individual or possibly an entire group, where specific issues are a marginal concern compared to the emotional climate surrounding these conflicts. For example, a disruptive mob may be engulfed in a climate of anger, that requires someone to manage the potentially violent nature of many angry people in crisis, or a couple may require someone to resolve an ongoing climate of jealousy, plaguing the couple with constant claims of indiscretion. Issues may arise and enter into the resolution of these conflicts, but changing the toxic emotional climate, may be the first step to reconciliation. Accomplishing this may require everyone's involvement at some emotional level.

Parents, teachers, employers and others who are responsible for peoples' emotional stability, seek interventions that normalize the emotional climate and look for alternatives, where emotions are less disruptive in everyday living. Some of us spend a significant portion of our day trying to reconcile the emotions of our children, students or employees. When this happens, we are practicing emotion-oriented conflict resolution (figure I.3).

Mediation and Conciliation

Our discussion has identified two characteristics of a conflict and the intrinsic connection between behavior and feelings. This was followed by organizing conflicts into three methods of conflict resolution focusing on issues, emotions and a combination of both. Understanding emotions in conflict resolution is the focal point for this book, so the task of deciding who best represents emotions in conflict resolution is simplified by leaving issue-oriented conflicts to others who have written copious information on the methods of; judges, lawyers, administrators and other issue-oriented professionals.

The next decision was, "Who represents those individuals involved in conflict resolution where issues and emotions blend together and are given equal importance?" The mediation movement over the past thirty-five years toward communication-based dispute resolution has made mediators increasingly popular, especially in conflicts where opposing viewpoints are given equal value (van Epps, 2013; MacFarlane, 1999). Mediators are aware of issues and emotions. They appear in mediated agreements, where both are needed for people to successfully talk to each other. We will look at skills mediators use in effectively balancing issues and emotions during emotionally charged mediations. The final decision was, "Who represents those individuals involved in conflict resolution, where emotions are the main focus. This task becomes more difficult when looking for professionals who leave issues behind and primarily resolve emotion-oriented conflicts. Much is written about emotions and from many points of view (Halperin, 2014; Schultz, 1987; Block, 1957). A sophisticated body of knowledge exists in the disciplines of counseling and psychology that explores the emotions of people in conflict, both inwardly and with others (Kutinsky, 2004; Kitayama & Marcus, 1993). Many religions have emotions at the center of discussions on spirituality, and many religious leaders give their followers directions on successful emotional and spiritual health (Hirschkind, 2010; Whitehead & Whitehead, 1994). Parents, teachers, coaches, and others involved with emotion-oriented conflicts can find books relating to anger management, coping with anxiety in the classroom and other theme-centered books offering emotional skills.

Our exploration approaches the emotions found in conflicts from a different viewpoint. We will work from the hypothesis that, "Understanding the *emotional climate* surrounding a conflict is one of the more effective methods in emotion-oriented conflict resolution" (Reyes et al, 2012; Rogers, 1956). With this hypothesis in mind, we will try to answer the following questions; "What are the emotional environments, or as we define them, 'emotional climates' created when people experience different conflicts?" and "How can these emotional climates change, so people continue their lives in a less disruptive manner?"

In answering these questions, professional conciliators or peacemakers have gained recognition in contemporary society as people who are capable of mending the emotional relationships of those in dispute. Even though conciliators or peacemakers increasingly have gained professional roles in our society, they also can be our neighbors, our relatives and our friends. We will look at conciliators who mend the relationships of people in emotionally charged conflicts by focusing on the emotional climate found in these conflicts.

Comparing Mediation and Arbitration

Mediation and arbitration are frequently confused, especially with non-professionals seeking out appropriate avenues for conflict resolution. This happens for a number of reasons. First of all, both mediation and arbitration are held in less formal settings than a court of law. They both give people in conflict an opportunity to present their side of a problem, and both are guided by a third party who directs a process set up to resolve the conflict. However, this is where the similarity ends:

- Arbitrators hear both sides of a conflict in order to make a judgment. Mediators help disputing parties hear both sides of a conflict, so they can make their own judgments.
- Arbitrators listen for issues that relate to predetermined rules. Mediators listen for issues and emotions that clarify the peoples' points of view.
- Arbitrators are responsible for the resolution of the conflict. In mediation those in conflict are responsible for the conflict's resolution.
- Arbitrators make decisions based on facts and their relationship to rules. Mediators empower people to share their issues and feelings, and make their own decisions.
- Final judgments are made by the arbitrator. Final agreements in mediation are made by the people in dispute.

In arbitration, emotions are kept to a minimum during conflict resolution. This makes sense if the final outcome is determined by pre-determined rules. People's behavior is judged based on these established rules—not people's feelings toward each other. During mediation it becomes impossible to avoid the impact of feelings on disputing parties. Actually, it may be feelings that are in conflict. For example, two friends may reach a final agreement in mediation, that resentment of each other has destroyed their relationship, and steps need to be taken for rebuilding their friendship. However, it is important to note that emotions of a disputant, in mediation relate only to the conflict, and not to their deep inner feelings as found in psychotherapy or counseling. This is also true of conciliation, which we will see in the next section.

Comparing Conciliation, Psychotherapy and Counseling

In this section, counseling and psychotherapy are used generically to represent all those practitioners who provide a service to people who have some form of ongoing emotional dysfunctional pattern in their lives, as established in many helping profession fields, with recognized experts and well known theories. On the other hand, conciliation is used in this section as a profession that is based more on intervention into actual conflicts but, at times, has been identified as informal mediation (Lande, 1987). Presently, the general consensus is that conciliators are those practitioners responsible for rebuilding relationships between people who are in conflict (Curtis, 1998; Terry, 1987). Keeping this in mind, there are times when psychotherapy, counseling and conciliating may seem quite similar, such as found in crisis counseling or in some forms of couple's therapy. Yet, differences do exist between conciliators, psychotherapists and counselors. Counselors and psychotherapists are more concerned with the inner emotions of individuals, where conciliators focus more on the negative emotional climate between individuals. (Note: *We prefer the term peacemaker over conciliator; however, the term conciliator is more professionally recognized in the field of conflict resolution. In this book, we state the terms conciliator and peacemaker as representing the same thing. This also applies to the terms dispute and conflict as being the same thing.*) The following compares those areas where conciliators, and counselors provide a different service to the general public:

- Counselors and psychotherapists focus on the specific emotions of their clients. Conciliators focus on the emotional climate found in a conflict.
- Counseling and psychotherapy is "a-situational." It focuses on dysfunctional patterns, no matter what the situation. Conciliation is "situational." It focuses on the conflict found in a specific situation that is in conflict.
- Counselors and psychotherapists are responsible for the wellbeing of clients. Conciliators are responsible for overcoming emotional differences and rebuilding emotional relationships within the climate of the conflict.

- Counselors and psychotherapists are successful when specific clients make positive changes. Conciliators are successful when the emotional climate of a conflict makes a positive change.
- Counselors and psychotherapists look for chronic dysfunctional patterns that disrupts their clients' lives. Conciliators look for specific conflicts that disrupt the lives of people in conflict with each other.

Looking at the differences between conciliators, psychotherapists and counselors brings out two points. First, counselors and psychotherapist may have considerable experience as peacemakers. Take, for example, public school counselors. In some circumstances, they may see students on a daily basis for counseling and do very little conciliation. However, there are those public school counselors who do not have the time to counsel, and spend part of the day reconciling emotionally charged conflicts. Secondly, there are many professionals who conciliate and are not employed as counselors or psychotherapists. This list includes; lawyers, law enforcement officers, administrators, correctional officers, social workers, principals, community activists, teachers, friends, spiritual leaders, drug and alcohol sponsors, employees, employers, coaches, parents and others. Practitioners in all of these roles may eventually face people in conflict, where rebuilding personal relationships and restoring the emotional climate is a concern. Finally, there are practitioners who make their living as professional conciliators. Schools, families, business and industry, communities, governments, and nations have hired conciliators to change the emotional climate found in their conflicts, and to begin rebuilding relationships among disputing parties.

The Connection between Mediation and Conciliation

Mediation and conciliation are two forms of conflict resolution that share an ongoing history. The first formally structured mediation service in the United States was in 1913, called the "Commissioners of Conciliation Panel," which mediated disputes between labor and management. In 1947 the panel became the Federal Mediation and Conciliation Service under the Labor and Relations Act of 1947. More recently mediation and conciliation have been used in alternative dispute resolution programs, commonly referred to as ADR, and along with arbitration, are the conflict resolution skills of choice—for many Multi-Door Dispute Resolution Programs found in our communities and legal systems (Nowell & Salem, 2004: Christian, 1981).

In the same vein, mediation and conciliation share a similar connection in actual practice. For example, there are times when a conflict becomes so emotional that the suggestion of mediating any form of agreement between disputing parties seems an unreasonable and untimely suggestion. In cases such as these, a conciliator may be needed to defuse the volatile emotional climate before mediation can take place. Our present world gives us examples of this happening at different levels of society. At the international level, conciliators may be used to defuse the emotional climate of two disputing countries, with the goal of getting their diplomats to the mediation table for bi-lateral negotiations. On a smaller scale, a conciliator may be asked to reconcile the different factions of a feuding family with the goal of calming down relatives and eventually having the entire nuclear family mediate their conflict. These examples demonstrate the connection between mediation and conciliation, with conciliation being used before mediation can take place.

However, the opposite also happens when practicing conflict resolution. Sometimes successful mediations are followed by a series of conciliations, when the mediated agreement partially or totally breaks down. When this happens, mediators are the initial practitioners in establishing a resolution to a conflict, and conciliators are given the responsibility of conflict maintenance. This connection makes sense for ongoing agreements to succeed. Take for example a successful mediation in the workplace. Employees agree to specific working conditions, only to have them break down at a future date because of some unforeseen conflict surrounding the mediated agreement. Under these circumstances, a conciliator may reconcile the conflict and restore the emotional climate of the workplace.

The third connection between mediation and conciliation may happen in an actual mediation session. Mediations that have disputants with a long standing emotional history, may have moments where emotions become overwhelming and require some form of emotional reconciliation. Such mediations, may call for a combination of mediation and conciliation skills, in order to complete the mediation session. In effect, the mediator considers two distinctly different goals namely; a conciliation goal of changing the unproductive emotional climate in the mediation session, and a mediation goal of successfully reaching an agreement between disputing parties.

Finally, it may be important to point out that mediation and conciliation do not have to be connected when resolving a conflict. Mediators conduct mediation sessions where issues and emotions flow freely and agreements are obtained without the use of conciliation and conversely; conciliators constantly reconcile conflicts in everyday living that do not require a formal conflict resolution process. Many times, reconciliation of these conflicts has little connection to mediators, arbitrators or negotiators. However, in our contemporary society, emotional conflict can happen to anyone, and disputes can arise without warning, and regardless of how they are connected or used, mediation and conciliation have value for those interested in resolving their conflicts.

The Emotional Climate Found in a Conflict

Before moving on to the chapters on conciliation and mediation, it may be important to clearly describe how the emotional climate can affect the outcome of mediated and conciliated conflicts. This is especially true in peacemaking where emotions run high and changing the emotional climate is one of the ultimate goals of any effective peacemaker. Here are some ideas to consider when trying to understand the emotional climate of a conflict.

An emotional climate is *not* the emotions that each person feels when involved in a conflict, but the emotion that surrounds people in the environment where the conflict is taking place. The emotional climate is the "ether" enveloping any given conflict (Ryan, 2006). This overriding emotion can dramatically affect how people feel, leading to how they resolve problems with each other.

For example, resentment may fill the climate surrounding employees and management when they try to resolve conflicts in a workplace environment, regardless of their personal feelings. The climate of resentment may be the driving force that inhibits employees and management from coming together in solving their problems. Parenthetically, a climate of compassion may have an opposite outcome by contributing to an environment of acceptance among the same employees solving the same problems. By a conciliator changing a climate of resentment to compassion, employees and management may find conflict resolution a distinct possibility.

This happens in both mediation and conciliation. In mediation, a shift in the emotional climate may change reluctant disputants into people who are ready to solve problems through some form of negotiation. Without the emotional climate having a positive change, mediations can deteriorate into intractable, polarized positions, where disputants are talking *at* each other, not *to* each other. In peacemaking (conciliation), the emotional climate becomes the actual problem needing resolution. Conciliators sometimes need to change the emotional environment of a conflict before any mediation, negotiation or other forms of conflict resolution can take place. How many mediations and negotiations have broken down because the conflict resolution professional could not reverse a toxic emotional climate?

Another point to emphasize has to do with the personal emotions of those in dispute. There may be many emotions found in the emotional climates of conflicts taking place between people. However, there is usually a central emotional theme that is recognizable to trained mediators and conciliators experiencing these conflicts. For example, an emotional climate of jealousy may generate anger or anxiety in others. However, it is the climate of jealousy that dominates those in dispute, and it is jealousy that requires reconciliation.

Finally, people solving conflicts tend to focus on the dramatic behavior found in problems, while letting the traumatic emotional climate remain in the background. Since emotional climates cannot be seen by people in conflict, it may require someone trained in conflict resolution to address them. They are the "elephant in the room" during any given conflict. They can have a serious impact on the outcome of conflicts, especially when emotions need equal consideration. For example, the emotional climate found in a mob may be as important for a conciliator, as the reasons behind the behavior of the mob. It does not matter to a conciliator the justifications for mob violence, or why the mob came together in the first place. That may be the role of judges or government officials looking for answers to mob behavior—the violence in 2014 in Ferguson, Missouri, being one example.

The peacemaker's job is to extinguish the climate of anger that controls the mob. By understanding how different emotional climates work, we can use different skills to change these climates. For example, there may be different skills when changing an emotional climate based on anger then one based on guilt. Different emotional climates require different skills. Much of the book focuses on learning about these emotional climates and the skills that will help mediators and conciliators resolve emotionally charged conflicts.

The Difference between Emotional Climate and Culture

At first glance, it may appear that emotional climates could easily be confused with culture, yet there are differences. An emotional climate can be felt when you enter any given situation. Some situations are filled with joy which can be immediately recognizable, while others are filled, for example, with resentment where frustration and feeling stuck is also subtly recognizable. In other words, the group's attitude surrounds us as it affects our state of mind. Some emotional climates are briefly experienced, like a family fight where emotions are intense but slowly wear off. Others can last for a long time, such as a workplace emotional climate that remains resentful no matter what day it is, or when brief moments of happiness break up the frustration. On a more positive note, emotional climates are less difficult to change, than any given culture. However, in some intractable emotional climates, conflict resolution professionals may need to help in the conflict resolution process.

Culture is a more ingrained phenomenon. Some cultures take years to evolve. For example, the culture of the United States is still evolving based on different changes and conflicts affecting both values and beliefs. This may be why the Declaration of Independence and the Constitution are important to Americans. They help people remember one's values and beliefs while giving us guidelines for a common identity. However, what happens when a toxic emotional climate lasts for many generations. It could be argued that an emotional climate of revenge has assimilated into the culture of Palestinian and Israeli cultures and could be seen as a cultural way of life. For the most part, emotional climate is based on actual experiences while culture is based on longstanding unspoken and spoken rules.

Emotional Climates Can Promote Violence and Mental Illness

In the revised edition of this book, we have added the possibility that people who are immersed in toxic emotional climates can be personally affected by such an environment. In contemporary society, speculation continues whether increases in violence are caused by those who suffer from mental health problems. When we hear of "lone wolves" who gun down innocent people, one issue that continues to be raised is the state of their mental health. Violence and mental health have received much notoriety in today's violent world. However, one part that has gotten little notoriety are those emotional climates that, we believe, promote violence and mental health problems. Sometimes the environment we live in is bigger than ourselves.

For example, if you are extremely happy, and you go to your family's break-fast table, where family members are filled with anger and resentment. How long do you think it will take before your happiness is modified, and feelings of anger and resentment slowly enter your thinking? People, places and things found in our environment can plant the seeds of violent behavior, along with promoting mental illness. They can also promote a life style leading to emotion-ally charged conflicts. In the following chapters, we address the possibility that toxic emotional climates are partially responsible for recent violence in our soci-ety, and these toxic climates also may be *as responsible* for peoples' mental health problems as genetics, severe trauma, and other problems from the past.

Over the years, we have observed these toxic emotional climates and have come to the realization that trying to change the emotions of people is more dif-ficult, than changing the climates these people are experiencing. However, it is easier to view the emotions of people in conflict than to view an emotional cli-mate affecting these people—unless you look for it, the emotional climate in a conflict remains invisible. Many mistakes in conflict resolution are made when trying to change the personal emotions of people, rather than, changing the emo-tional climate surrounding these people. For better or worse, the emotional cli-mate in a conflict is the common ground that holds the conflict together. Even when people hate each other, it is the climate of hatred where people can reject, alienate and inflict violence on each other. Without the climate of hatred these people cannot justify their feelings and behavior to themselves or to the outside world. That may be why terrorist are so determined to get moderate people to join the climate of hatred and violence. An emotional climate of hatred becomes legitimate when others behave in similar destructive ways.

Our present climate of violence against each other through terrorism, politi-cally defaming opposing candidates, cyber-bullying, and the polarizing of peo-ple with differing points of view, are threats to societies where democracy is viewed as a value and a belief. Beyond any one person's emotions and behavior are those emotional climates made available to others who now can justify simi-lar behavior. Thus, allowing an emotional climate to establish itself within our human experience—take for example, the emotional climate created in the 2016 political campaign for the President of the United States.

Hopefully, the revised edition of this book will establish an understanding of emotional climate in the conflict resolution process, and more specifically in the fields of dispute resolution and mental health. We believe those people trained as conciliators and mediators need an understanding of emotional climate. Fur-thermore, those in the mental health professions of; mental health counseling, psychology, psychiatry, social work, and many others, need to expand their per-spectives when looking at mental illness beyond a medical model. It may be the emotional climate has a direct effect on numerous mental health disorders.

Part I:
Emotional Climates that Promote Violence

Chapter 1

Anger and Conciliation

Anger is an emotion that remains a part of our DNA, and has protected us through our long history as human beings. It is connected to a series of neuropathways in our brain, eventually leading to our crisis center called the amygdala. When we experience danger, or feel overwhelmed or are simply having a bad day, anger may kick in saying to us that the present state of affairs has become unreasonable. This sets the amygdala into action by preparing us to either fight or flight our current situation. This is most prevalent when in conflict with others. We reach a critical mass of being reasonable where the threshold of logical interaction is unsustainable. We let loose adrenalin preparing us for some type of explosion, sometimes through words, sometimes through behavior, and sometimes both. Anger is our safety valve when reason and logic cease to help us, and defending ourselves becomes a higher priority than solving a problem.

The irony in conflict resolution is that anger might be viewed as a taboo, as bad, as undesirable, and as a dangerous outlet. However, in conflict resolution for those who understand the emotional component of the process, anger is not necessarily any of those things. It is when anger turns to violence then the above negative attributes become an issue. The violent side of anger seems to define it as a rule but in the fields of mediation and conciliation there is a place for it. When a conflict becomes highly emotional and dangerous conditions arise, skilled conflict resolution professionals may want to consider the "safety valve" of anger to benefit a successful resolution.

In conflict resolution, perceiving anger as a safety valve may change how we approach it. For example, when anger erupts an inexperienced person might attempt to shut it down by yelling "calm down" or "control yourselves," but these commands are unreasonable in this environment. Clearly the situation requires another approach. What about when a situation turns violent and forceful intervention seems the only option? When we think about it, using such expressions do not make sense. Being reasonable has reached that critical mass and angry people are getting ready to either fight or flight. Not exactly the most opportune time to express logical, reasonable commands. How about when an angry conflict has become violent and the use of force seems inevitable? To respond with force is adding fuel to the fire.

In the rest of this chapter, we will describe how anger can be effectively expressed in conflicts, along with ways to defuse anger before it turns violent. In our present-day world where anger is being acted out through violence, it may be important to reiterate that anger is neither good nor bad. It is a safety valve that remains a part of our DNA, and by perceiving it this way, we have a better chance of resolving its violent effect on our society. For those who practice conciliation, anger has predominately been one of the most feared emotional climates. However, you will see in subsequent chapters that anger may be the clearest emotion to conciliate.

Case Study

John was an assistant dean at a small liberal arts college in northern New York. It was the perfect job for a twenty-eight year-old with aspirations of getting a PhD in psychology. The school provided a campus residence, free meals at the cafeteria, a stipend, and was near a neighboring university where he was pursuing an advanced graduate program.

On a Tuesday night in early November, a loud knock on his door brought him out of a peaceful sleep. When he opened the door, the local campus police rushed into his living room and demanded he call the New York State Police to control an angry mob that had formed in front of a college residence hall. They also showed John the crumpled remains of a police identification badge, telling him that an angry student had destroyed it when they tried to identify themselves.

John followed the police and five minutes later he arrived in front of the residence hall where approximately three hundred people were watching a student screaming at a dozen other students. The student was demanding they give back the keys to his car. John thought for a moment then slowly walked toward him while the other students in the argument became silent and moved away.

John recognized the angry person as a biology student from the science department, and realized the people arguing with him were his roommates. He knew there was little time left to do something, especially after the police threatened the crowd with retribution. The crowd was beginning to show signs of stress and he knew they could turn into a mob at any moment. His personal feelings of anxiety made him consider asking the question, "What is going on here?" but such a statement seemed dangerous. His uncertainty was a minor matter compared to the growing tension in the crowd. He finally decided to say nothing and simply walk toward the angry student.

The student was saying, "I will hurt you if you come any closer!" and he began swinging his arms as a gesture of his intentions. John cautiously walked up to him. The student stopped swinging, and John pointed to a quiet area on campus and said, "Let's get out of here." The student looked around at all the people and reluctantly said, "Ok." They walked to a secluded bench on the perimeter of the campus where the student told John he was upset over the loss of his mother that morning. He apologized for creating a scene, and thanked him for removing him from an embarrassing moment. John said he was the assistant dean and to stop by his office the following day.

The student returned to his dorm room and John went back to the waiting crowd. He said, "Everyone go back to your dorms," and asked the student's roommates to check on him during the night. The crowd dispersed and the campus police helped John direct people to their dormitories. The next day, the student came to John's office where they discussed time off for the funeral, and how the college had made arrangements to send flowers. He also asked the student to meet with the head of campus police at a later date to discuss payment for the identification badge, and that he would inform the head of security that the student was coming. When the student was leaving, he said to John, "Thank you for not charging me with disciplinary action." John replied, "Many traumatic events happened yesterday. This is not the time for college administrators to become unreasonable." The student listened to John's remarks, then turned away and closed the door.

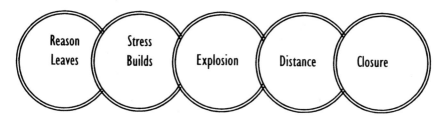

Climate of Anger
Figure 1.1

Understanding an Emotional Climate of Anger

Reason Leaves

Anger can be an illogical reaction to an emotional climate that has become unreasonable. The crowd in front of the residence hall felt it, when they saw campus police exerting their power. The student in distress experienced it, when his roommates took the keys to his car. The campus police experienced it when, one of their identification badges was destroyed. All of these people had one thing in common—an emotional climate they perceived as reasonable now had changed. When reason leaves, the potential for anger increases and in disputes, it can reproduce quickly.

That is why disputes resolved by mobs can become dangerous events. People are swept away by a chain of perceived unreasonable behaviors where logic and reason may have little impact on the mob (Bar-Tar & Spitzer, 1999). In our case study, the behavior of the campus police illustrates this point. The emotional climate was extremely tense and uncertain. A student was creating a disruption at a late hour of the night while others were sleeping, and the campus police

accurately viewed his actions as unreasonable. They saw the incident as an issue-oriented conflict, where someone had broken the campus rules on noise and
disorderly conduct.

Yet, there was a larger and more dangerous conflict slowly growing in the
emotional climate surrounding the noise and disorder. The crowd was tense and
restless, the student was drunk and unreasonable, and his roommates were in no
mood to accept alternative solutions based on the rules of the college. The emotional climate had become a larger issue than violations of the rules, and the
police became a part of this angry climate when they demanded John call the
State Police. In this particular case, enforcing college rules became one more
unreasonable event in a series of unreasonable events (figure 1.1).

Stress Builds

When reason leaves, angry people replace it with something else. A neurological
explanation of this process can be found in the limbic portion of our brains. The
cerebrum portion of the brain controls reasonable thinking, and functions as a
logical problem solver when emotional conflicts arise (Salzano, 2003). But,
what happens when the emotional climate surrounding a conflict becomes unreasonable? The amygdala in the limbic system is the primitive portion of the
brain that prepares us to defend ourselves. The amygdala is our crisis manager
and acts as a "safety valve" when we experience danger. It sends a message to
the pituitary glands to shoot adrenaline through our bodies as a strategy of defense against crisis (Harmon & Sigelman, 2001). The normal reaction is stress,
and a readiness to freeze, fight or to flight.

In our case study, the police, the crowd, the student and his roommates became stressed, when the emotional climate was filling up with tension. When
reason is abandoned, stress increases and effectively solving problems becomes
a challenge. The emotional climate has become stressful and unreasonable. John
reconsidered asking the crowd, "What is going on here?" It was an intervention
based on logic that did not fit the emotional climate confronting him. Actually, it
had the potential for causing more stress and more unreasonable behavior. When
a situation has already progressed to this stage an angry mob is in no position to
listen to logic, fact-finding or issue-oriented investigations. Many times, these
activities will make resolution of the conflict more difficult (figure 1.1).

An Explosion

In an angry climate, explosions occur when a culmination of unreasonable perceptions and the resulting stress that accompanies it look for a suitable outlet for
discharging the mounting tension. In disputes filled with anger, explosions are
usually the next expected event. Predictably, in our case study the expectation
was one of an explosive climate, from the campus police to the assistant dean
who was called in to assist. The people in these examples anticipated an explosion, and either prepared themselves to meet it, or let the explosion happen.
Outward explosions as an outlet for stress are a normal physical phenomenon

but not considered a socially acceptable one. The effect explosions have on others leads to angry conflicts. Even though the student's natural response was to explode, it was unacceptable to those around him and it led to a series of related explosive outcomes. Furthermore, a disruption to social order occurred and this is where many angry conflicts materialize (figure 1.1).

Distance

The crucial step in an emotional climate of anger is distance. Without getting distance from angry explosions, people have difficulty returning to more reasonable surroundings. Distance from an explosive situation allows time to diffuse some of the anger so that a resolution can be reached without further disruption. In the case study, without fully understanding the reason for the student's anger the friends reacted to his explosive behavior without knowing its cause. The arrival of John, who approached with a calm demeanor and offered guidance to a safe place, was enough to bring the angry student back to a reasonable state of mind. He was physically exploding, and when John approached, he was acting on the stress and unreasonable happenings of the day.

Without distance, his behavior might have been misinterpreted, causing an escalation of everyone's anger into a more intense and unreasonable emotional climate but also gives time for someone to process thoughts and feelings so that reason returns successfully. John told the student to go back to the dorm room and to stop by the office the next day. By doing this, John gave him both temporal and spatial distance to cope with his mother's death (figure 1.1).

Closure

An emotional climate of anger has ended when reason returns and some form of closure marks the end of the dispute. In the case study, John's work was not finished with the students going back to their dorms. He called the student to his office to bring closure to the unreasonable events that happened the night before. First, John acknowledged the death of the student's mother by sending flowers, and informed him that no disciplinary action would be taken. Then, he asked for a meeting with campus security to discuss reimbursement damages. Distance without closure, may create the possibility for future unreasonable behavior, and for other emotional climates to evolve.

For example, if John does not provide closure for all of the conflict's affected parties, resentment could cause further tension. The lasting result could be an ongoing climate of anxiety on the campus in regards to tensions and security. Conflicts without a beginning, middle and end are not resolved. There is no end in sight (figure 1.1).

Conciliating Anger

Angry conflicts begin when people decide their emotional climate has become unreasonable. Stress builds, explosions take place, and distance gives us a reprieve until reason returns. In all stages of anger, we find a series of events connected together by an underlying pattern that is not remarkably different from one angry conflict to another. For example, our case study has similar stages of anger compared to a family conflict where parents are angry about their teenager's radical behavior, or a conflict between neighbors where one is driving across the other's lawn. In all of these, someone seems unreasonable, and the stress levels of their anger leads to potential explosions, and distance may be needed for reason to return. The importance for conciliators is that angry conflicts, along with other emotional conflicts, have an underlying pattern or phenomenology that can be recognizable regardless of the conflict or dispute being conciliated. (LeVasseur, 2003). Conciliators who understand the underlying pattern of; anger, resentment, revenge and other emotions are better equipped in resolving emotion-oriented conflicts. In the following, we will describe strategies a conciliator uses when facing an angry conflict (Stevick, 1971; Allred 1997). Subsequent chapters will cover strategies for other emotional conflicts et al.

Understanding Unreasonable Thinking

In the initial stages of an angry conflict, people may believe that something has become unreasonable. In our case study, the death of the student's mother prompted his explosive behavior with the campus police. He found their behavior as unreasonable as his mother's death. The police saw the student's behavior as equally unreasonable, but were ineffective in defusing the emotional climate of anger brewing around him. Their decision to uphold the rules made the dispute bigger and angrier. Conciliators view unreasonable thinking differently. Their responsibility lies in the emotional climate, where unreasonable thinking and behavior are a part of that climate.

Conciliators can make a mistake when they view the unreasonable thinking, found in angry people, as "wrong." It may be unreasonable, but from their perspective, it is not wrong. If unreasonable thinking is judged as wrong, then most angry disputes may become angrier and more unreasonable. John, in our case study, viewed the student's behavior as unreasonable but not necessarily wrong, and guided him to a spot on campus where more reasonable thinking took place. It doesn't matter what the reason behind the anger is, what matters is how it is approached. The goal is not to polarize the person against you. Any form of resistance or judgment can be detrimental to the process of conflict resolution.

Fact finding can be another mistake inexperienced conciliators make when peoples' thinking has become unreasonable (Rothchild, 2006; Hankins & Hankins, 1988). On a Native American reservation in the Northeast, a group of fact finders were called to defuse the anger between two disputing factions of the tribe. The fact finders were immediately struck by the unreasonable thinking both sides displayed in trying to present their points of view. They tried getting people to give only facts, and said their anger was causing unreasonable thinking that was counterproductive. Unfortunately, they left discouraged with no reconciliation of the conflict.

Fact-finding is a method for gathering information in order to render a judgment, and may have little effect on angry people. Another group of conciliators were called to help the same group of Native Americans, except they allowed them to express their anger, and guided their unreasonable thinking to a place of reason, and only then gathered facts for resolution of the conflict. The conciliators, in this example, were not ahead of themselves. They first defused the emotional climate before their information gathering had any meaning.

Finally, consider a few thoughts on more permanent unreasonable thinkers. We all know of people who seem angry most of the time and their unreasonable thinking is present long before disputes arise. Psychologists can provide many examples of people like this from a psychological perspective but from a conflict resolution point of view, certain groups stand out. Racists, bigots, fanatics, terrorists and other prejudice people have incorporated unreasonable thinking into their lifestyle. For conciliators, this is problematic, because of the difficulty in facilitating reasonable thinking into lifestyles already determined to be unreasonable.

Reducing Stress

Meditation, yoga and exercise are terrific methods of stress reduction but are obviously ineffective in the middle of an angry conflict. The reason for this is time. In angry conflicts, conciliators have a limited amount of time before an explosion takes place and must look for methods to quickly reduce stress (Schaeffer, 2001). Behavioral methods of stress reduction may be more successful, because of the time factor. Here are common behavioral methods of stress reduction in angry conflicts.

Pacing

People in angry conflicts abandoned reason and are prepared to argue, fight or act out some other form of explosion. Stress is the neurological byproduct of all this activity, and conciliators are susceptible to it like anyone else—not to mention how quickly stress reproduces in an emotional climate of anger. A conciliator's first responsibility may be in controlling personal stress before controlling the stress of others in a conflict.

That may sound self-centered, but the rapid movement of stress through an angry group of people may require someone to manage their own stress prior to managing other's stress. For example, how long does it take to feel stress in a workplace setting when other workers are exploding with anger? The answer is, not long. Stress can reproduce quickly and some people observing angry disputes find themselves caught up in "mob" behavior, when they had little intention of getting involved.

In our case study, the student's stress had reproduced in a crowd of over three hundred people, and eventually reproduced in the campus police. However, John controlled his personal stress and the crowd slowed down waiting to see what would happen next. Ironically, John, focusing on personal stress, helped others focus on their personal stress. From a neurological point of view, mirror neurons in John's brain connect him with the neurotransmitter reactions of the crowd (Heyes, 2010). As John paces himself down, the crowd begins to do the same neurologically.

The outcome may have been quite different if he arrived on the scene, visibly stressed and shouted at the crowd, "Everyone calm down!" Whether he knew or not, John had paced the crowd down to a reasonable level of stress and that allowed him to approach the troubled student effectively. Pacing yourself in angry disputes can be more effective than asking others to pace themselves. By modeling an appropriate pace when approaching angry conflicts, conciliators can set the pace for effective conflict resolution.

Slow, Shallow Breathing

What can conciliators do in angry conflicts to slow the pace, thereby reducing stress to a workable level? Conciliators have numerous ways of slowing the pace in angry disputes, but knowing the importance of slowing down may be as significant as any specific method. The slow, shallow breathing mindfulness technique is used in crisis counseling for slowing angry conflicts, and it was selected because of its neurological implications (Bauer-Wu, 2010). When stress builds, people shift from slow, shallow breathing to rapid, shallow breathing. It is one of many neurological changes that happen when we feel stressed (Poster, 2003). Somewhere between slow, deep breathing, found in sleep, and rapid, shallow breathing, found in angry conflicts, is slow, shallow breathing found in reasonable forms of conflict resolution.[1]

For example, a law enforcement officer approaches an angry group of neighbors who want to attack a "crack house" that has decimated the climate in their community. The goal is to stop them from exploding into acts of violence. As a conciliator, the police officer focuses on slow, shallow breathing, as she approaches the angry neighbors. They are highly stressed and want to do something about the people in the house. While talking to them, she is aware of slowing the pace down by breathing more slowly, helping her to speak more slowly. When the neighbors slow down to her pace of talking and breathing; the stress drops to a reasonable level for resolving the conflict, and the emotional climate of anger is less likely to explode into a violent event.

Understanding Angry Explosions

Consider an angry conflict where unreasonable thinking has filled the climate with stress and tension, and an explosion appears inevitable. The conciliator thinks, "Should I stop the explosion or let it happen?" This may be a valid question because there are popular physical methods for stopping angry explosions. For example, strategies are available for stopping two students fighting in the hallway of a public school where someone approaches them from the back, wraps their arms around them, and moves them a safe distance from each other.

Subsequently, the conciliator can find additional methods that forcefully bring them to the ground until help arrives. Using force in stopping explosions during angry conflicts can be a legitimate choice made by people who want to curtail violence before it happens. However, these approaches may have their limitations in a climate of anger plagued by frequent explosions. Look again at the example of students fighting in the hallway of a public school. If someone frequently intervenes with force, a higher probability exists for explosions to increase in the school. Constantly trying to "keep the lid on" angry explosions, can increase unreasonable thinking, and exacerbate peoples' levels of stress (Elbogen & Johnson, 2009). In angry conflicts, forceful interventions may curtail peoples' behavior but the effect is short term and are less effective in improving the emotional climate long term.

Venting

For conciliators, force is a last resort. Keeping "the lid on" angry explosions may be less desirable than "taking the lid off skillfully." Sometimes, conciliators can avoid explosions by helping people with their stress levels, and other times explosions are the next step in emotional climates filled with unreasonable thinking and high levels of stress. So, preparing for imminent explosions may give conciliators choices to either reduce stress or let explosions happen. Venting can be a productive method of exploding in angry conflicts. It can give explosions a purpose in the conflict resolution process. When conciliators tell angry people to "Let it go!" or "Get it out!" they are establishing an unspoken rule in conflicts that says venting feelings can be an acceptable and productive part of the resolution process.

For people in danger of exploding, this seems more reasonable than putting "the lid on" expressions of deeply felt feelings. Consider the following example. A community meeting took place in a public school auditorium to discuss a recent suicide by a student in the school. Community members were invited along with public school teachers and administrators. The auditorium was split in the middle. On one side of the auditorium sat school personnel and on the other side sat members from the community. A microphone stood between them. The first person from the community approached the microphone and exploded with profanities saying how little the school had done to prevent the student's death. The moderator said, "We are not here to blame the school but to discuss the death of a student." That sent the community member into a rage, "How dare you cut me off!"

Fortunately, a conciliator was invited to oversee the process and asked the moderator for the microphone. "You have a right to ask that question and to be angry but one request—no foul language." The community member vented his feelings, without foul language, and was the first of many who vented their feelings throughout the evening. By the meetings' end a plan was devised for prevention of suicide in the community.

Climate Problems vs. People Problems

In the above example, and in our case study, someone initially ignores the angry climate leaving everyone vulnerable to further explosions of anger. Take for example our case study, an angry student personally felt attacked by the campus police. They, in turn, felt attacked when he destroyed one of their badges. They retaliated by asking for a full-scale attack on the observing campus community. In all of these escalating personal attacks, no one had recognized the immediate underlying problem. The dispute was endangering the emotional climate of three hundred or more stressful people. The explosive nature of angry disputes can make conciliators vulnerable to focusing on peoples' personal explosions and not the underlying dangers affecting the emotional climate.

On the other hand, John approached the incident differently. He walked up to the student and gave the option of going to another place on campus. As an effective conciliator, John's first concern was the emotional climate surrounding the angry conflict, and the climate started improving when the student accepted his offer. Only after resolving the climate issue did John help the student attack the problem of his mother's death, by venting his feelings and sharing his remorse. For conciliators, peoples' personal problems are important, but the emotional climate may hold priority in emotion-oriented conflict resolution. The climate, in angry conflict, can be vulnerable to explosions and may need reconciliation skills to protect it.

Directing Explosions to the Conciliator [2]

Experienced conciliators may tell you the value of directing angry explosions toward themselves and away from others in the conflict. By re-directing the conflict, conciliators may be in a position to set up ground rules for acting out angry explosions. In our case study, John was prepared to re-direct the explosion when he approached the swinging arms of the student in front of the campus dormitory. In this case, the conciliator took control of the angry explosion and absorbed the shock directed at others. Being a "shock absorber" to reconcile angry conflicts may be seen as the conciliator's personal responsibility to gain control over the emotional climate. Success in such an arduous task may require depersonalizing the explosions of others. Highly stressed people have left reason behind and could direct their explosions at *any one* or at *any thing*. It makes sense to direct explosions to someone who is protecting the emotional climate surrounding the conflict. Even though some professionals have criticized such an intervention, conciliators may be the most qualified professionals to intervene when a climate of anger erupts into some form of explosion that may lead to violence. Law enforcement, violence negotiators, and in the case study, an assistant dean of students can defuse violence through reconciliation by directing angry explosions to themselves.

Spatial and Temporal Distance

Question: "Why is a couple verbally arguing with each other in a moving car not a great idea?" Answer: "Unless you stop the car and walk around, not enough distance may be provided for calming down and resolving the verbal argument." Getting distance can be an important part of anger-oriented dispute resolution. It acts as a bridge between angry explosions and reasonable closure of the conflict. In our case study, removing the angry student from the on-looking crowd helped everyone gain composure. Spatial distance separated the person exploding from everyone else. Parents understand the need for spatial distance when they put their angry children into "time out" until reason returns, and many of us have taken a walk to calm down after a bout with explosive anger. Also, discussing problems with angry people may require moving to other locations to create different roles for different emotional climates. John went from conciliator to counselor, when he and the student moved to another location, and began talking about the death of the student's mother.

Yet, a secondary problem looms under the surface of explosions in angry conflicts, especially when conciliators attempt problem solving while people are exploding. Reason has left, people are under stress, and explosions are taking place—not exactly the most effective moment for solving problems. Attempting conflict resolution during angry explosions can be counterproductive. The possibility for other conflicts exists in this climate. In our case study, John walked the student away from explosive conditions and discussed his problems at a distant location. What if John chose to find out what was wrong in front of three hundred people? Talking about the death of the student's mother could be secondary to the embarrassment of talking in front of the on-looking crowd.

Temporal distance acts as another method for handling angry explosions. Consider this example. Two conciliators were rushed to the scene of a public school where parents of disputing students were confronting the principal and superintendent about what they perceived to be a racial incident between opposing groups of teenage boys. The conciliators separated the parents, and established spatial distance by each going to a different room in the school while the opposing students went with their group. Both groups vented their anger about the presumed racial event that had taken place. This went on for an entire morning, and proved so successful that the principal and superintendent wanted to bring the boys together and mediate the conflict that afternoon. The conciliators however, felt that was too soon. A compromise was reached and the students returned two days later to resolve the issue that turned out not to be racially motivated, but a fight about starters on the football team.

This particular dispute had a "window of opportunity" where too early would interfere with continued venting and too late would allow the racial perception of the conflict to fully develop. Many angry conflicts have a window of opportunity where the exact amount of temporal distance may need consideration. Guidelines, for such a window, are difficult to generalize, but it should be at least after the explosion has calmed down and before people develop conclusions, and make their own closure. How many acts of violence have taken place because someone did not intervene and missed the window of opportunity? In our case study, John was wise to have the angry student meet the next day to talk about the events of the previous night. If they met five days later, the discussion may have a different emotional impact where violence becomes justified based on a lack of closure.

The Importance of Closure

Creating distance without some form of closure in angry conflicts can open the door for conflict to return or evolve into a different emotional climate such as, resentment or anxiety. Take for example the angry parent who continually yells at the children. After each outburst, the parent may believe the problem has ended and it is time to move on. The children may have a different point of view. Without some form of closure, they still may be waiting for the conflict to end. Getting distance from the outburst alone may not reassure them the conflict is over, especially if other outbursts begin with a new conflict before closure happens with the initial one (Coughlin, 1993). Family therapists know how easily chronic patterns of communication develop where outbursts become a part of a patterned life style—way beyond explosions found in angry conflicts.

In our case study, John asked the angry student to come to his office the next day. He knew the conflict had established distance but it still needed some form of mediated or negotiated closure. There were issues of disciplinary action, reimbursement for a broken badge and even closure on sending flowers to his mother's funeral, the latter representing the college's compassion towards the student. Even the ritual of shaking the hand of another after a disagreement shows closure to an event. Too many conflicts have turned into ongoing feuds, only because someone forgot to obtain a proper form of closure (Meyerhoff, 2001).

When people experience any conflict, we are looking at a phenomenon with a beginning, middle and an end. Counselors, psychologists, and psychiatrists make a living in the treatment of conflicts that may have never obtained proper closure, which eventually cause chronic problems and sometimes acts of violence. A counselor may see a client who has chronic anger problems that are present at work, at home and with their friends. Anger is present regardless of the circumstances. A counselor may recommend learning forms of anger management, to stop these internal outbursts of rage. He or she may look into the client's past, for clues for the anger, or may develop cognitive-behavioral strategies for rethinking the anger before someone gets hurt (Henwood, 2015).

This is not the role of most conciliators. Counselors and other professionals make excellent referral sources after angry conflicts have ended, but it is the responsibility of conciliators to end conflicts. Conciliators are concerned with disputes taking place in certain settings, under unique conditions, with a specific group of people. Unlike other helping professionals who treat chronic ailments, conciliators interact with the emotions happening specifically in emotion-oriented conflicts. With that in mind, anyone can act as a conciliator. When you take the responsibility for defusing an emotionally oriented conflict, you may want to unofficially consider yourself a conciliator.

A Peacemaking Alternative: A Climate of Reason

Summer school classes were being held for classroom teachers interested in furthering their education, in an urban college in South Florida. Two teachers from the same school, teaching the same grade, started debating the problems and attitudes of students today, as opposed to years ago. One teacher was a small, unassuming woman in her early forties who defended her students by saying, "My kids have normal problems and are not very different than other students I have taught over the years." The other teacher was a large, boisterous man in his mid-thirties who stated, "You are wrong about that. Students today are filled with anger and I know by the fourth week of school who they are, and who will be repeating my course next year." The college professor found this discussion intriguing. Here were two teachers, teaching the same students, but with totally opposite points of view. Finally, the professor interrupted and said, "In October, how about if I come to your classrooms and see if I can shed some light on this debate?"

School was in session for a month when the professor showed up at the teachers' school. The first stop was the woman's English class where a calm, engaged group of students were interacting in a discussion of Shakespeare's play *Hamlet*. When students were confused, they raised their hands and she quickly cleared up the confusion. If the noise level became too loud, she would say, "Quiet down, it is too noisy in here." The climate in the classroom seemed typical of any well-functioning group of students, and she presented herself as a reasonable, intelligent teacher.

That all changed when the professor followed the class to the boisterous man's social studies classroom. He began by asking the class to start reading a certain page in the textbook. One boy was confused and started asking the student next to him for the page number. The teacher became inflamed and challenged the boy to justify his behavior. The boy said, "I was asking for the page number." "Sure you were," said the teacher. "If you think you're going to get away with that behavior in here, you're wrong!" Interchanges similar to this happened constantly during the classroom period.

The social studies teacher had a free period after class, and met with the professor in the teacher's room of the school. The college professor looked at the teacher and said, "Now I also know who will be repeating social studies next year: the boy in the back of the room wearing the green shirt, the girl near the window with the blonde hair, and the big student in the front row." Surprised, the teacher asked, "How did you know that?" The college professor said, "Tell me about the big student in the front row." The social studies teacher replied, "Oh! I had his brother last year in class and he was big trouble. Actually, this school has a history with that family and they are all trouble." The college professor answered him by saying, "Here is how I know that student will fail this class." When you caught him asking another student for the page number in the textbook, he appeared confused, but your response to him was filled with anger. Actually all of your responses to him during the class period were filled with anger until he eventually responded back with anger, and at that moment you smiled. Your student was set up to fail. He became your self-fulfilling prophecy for eventually doing violent acts." The social studies teacher exploded, "How do you know anything when you sit in an ivory tower? Until you have been in the real world of public school you couldn't possibly understand. There are a lot of angry kids in this school, and you need to stop them before things turn violent!"

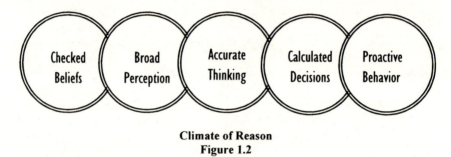

Climate of Reason
Figure 1.2

Let us compare these teachers and the emotional climates they have established in their classrooms.

Checked Beliefs

The English teacher made no unchecked beliefs about her students that would cause them to view her as unreasonable. If a student was confused, she responded to it, and if she became annoyed, she let them know of her discomfort. The beliefs she had about her students developed by knowing them over time. Compare this to the social studies teacher who already made assumptions about students before they arrived in his class. Maybe the big student's brother was trouble for him in another class, but it requires an unchecked assumption to believe his brother also is trouble (figure 1.2).

Broad Perception

How did both teachers view their classroom students? The English teacher saw a broad range of potential. She made an effort to know them as the year went on. The social studies teacher's view of his students was narrowed by his unchecked beliefs, especially his views on potential troublemakers. He believed certain people would cause him trouble. He saw trouble and not much else. Notice that both teachers' beliefs about students influenced their perceptions of what they saw happening in their classrooms and this formed their thinking about students in general (figure 1.2).

Accurate Thinking

The English teacher saw normal students who were about the same as others during her career. Her thinking was based on checked beliefs and broad perceptions of student behavior. The social studies teacher's unchecked beliefs and narrow view of students made his thinking uninformed. He assumed too much and saw too little to accurately know the students in his classroom (figure 1.2).

Calculated Decisions

The English teacher made calculated decisions in the classroom. Her thinking analyzed the needs of the students, along with her needs. Both students and teacher's needs were met by calculating what was best for classroom learning. The social studies teacher made random decisions based on inaccurate thinking, narrow perceptions and unchecked beliefs. The capricious nature of his decision-making became unreasonable to certain students in his class (figure 1.2)

Proactive Behavior

When a problem developed in the English teacher's classroom, she became proactive and resolved it quickly. However, the social studies teacher was highly reactive to problems in the classroom, causing unreasonable behavior to grow during the classroom period—especially in students assumed to be troublemakers. He reacted with anger based on his unchecked beliefs concerning troublemakers, and he smiled when students eventually caused him trouble, reinforcing his unchecked beliefs as accurate (figure 1.2).

The English teacher created a climate of reason where beliefs about others remained irrelevant until she acquired more accurate information. This opened a much broader view of her students—a perception that most people would consider reasonable in a public school classroom. Her thinking about students in general was more accurate, and her thoughts reviewed the needs of all her students, not only a troubled few. She thought about them from a broad spectrum of student behavior. When she made decisions in the classroom, her thoughts and perceptions were accurately portrayed in her calculated decision making. Her behavior was proactive, and the students in the class found it reasonable. She had established a climate of reason, where conflicts were resolved and effective learning was taking place.

The social studies teacher created a different classroom climate. It was one where angry explosions were a common occurrence that came not only from the students but from him as well. His unchecked beliefs about specific students narrowed his perceptions of them. This turned his thinking into a series of guesses concerning their behavior. When he decided to discipline students, the decisions were made in a random manner based on unchecked beliefs, and a narrow point of view. In such an emotional climate anger seems inevitable. He had created a climate filled with unreasonable thinking, high stress, frequent explosions, and some unlucky students who would take the blame by failing the class. The social studies teacher was not concerned with the emotional climate in his classroom but the behavior of a few chosen students, who he believed would give him problems. His beliefs were unchecked and his behavior was reactionary. He created the potential for a climate of anger that could lead to violence. How many school shootings over the past fifteen years started with someone being unreasonable? How many shooters have become self-fulfilling prophecies based on a climate of anger turning into violence?

Cultural Implications

For people raised in some collectivistic societies, it is not enough being logically correct when in conflict with a person or a group. For them, it is more important that they deal with a conflict in a most undisruptive manner. Some cultures advocate that people should be warm and benevolent to others and live in harmony with one another. When in conflict, these people tend to sacrifice their own interests, in order to satisfy the well-being of others. Consequently, they tend to restrain their anger.

However, in some Asian cultures and sub-cultures people tend to hold the powerful class in awe, and in those societies anger can function as a signal of high status and privilege. In the United States, expressing anger seems to reflect the degree to which people experience negative events, while in those cultures it may reflect the degree to which people feel empowered and entitled. For instance, last year during a flight, the daughter of a South Korean Air chief executive made the news when she threw a tantrum over a bag of macadamia nuts being served in a bag instead of on a plate. She ordered the plane back to the terminal and kicked off the head steward (Sang-Hun, 2014).

This seems in stark contrast to Western culture where anger is based more on what seems logical to individuals in any given conflict. For example, the police in the case study were responding to what they believed was reasonable by their standards of reason, and not to what culture dictated as reasonable. A conciliator would have to take culture into consideration when approaching people from certain areas of the world, where only understanding an underlying pattern of anger may not be enough for reconciliation. This especially may be important when the conciliation of disputing parties is affected by culture, and where venting and exploding with anger is a privilege found in the culture and not in one's feelings. So, culture influences attitudes towards anger whether seen as positive or negative expressions, and cannot be overlooked.

Notes

1. Powers, D. (2008). Life stress and effective well-being. *Journal of Psychology and Theology, 3*(3) 235.

2. Some people find directing the conflict toward the conciliator too dangerous. Purkey, W. (2010). *Conflict to conciliation.* Thousand Oaks, CA: Corwin. 91–102.

Chapter 2

Resentment and Conciliation

In contrast to anger, resentment seems a more acceptable emotion in a civilized society. Resentment is partially based on buried anger where implosions of frustration and feeling stuck are more permissible than explosions of intimidation and rage. Yet, in a civilized society, a climate of resentment may be the breeding ground for a particular form of violence. Lateral violence or indirect violence can be an everyday experience taking place in our families, schools, workplaces and communities. Anywhere frustration and feeling dominate our emotional experience, resentment may be accumulating just under the surface of our consciousness. A frustrated staff working under an incompetent boss, a dysfunctional family feeling the oppression caused by other family members, a racist community finding a scapegoat for their own shortcomings, or a school promoting success while under the surface students and staff are experiencing frustration and discontent: these are all examples of the subtle yet harmful nature found in the emotion of resentment.

Yet, a climate of resentment survives and becomes the solution for many highly emotional conflicts. For some, it appears more prudent not to "make waves" or bring conflicts out in the open, fearing the consequences awaiting one's assertive behavior. The indirect violence caused by resentment unfortunately can exacerbate one emotional problem into a web of emotional problems through gossip and secret alliances. Sometimes such indirect behavior can be masked by a person or group of people putting on an "illusion of harmony." On the surface people interact in a civilized manner while under the surface they may be seething with many of the characteristics of frustration and buried anger found within a climate of resentment.

In this chapter, we try to answer in detail the question, "Why is the emotion of resentment utilized so readily within our civilized society?" Let us start by briefly saying, "It works." Here is a comparison. If you have many problems and you take a drink of alcohol and it "takes the edge off" your problems, our immediate gratification would conclude that it works. However, it does not solve your problems but only masks them. In some cases, it may cause numerous other problems. When people indirectly gossip or secretly form alliances behind the scenes of a workplace, school, family or community, it also may take the edge off of many types of problems. Unfortunately, it may exacerbate more resentment while increasing the number of problems facing these different groups of people. Brief moments of anger where problems are directly and civilly addressed may be more productive than frustration and buried anger experienced over time. Multiple problems created by an emotional climate of resentment may be the toxic elements that separate open transparency from indirect forms of lateral violence. In the following chapter, we map out how resentment works, and how an effective conciliator can intervene when emotional problems based on a climate of resentment go underground.

Case Study

Anne was excited about her new appointment as assistant director of services for a community mental health agency in a large metropolitan area in Southern California. Her interview for the position felt right and the director of the agency gave her a warm reception when she arrived at work the first day. Her position included supervising a staff of mental health counselors, typical administration duties, and networking between community mental health and outside referral sources. In her first week, she talked to the counselors in several group meetings and within two weeks had completed a successful orientation to her new job. For the most part, the staff seemed committed to their work, and she found talking to them a pleasant, uneventful experience.

All of that changed when she overheard a group of counselors secretly talking to each other in the agency's lunchroom. They were gossiping about other counselors, and made jokes directed at their oppressive working conditions. Anne decided to approach them, but they grew quiet as she advanced. "How is everybody doing today?" she asked. They all became silent and with forced smiles, said, "We're fine," and walked away. The next day she gathered together the staff of counselors and started the meeting with these comments:

> In the last month, I have realized that all of you are dedicated hard working professionals, so this meeting is not about your work. Our profession is frustrating and exhausting and any normal person would expect eventually some type of "fallout" to take place. You have remained dedicated to the clients, and their evaluations of your performance are excellent. The "fallout" has come in the climate we formed between each other, where blaming others has only caused more frustration and pain. We are all trained professionals who advocate for the health and well being of dysfunctional people. Our emotional climate is dysfunctional, and I am asking you to join me in changing it. A counselor resigned yesterday because of this "fallout." Let us look for other alternatives, so quitting the job is not our only resolution of this problem.

The group was taken aback. People started looking at each other, waiting for someone to say something. Finally, a veteran counselor said in anger, "No administrator has ever recognized our different areas of expertise. The secretaries give us whoever comes through the door. A medical clinic directs many patients to the specialist treating a particular ailment. Here our training is ignored!" Anne replied, "Thank you for expressing that very revealing statement. As counselors we are smart enough to know the importance of getting our resentments out in order to solve problems." The rest of the meeting was a highly emotional venting of personal feelings about activities, causing frustration in the agency.

Several meetings followed where the emotional climate was viewed from countless points of view. As feelings were released and issues were uncovered, the climate of the meetings changed from highly emotional events to discussions concerning procedural agency improvements. With time, counselors began supporting each other, especially when frustration became an apparent problem. In the final analysis, Anne concluded that, mental health counseling could be a frustrating and painful profession. However, being a victim of frustration had viable alternatives, and the answers were found in the emotional climate of the agency. In effect, Anne had convinced agency professionals that they were subtly involved in experiencing a long history of resentment-oriented disputes, and were slowly becoming the victims of these disputes.

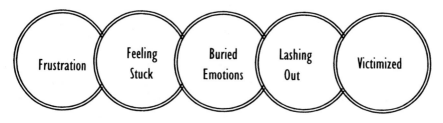

Climate of Resentment
Figure 2.1

Understanding an Emotional Climate of Resentment [3]

Frustration

Unlike anger's dramatic and unreasonable nature, resentment begins with subtle frustrations that build over time. At first, people in a climate of resentment may not recognize any clear examples of emotion-oriented conflicts. Usually, a series of unchallenged small frustrations accumulate over time, making the beginning stages of resentment less noticeable. For example, the counselors at the mental health agency probably experienced similar cordial feelings as Anne did upon their arrival. Only with time, did they become frustrated with the working conditions and began experiencing the oppressive side of resentment. People in resentiment-oriented conflicts have a tendency to accept their circumstances as an *oppressive way of life,* and ignore any chances for successful conflict resolution.

By accepting this premise, over time, resentment subtly may erode feelings of personal power and free-will. A series of resentment-oriented conflicts can begin to blend into an oppressive lifestyle, and unresolved conflicts may create feelings of frustration. These were the circumstances facing Anne, when she joined the mental health clinic. The counselors and the director cordially welcomed her to the Agency, and gave her no indication of any raging conflicts needing her attention. Their feelings of frustration had fallen into a background of subtle resignation. They believed it was associated with mental health counseling. Only with time, did Anne understand the serious consequences existing in the climate of resentment at the agency, and only when she started feeling personal frustration did she take steps to change it (figure 2.1).

Feeling Stuck

Before Anne's intervention, others at the agency may have faced the same dilemma. At some point, each one of them could have come to the realization of being stuck in a working environment that felt frustrating and oppressive. The difference between Anne and the others was that they realized their frustration, but unlike Anne, they accepted it. The only alternative for "un-sticking" yourself at the agency was quitting your job, and that created more frustration and stress for those left behind. A climate of resentment can begin with subtle frustrations that develop into not-so-subtle realizations of being stuck, in an emotional climate filled with an oppressive lifestyle. No matter how professional the counselors acted in their work or professionally performed their duties, they still had to face each day with the realization of being stuck—a realization that eventually drove some competent professionals to leave the work they enjoyed. For those who stayed, they had to endure a climate of resentment and devise methods for tolerating accumulating levels of frustration. Whatever the counselors' reasons were for staying, they had justified these reasons and sought out ways of coping with the frustrating environment (figure 2.1).

Buried Emotions

Frustrated people must go somewhere with their feelings when stuck in a climate of resentment, and their decision to tolerate resentful feelings can leave outward explosions of anger an unacceptable option. Resentful people may substitute outward explosions of anger for inward *implosions* of frustration. In our case study, we witnessed agency personnel covering up the frustration by creating an "illusion of harmony" that comforted Anne when she considered the job as assistant director. For example, the director welcomed her and made an effort to explain the responsibilities of the job, and the counselors, under her supervision, talked openly in meetings giving her no indication of any problems. On the surface, people tried to get along as dedicated professionals, while buried under the surface was resentment accumulating with each passing day.

Buried emotions can give civilized people a way of continuing with their lives, in spite of their conflicts. Unfortunately, the buried emotions found in resentment can cause people to disregard important conflicts and reinforce an already frustrating lifestyle. The complacency of resentful people toward buried emotions can cloud peoples' understanding of these emotions, and may open the possibility for more frustration when emotions indirectly begin to surface (figure 2.1).

Lashing Out

Buried emotions in a resentful climate can eventually surface and peoples' "illusion of harmony" can have its moments of hard reality. In a climate of resentment, people find ways to relieve buried emotions by indirectly lashing out at each other. Anne overheard counselors sarcastically gossiping about their colleagues in the lunchroom, and when she approached them, they said they were fine and walked away. In all of these examples, people were coping with their underlying feelings by periodically lashing out. Common sense would tell us there must be reasons for lashing out indirectly. The answer may be found in the rationale that by indirectly lashing out people are able to cope with buried frustration, yet avoid any conflict that draw attention to their behavior. Sarcasm, mean-spirited joking, the "silent treatment," and different forms of gossiping can become established patterns of communication that relieve frustration, yet do little in resolving conflicts. The closest anyone came to resolving a resentment-oriented conflict at the agency was when a frustrated counselor finally quit the job. Unfortunately, this also was a form of indirect lashing out. In a climate of resentment, people may bury emotional conflict, where it simmers over time. Some people, when they have had enough indirectly lash out by exploding like a volcano, leaving everyone around them wondering what the reasons were for their explosions. In our case study, we see this clearly when the counselor had enough and quit the agency (figure 2.1).

Victimized

Resentment-oriented conflict resolution seems an improbable alternative for people who have a history of indirectly lashing out at each other. As a coping mechanism, resentment has proven itself a successful method for relieving frustration—or current levels of gossip and innuendo would be on the decline. Where "lashing out indirectly" fails, is in its inability to resolve conflicts. Frustration may be relieved, but conflict may continue to accumulate over time, making people the end product of a victimizing experience. When people perceive themselves as victims, resolving conflict may seem an irrelevant exercise that offers little hope for change. That accounts for the sarcasm and mean spirited joking Anne received when she asked if the counselors were having problems.

Resentful people usually focus on frustration reduction not conflict resolution, where lowering peoples' frustration reinforces resentment, not a healthy emotional climate. The counselors' remarks to Anne did not improve the emotional climate, but tried to make her the climate's next victim. If Anne had allowed herself to become a victim of their remarks, she would have joined a cycle of resentment, where being a victim reinforces resentment and being resentful reinforces a person's perception of being a victim. That is why the counselors were taken aback when Anne directly declared war on the resentful climate, and not them. As victims, they were used to indirectly declaring war on each other through sarcasm, joking and gossip, but had little understanding for resolving a resentment-oriented conflict. The constant cycling through the stages of resentment can make it dangerous, and fortunately for the agency, Anne was not about to get caught in this vicious cycle. She saw the agency's problems as a resentment-oriented conflict, and as a conciliator, took measures in emotion-oriented conflict resolution (figure 2.1).

Conciliating Resentment

Unlike conflicts based on anger, resentment-oriented conflicts accumulate. They do not explode. For conciliators, this can create an initial problem because many disputes found in a climate of resentment come from the past, and may be subtly lingering into the present. Frustration over time seems a less likely candidate for immediate action than an angry conflict, where circumstances are explosive. Adding to a conciliator's problems with resentment-oriented conflicts are that many problems remain buried, and alternative solutions are adopted that allow people to continue, for example, tolerating a frustrating family system or working in an oppressive environment (Howse, 2003; Scheler, 1961). In addition, changing obvious, unacceptable problems may seem more crucial than changing solutions to these problems and gossiping or sarcasm can be tolerable solutions in a resentful climate. Under these circumstances, resentment accumulates over time, filling the emotional climate with frustration, indecision and indirect communication. For conciliators, this calls for different strategies than found in anger-oriented conflict resolution. Strategies that capture the subtle phenomenon of resentment may require an understanding of the perils in living a resentment-oriented life style (Petersen, 2002; Von Eckartsberg, 1970; Scheler, 1961).

Problems vs. Predicaments

Conciliators should not assume that resentment-oriented conflicts are resolvable all the time. Making that assumption requires a belief that "people have the power and free will for change, all the time." Even existential scholars declaring the power of free will know control is in ourselves, and we are not in control of all circumstances, and people experiencing resentment cannot be responsible for resolving every resentment-oriented conflict (Neitzche, 1967; Polanyi, 1964). There are countless stories of people suffering from resentment where the climate was too powerful to overcome, and these stories have left their mark on our recorded history (Stack, 1993).

Keeping this in mind, the first question conciliators might ask in a resentment-oriented conflict is, "Am I in a position to resolve this conflict?" Or, more specifically, "Has the frustration in this resentful climate created a problem I can resolve, or am I facing a predicament that must be endured?" Answering these questions may involve a delicate balance between peoples' willingness to change and the conciliator's power to facilitate change. In our case study, Anne asked the counselors about problems at the agency, but they ignored her requests. The director reluctantly gave permission for change but believed agency problems were symptomatic of mental health counseling. The emotional climate at the agency was not perceived as an immediate problem. It was perceived as a part of their lifestyle at work. There was no enthusiasm for solving agency problems, yet they solved problems for a living. Anne refused to accept the agency's emotional climate as a "predicament that must be endured" and that with the others support and cooperation gave her the power to facilitate change.

In fairness to readers who find little power in changing *their* climates of resentment, let us play "devil's advocate" for a moment. If Anne's director had an oppressive, authoritarian personality and under any circumstances refused to make changes at the agency, then she might endure the emotional climate like everyone else, or decide the climate was too frustrating and leave. People quitting their jobs, getting divorces or "moving on" in some fashion are popular ways of relieving frustration in climates of resentment, and who is to judge under what circumstances people should endure frustration in their lives or when they should admit, "I've had enough!"

However, oppressive authoritarians are not the cause of many resentment-oriented conflicts, even though that is a common viewpoint with some people (Wade, 2001; Adorno, 1969). In a resentful climate, people in positions of authority may feel frustration like everyone else. They also may see their condition as a predicament; even though, they are presumed to hold the power. Many bosses, parents, school administrators, and others in positions of power, can feel as stuck and frustrated as their, employees, children and students. In effect, the emotional climate becomes more powerful than the people in it. Conciliators can offer hope for these people by refocusing the problem away from their frustration with each other and onto the resentment found in the emotional climate. In our case study, the indirect lashing out of the staff was symptomatic of the real problem that stayed hidden in the emotional climate at the agency. Anne recognized this, and as a conciliator, set out to facilitate changing the climate, not the people in the climate.

Negotiating for Change

One of the first steps effective conciliators make in resolving resentment-oriented conflicts is to establish negotiations with whoever holds the power in the emotional climate. Anne found herself in the role of conciliator when she realized personal frustration with the mental health agency. She also realized changing the climate required getting permission from someone. First, she negotiated with the director who offered little help but little resistance. She then negotiated with staff members, discussing different strategies for resolving problems emanating from the resentful climate. She realized the best negotiation strategy was identifying the climate as a series of resolvable resentment-oriented conflicts, if agency staff were willing to help.

Anne's negotiations raise obvious questions. What if the director resisted Anne's assertive request? Or, the staff refused to help her? Such negotiations hold no guarantees; however, negotiating to change an emotional climate may have more bargaining power than negotiating to change the personalities of resentful people, especially if the person in charge is one of those resentful people. For conciliators, a vital goal in negotiating changes to a climate of resentment may be in empowering people to make changes in the emotional climate—not personal changes in each other. This avoids the inevitable trap of resistance associated with personal change. As we saw in resolving anger-oriented conflicts, climate change and personal change can be different phenomena. Negotiating for climate change can be an effective strategy, especially when people realize the climate is at the root of their frustration.

A Climate of Choices

Offering choices to resentful people may have importance, no matter how insignificant the choices may appear in the conflict resolution process. Resentment may begin to fade when choices become a common occurrence (Neu, 2008; Schaeffer, 1988). For example, a group of troubled high school students were meeting with the school counselor every Tuesday for an extended period, as punishment for writing sarcastic graffiti on bathroom walls. The first few meetings were filled with indirect talking, joking and sarcastic comments— very similar to the bathroom graffiti only in verbal form. Wherever the students went, a climate of resentment followed them. The counselor's mandate was in changing their behavior, so they would become upstanding citizens of the school.

At first, the counselor focused on their behavior, pointing out strategies for acting differently. This approach had little effect, except on the behavior of the counselor who was becoming more frustrated with each meeting. After a few sessions, the counselor decided to conciliate by refocusing efforts onto the emotional climate surrounding these students. They were shocked when he negotiated with them a different meeting place, the length of sessions and allowing food at each session. Most troubled students have choices taken away as punishment for unacceptable behavior, but the counselor eventually realized these students were frustrated with the school climate, and expressed their frustration through graffiti. Giving choices became an effective way to "unstick" their behavior. They met at a picnic table on the outskirts of school property where they negotiated meeting for an hour and a half and enjoyed numerous snacks. The counselor discussed ways of fitting into the school climate, and not their dysfunctional behavior. After several meetings, the groups' communication shifted from indirect banter to straight talk about frustration with school, their families and growing up feeling stuck. From that point on, no one missed a meeting and the indirect sarcasm of a few weeks earlier stopped. The students and the counselor negotiated simple choices that significantly empowered their behavior, and helped in unraveling a resentful climate that was accumulating over time.

Challenging Buried Emotions

Students, in the above example, were given choices that directly affected their resentment, but other resentment-oriented conflicts may not be affected as easily. In our case study, Anne was ignored when she first asked about problems at the agency. She needed a strategy to bring resentment to the surface. Her strategy was in challenging colleagues to unleash their buried emotions in a systematic and professional manner. Without a formal challenge the mental health counselors indirectly avoided all her efforts. Challenging buried emotions through being assertive can be a crucial step in resentment-oriented conflict resolution. It can stop people from lashing out indirectly and can force them to resolve issues surrounding their accumulated frustration.

Anne's challenge was successful the first time she tried it, but resentful people's buried emotions might not surface with only one challenge. As a conciliator, if the mental health staff did not respond to Anne's challenge, she would challenge them on other occasions until their buried emotions came to the surface. Buried emotions can accumulate over time, and successful conciliators may want to challenge these emotions even when time makes them resistant to change.

Take for example, the mother who was resentful of her husband for not helping with their four children. For years, she complained about him to her friends, relatives and anyone else who would listen. She loved him but resented his behavior, and used gossip as her method for relieving her buried emotions. Talking to others, relieved her pain but little changed—except, her children were becoming frustrated with her behavior. Finally, a friend pointed out that she had plenty of resentment but little change in her marriage. The friend challenged her to take action, but the type of appropriate action was her decision. The distraught woman continued to gossip about her husband, and her friend continued to challenge her. One evening, her buried anger surfaced and she shouted, "If you don't start helping me, then I am leaving you!" A huge argument took place, but the next day he was helping with all facets of child rearing.

We might conclude that the husband's dramatic behavior change is only a small portion of their relationship problems, and professional counseling may be a consideration. This may be correct. The couple's personal problems are not intended to be within the scope of a conciliator's responsibilities. Her close friend acted as a conciliator when gossip created resentment in the emotional climate surrounding friends and relatives, and she forced change by challenging this climate. Challenging her friend's buried emotions was a neighbor's attempt at emotional climate change, not an amateur's curiosity with professional counseling.

The Dilemma with Buried Anger

As stated previously, most people seem afraid of anger and buried anger seems more acceptable than angry explosions. This causes a dilemma for conciliators, because unleashing peoples' buried anger may become a common goal in resentment-oriented dispute resolution. However, others may view unleashing anger as a violation of existing rules and regulations. Frequently this occurs in public high schools, where teenagers express anger as a method for coping with their resentment. When resentful students, who have not broken any school rules, are punished for their angry points of view, it can cause more resentment in the school climate. In this case, angry explosions are a dilemma because they are viewed from differing points of view. An administrator's view may be negative. Students seem to be acting out on school property. However, a counselor/conciliator's view may be positive. They may value angry explosions and see their role in resolving resentment-oriented conflicts. This dilemma gives most conciliators an opportunity to educate people in authority about different forms of anger. For example, anger that leads to violence may be detrimental to an emotional climate. It breaks established rules in our society. However, anger emanating from peoples' resentment, can create direct communication, leading to positive changes in an emotional climate—an obvious benefit to our society (Retzinger, 1991).

The Importance of Direct Communication

If you want to understand resentment in institutions such as work, school or neighborhood communities, listen to the information discussed on the underground network of communication euphemistically called the "grapevine." Established networks of gossip are natural outlets for peoples' resentment. They allow venting of frustration without confronting problems. Gossip and other forms of indirect communication relieve frustration but may do little to change a resentful climate. In many cases, indirect communication may increase levels of frustration, as we sometimes experience through the internet (Sandberg, 2003; Nicholson, 2001).

In a climate of resentment, indirect communication can be used as a coping mechanism for tolerating accumulating levels of frustration. Ironically, resolving resentment-oriented conflicts through indirect communication can add to the frustration levels, where one conflict can turn into numerous conflicts and beyond. Direct, assertive communication may stop the multiplication of problems in resentment-oriented conflicts.

Victims of Mediocrity

Here is a quote from a Native American drug and alcohol counselor, who chooses to remain anonymous. He said, "Resentment is anger without an explosion and revenge without a plan." This quote captures an essential nuance of the phenomenon of resentment. Unlike anger with its dramatic explosions or revenge with its plans of intrigue, a climate of resentment suffers from a subtle mediocrity where emotions are buried, communication may be indirect and people are left as victims with little motivation for change. Consider this example:

> Two men are driving in a car along the streets of Washington, DC, when they notice a number of men standing on the corner. The one man turns to the other and says with racial overtones, "Look at all those poor people costing taxpayers money with their lazy behavior. They should go find a job!" The other man thinks, "How many times have I heard that comment made about so-called lazy people. They are probably not lazy at all."

From a conciliator's viewpoint, the second man's assumption seems far more accurate. Chances are they suffer from frustration over time, realizations of being stuck, buried emotions and indirect methods of relieving their frustrations, and have fallen into the mediocrity of cycling through these stages of resentment countless times. Being with other resentful people has more meaning than seeking employment. The men on the corner are not exploding with anger, and most likely, no plans are being made to get back at others. The familiar phrase "misery loves company" may be more in line with their thinking. They might be experiencing the mediocrity of a resentful climate and have become victims of this mediocrity. Motivation, personal power and self-esteem may all suffer when resentment-oriented disputes become a resentment oriented way of life.

Conciliators may have an opportunity to educate critics about the difference between being victims of mediocrity and intentional laziness. The great conciliator, Dr. Martin Luther King Jr., understood the difference when he said, "I have a dream!" However, Dr. King also had a plan to challenge victims of oppression in not accepting the condescending judgments of their oppressors. He understood the dangers of mediocrity, and educated others to face their resentments directly. The challenge may be the same whether you are Dr. King, or a special education teacher tired of the stereotypical judgments of laziness, that frustrate so many children with learning disabilities. Empowering victims of mediocrity, into action, can be another important step in resentment-oriented conflict resolution, and it may bring resentful people a step closer to realizing a climate where being empowered is appreciated and understood.

A Peacemaking Alternative: A Climate
of Empowerment

It was months since the graduate school of education faculty met as a group concerning the future of academic programs in the education department. Tension remained high in the meeting room when faculty members met for the second time. They were disputing over how to discuss different graduate programs for future years. The faculty already was filled with frustration; even though, an illusion of harmony seemed to fill the air. For months, certain plans were being secretly discussed in small groups. The members of the department were forming alliances with each other against those that disagreed with their positions. However, there was an attempt at being pleasant and cordial as they went through the agenda.

Among those present, a single critic assertively stated to everyone that the department had developed problems by failing to involve everyone in discussions going on, behind the scenes. Juan, was a tenured professor who was in the department for many years, and saw at the first department meeting the emotional climate slowly deteriorate into frustration and buried anger. He stated that the department was having serious problems during that first meeting, yet at the time no one was willing to listen.

They were listening now. The emotional climate in the graduate school of education was frustrating everyone: the faculty, the staff, and the students. The faculty chairperson went around the conference table asking faculty members to voice their opinions, but no one was willing to speak up. Finally, Juan said, "You want to meet for lunch and have special outings, acting as if we do not have any problems. There is silence when we discuss the transitions being proposed within this department by the administration of the university. We have a responsibility to the graduate students and the graduate alumni to make an effort to critically think about the future of our programs. I am asking you to discuss this issue openly and candidly with each other." The room fell silent as faculty members listened to his words. Finally, one faculty member said, "Juan is correct. We do have a responsibility to openly discuss this issue regardless of our disagreements."

Many meetings followed, where they talked face to face with each other, and where an invited representative of the administration was present at the meetings. Together they looked for options that appealed to the administration of the university, expertise of the faculty, along with the cultural and emotional needs of the students and alumni. All parties made suggestions as a matter of conscience, according to their beliefs. They agreed that each other's expertise was needed to make any future transitions a success. Sometimes they agreed with each other. Other times they agreed to disagree, and made creative compromises. In all cases, they assertively stated their points of view. They knew they were equally responsible for the consequences of their decisions.

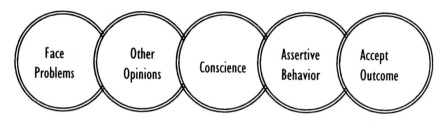

Climate of Empowerment

Figure 2.2

Face Problems

Juan directly faced the problem regarding changes to the graduate school, but faculty members were not listening. He was advocating for faculty involvement by describing the problem as he saw it. In developing a climate of empowerment, it may require someone to directly face the issues in dispute. However, the graduate faculty had little understanding of this phenomenon. They saw changes in the graduate school from their self-centered and self-serving perspectives, and were unwilling to consider conditions beyond their personal beliefs. Juan initially challenged them to look beyond their self-interests and engage each other in a discussion of the issues. He faced the problem again when no one else would give an opinion. He continued to uphold his position, by directly facing a problem that others overlooked (figure 2.2).

Other Opinions

In the beginning, the graduate faculty and the administration were viewing the possible changes in the graduate school as though, no one else was effected by these changes. Their viewpoints changed when Juan asked them to openly state their opinions. The faculty considered other points of view, only after becoming frustrated and wasting a considerable amount of time, in acting as if there were no problems. Juan realized that considering each faculty member's point of view along with the point of view from the administration, would make any outcome more accurate and fair, and would also reconcile an emotional climate filled with resentment. Sometimes, people are consumed by self-interests and fail to recognize opportunities associated with empowerment. Faculty members' lack of consideration for everyone's point of view eventually created more frustration in both the graduate faculty and in the graduate school (figure 2.2).

Conscience

Juan was not the only person with an opinion at the crucial department meetings. Why did others remain silent? They had an equal opportunity to make a difference. An old proverb may help in answering the question, "There is doing the *smart* thing and there is doing the *right* thing and life involves less conflict, when the smart thing and the right thing are the same thing." But, what happens when they are not the same thing? How many people remain silent, because they are trying to do the *smart* thing, yet they know it is not the *right* thing to do?" Who is to say how many faculty members kept silent at the faculty meetings, knowing that an open discussion of the issues was important? A climate of empowerment may require an act of conscience where a person or a group of people do the *right* thing; even when others consider their actions imprudent and unwise (Merleau-Ponty, 1970). Juan told the truth, as he perceived it. He did the right thing, and eventually acted as a conciliator by putting into motion a climate of empowerment (figure 2.2).

Assertive Behavior

Juan's act of conscience required him to assertively convey his opinions to others. Others involved with changes in the graduate school were less assertive. The graduate faculty demonstrated insensitive behavior regarding the graduate school community, and students and alumni we treated with indifference by the indirect behavior and silence of graduate faculty members. It was only after Juan established a climate of empowerment between the faculty members and administration that assertive behavior was recognized as a viable option. However, assertive behavior has its risks. Juan's behavior might have threatened others in power, making his point of view irrelevant, or he may have offended a group of faculty members where "making waves" was viewed with contempt. People, frustrated in a climate of resentment, may lose sight of taking risks. Indirect methods of behavior may seem less risky. Creating a climate of empowerment requires someone to take a risk, and Juan accepted this challenge and assertively upheld his position (figure 2.2).

Accept Outcome

If people directly face their problems, considering different points of view, with the intention of doing the "right thing" and assertively take risks, then the consequences of their efforts can be more acceptable—even when problems are not entirely solvable. As stated in the Introduction to this book, conflicts are part behavior and feelings, consisting of issues and emotions. In a climate of empowerment, it is possible to disagree on issues, yet keep the emotional climate intact (figure 2.2).

Juan understood the faculty would gain power if they shared with each other and the administration. This seems especially true when people are living in an emotional climate of resentment. A climate of empowerment can be seen as an attractive alternative to people who feel frustrated and stuck. It may offer an opportunity to cast away the chains of victimization, and engage in creative problems solving. Juan considered the goals of the faculty, but he also understood the emotional climate of the graduate school. He was responsible for setting in motion a climate of empowerment that benefited those involved.

A climate of empowerment may not only benefit the future of graduate schools. Families, schools, and places of business may find equal value in sharing power; especially when, the emotional climate feels oppressive. However, empowering people to do the "right thing" is not always easy. However, for people caught in a climate of resentment, the sharing of power can have a healing effect. It offers choices and free will. Yet, a climate of empowerment may not be for individuals seeking indirect methods of conflict resolution. It requires direct, assertive behavior and a willingness to take risks. Those who ignore such characteristics may find themselves resenting authority based on ineffective leadership.

Cultural Implications

Here is a cultural reference to an emotional climate of resentment from a teacher who worked in the New York City school system. He was called to the school counselor's office because a Guatemalan student in the seventh grade, a recent immigrant, was accused of being rude to his teacher. As he listened to the teacher scold the student, he heard the teacher shout "Look at me while I am talking to you!" In Latin America when an elder punishes you, it is considered rude to look in his or her eyes because that might be interpreted as a challenge and as disrespectful to the elder. The proper etiquette is to look down, bow your head, and not to answer back. In the United States, making eye contact with someone older may indicate that you are listening to what he or she is saying. Unfortunately, over time, the uninformed teacher along with other teachers with a limited cultural understanding, could create a climate of resentment where Latin immigrants are viewed as disrespectful. In this situation, the lack of knowledge regarding differences in culture may be at the heart of a conflict where the possibility for resentment is based on cultural differences.

This is not the only cultural phenomenon connected to resentment. In numerous societies, people assume that members of the community in general and family members in particular are interdependent. Family members can be highly involved in one another's lives when it comes to making major life decisions. In a more collectivistic society where duty, sacrifice, and compromise are considered desirable, shame can be a powerful tool to control one another and can develop resentment in a person who is controlled by this tactic and this may cause serious problems.

In some Asian cultures, feelings of status and prestige are derived from strong identification with a family's reputation and honor and not from individual achievements. For instance, the tradition of arranged marriage fits this concept. A compatible match chosen by the parents or elders of the family is preferred over a personal choice based on feelings of romantic love. Similarly, children are forced to follow the career path preferred by their parents over their personal interests. Even though their primary loyalty is to their families, many young Asians may feel resentful. Again, these are the examples exemplifying how cultures can enter into conflict resolution and the importance of considering them when they are presented in the process.

Notes

3. The original ideas for mapping out emotions came from the doctoral dissertation. Ladd, P. D. (1976), *Resentment of authority: A phenomenological approach.* (Doctoral Dissertation), San Diego, CA: U.S. International University 1–15.

Chapter 3

Revenge and Conciliation

To some, revenge is perceived as a solution to many disputes where emotional upheaval affects an individual, a group and even a society. Furthermore, it is the justification of revenge that helps many conflicts turn violent. In numerous cases, the emotion of revenge evolves into a pre-meditated plan based on violence and retaliation. Dylann Roof, the shooter responsible for the church shootings in Charleston, South Carolina, poses before a rebel flag while planning an act of violence against innocent, God-loving people, while a church community, also feeling violated by the deaths of church members, develops a plan to do the opposite, by attempting to stabilize the emotional climate surrounding them. They advocated for a plan based on justice, not revenge, by facing Dylann Roof at the county court house and forgiving him. Through their actions they became a model for justice in America.

In many acts where people feel violated and are thrown emotionally out of balance, some form of response seems justified. When people retaliate after being violated, the act of "evening the score" seems a natural response, and violence seems an effective alternative to doing just that, "evening the score." Yet, in an emotional climate of revenge, violent retaliation rarely evens the score. What is one person's retaliation can become another person's violation, escalating a conflict where violence and retaliation seem more justifiable. How many conflicts have escalated based on this premise?

In this chapter, an attempt is made to understand an emotional climate of revenge. You will see that a fine line differentiates a climate of revenge compared to a climate of justice. In other words, revenge is a phenomenon based on being violated, leading to different forms of retaliation. Justice, on the other hand, is a different phenomenon based on clearing up the original violation. Attempts by Sandy Hook Elementary School survivors to have Congress legislate gun control measures was based on clearing up what they felt was an emotional violation to their community. Whether one agrees with such legislation or not, their plan was not based on retaliation but on clearing up the emotional violation caused by an act of violence.

This chapter also tries to point out that revenge may be more prevalent than some of us believe. The case study that follows this brief commentary is not about two people who develop conscious, pre-meditative plans based on retaliation. It is about a couple who are trying to survive a divorce where an emotional climate of revenge unconsciously begins to develop its own plan. It is an unconscious plan where friends and other family members join the emotional climate and begin feuding with each other. Sometimes the emotional climate is bigger than the people in it. Unlike anger, revenge has a pre-meditative element to it both consciously or unconsciously. It may be a conciliator's job to help violated people understand the difference between a climate of revenge and one based on justice. This becomes a paramount issue when violence becomes an alternative in resolving a conflict.

Case Study

The problems between Frank and Martha were not new to James. For the last six years he observed their relationship in decline, and for most of this time he acted as an outsider, choosing to let their family business be a private affair. This position seemed an uncomfortable but acceptable alternative until their divorce. It was during this period of time that both of them contacted him, seeking advice.

Martha met James one afternoon and told a story of Frank's constant sabotage of the relationship with her son. According to Martha, "Frank feeds Michael crazy ideas about me, and when Michael comes home after visitation, he is loud and disrespectful. James listened to Martha's story and told her that Frank was going to meet him later in the week. Martha said, "Good! Maybe you can knock some sense into him."

Frank and James got together three days later and James told Frank that he had met with Martha, and agreed to get involved. Frank welcomed his input and described the cruelty Martha had inflicted on him. He shared the latest injustice by describing how Martha's constant pressure had eventually ruined his relationship with his girlfriend. He vowed to get her back for wrecking this great chance at happiness.

Adding to their problems, Frank and Martha's families had taken sides, adding more fuel to an already raging fire. They also started contacting James and told of the atrocities the "other side" had committed. They said that in the last three years the problem was getting worse where both families were retaliating at any chance to violate the other side. James felt obliged to do something. James invited Frank and Martha to his home and told them he wanted to talk about the ongoing feud between both families, and if they would be willing to discuss this issue. Reluctantly, they both agreed. The following is what James told them when they came for the meeting:

> I have been your friend for many years and have always cared equally about both of you. So, I don't plan to take sides when talking to my friends. However, I have some things to say and I hope you will

hear me out. First, I believe you both have a right to start a new life after the divorce, but not by retaliating against each other, and I realize both of you feel violated and getting even seems a normal response. At times, I have felt that way myself. What concerns me are your methods for getting even. They are hurting everyone around you. This has been going on for three years and I don't see you or your families moving on. Your families keep waiting for some form of retaliation to take place, but this waiting is hurting everyone. I don't care if you want to start a new life, but at least come up with a plan that doesn't hurt so many people. Have you considered going to a mediator? Here is the address and phone number for a community mediation center. Why don't you call and work through this terrible situation?

A few weeks later, James ran into Martha at the supermarket and asked how everything was going. Martha replied, "Well, we still are not the best of friends, but we did go for mediation, and that at least stopped the feud." James told her it was good to hear things are better and encouraged her to stop by sometime. Martha thanked James for his help and then continued with her shopping. James felt his intervention was worth the effort, and that Frank and Martha were good friends who needed someone to reconcile a difficult moment in their lives.

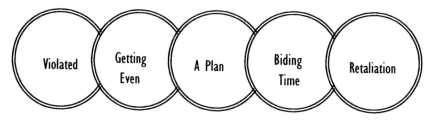

Climate of Revenge
Figure 3.1

Violated

In a climate of revenge, people initially feel violated by some act that is so disruptive that the relationship with the violator seriously affects another's emotional stability. In the case study, Martha felt violated by Frank when their son, Michael, came home from visitation days demonstrating disrespectful behavior. In her mind, Frank violated her and seriously disrupted her emotionally. Frank also felt violated when pressure from Martha threatened his budding relationship with another woman. Frank blamed Martha, and felt she was the cause of the relationship's failure. In these examples, Frank and Martha's feelings of violation severely affected how they perceived each other, what they said to each other and how they behaved when in the company of each other. When Frank and Martha looked at each other, they saw a "violator" looking back at them. When they talked to each other, their words could not escape previous violations. They chose not to be in each other's company, as a behavioral statement of how deeply rooted being violated affected their feelings, and how disruptive these feelings became when in the other's presence. Feeling violated, in a vengeful climate, becomes a mind-set that can affect anything or anyone associated with these feelings, and the mind-set is not easily forgotten, no matter how insignificant others may rank its importance. In a climate of revenge, violations are the disruptive events setting the climate in motion, gathering other violations along the way. Whether they are between family members disputing a divorce, or on a larger scale, where violations occur between disputing cultures, feeling violated can be traumatic, memorable and disruptive to peoples' everyday experience (figure 3.1).

Getting Even

Feeling violated establishes a climate of revenge, but wanting to get even with the violators sustains the climate once peoples' everyday experiences have weathered the initial shock. In the case study, Martha states, "I am not going to let Frank get away with this!" and Frank has similar feelings when he vows to get back at her for wrecking his "one great chance at happiness." In a climate of revenge, the natural tendency is to make a definitive response in some way when violations occur and peoples' emotions are thrown out of balance. Within such a response are choices. Violated people can choose to clear up the violations and get emotionally back in balance, or get even with those who committed the violations in some retaliatory manner. Frank and Martha's decision was not connected to the first choice of clearing up violations. They both ignored their violated feelings, and directed their energy to retaliating against each other. This is too common a decision made by people caught in a climate of revenge. They confuse clearing up violations and getting emotionally in balance with getting even, where one leads to emotional stability, and the other creates escalating forms of retaliation

In the case study, both families were eventually drawn into getting even. It was only James who understood that restoring emotional balance for Martha, Frank, Michael and both families was an obvious goal to pursue. In a climate of revenge, the confusion lies in, "getting even" appearing as a more satisfying choice, than "clearing up violations and getting in balance emotionally." Unfortunately, violated people can justify retaliation; even though, it may eventually cause more serious emotional imbalance. Herein lies the dangers associated with an escalating climate of revenge (Fang, 2003) (figure 3.1).

A Plan

People who feel violated and decide to get even with others form a plan based on retribution that satisfies their violated feelings. The formation of the plan can be highly calculating, as in scheming an elaborate series of events that attack the violator. Unfortunately, many examples of this can be seen in our current society, where one culture feels violated by another and forms elaborate plans carried out through embassy bombings, car bombings, suicide bombings, sniper shootings and other violent methods of retaliation. However, a climate of revenge can produce less calculated plans that are formed in vague and less elaborate ways. In our case study, Martha tells James, "I am not going to let him (Frank) get away with this," and, "Maybe you can knock some sense into him." Frank confronts James with similar threats when he says, "Her behavior is inexcusable," and he vows to get her back for wrecking the relationship with his girlfriend.

In both of these examples, no elaborate plans exist, but the *intent* of getting back at the other is formulating just below the surface of their consciousness. They have set into motion the formation of plans to get even, one way or the other. It is the pre-determined formation of a plan to get back at others, and the specific justified beliefs accompanying these plans, that can make a climate of revenge significantly different from a climate of anger or a climate of resentment (Scheff, 1994). Angry people may explode when the climate becomes unreasonable, and resentful people may eventually lash out from frustration, but neither anger nor resentment have pre-determined, calculated plans that are primarily based on getting even, and neither have strongly held justifications allowing for the pre-meditated behavior associated with a climate of revenge (figure 3.1).

Biding Time

Having formed a plan to get even, violated people bide their time and wait for the moment when they can put their plans into action. To some, this may appear a more dormant and less dangerous stage in a climate of revenge. Yet in some ways, it may become the most destructive. It is during the period when people are biding their time that intensified feelings of violation may occur. With the passing of each day, vengeful people may feel the violation being repeated in their memories, continuing their experience of being emotionally out of balance. The accumulation of repeated feelings of violation and emotional imbalance can increase the severity of the initial violation.

In our case study, Frank and Martha were biding their time for three years. They never successfully got back at the other, yet held on to plans of retaliation that eventually consumed their son and both of their families. In a climate of revenge, people biding time have an opportunity to recruit others into their plans, no matter how vague their plans may appear. Biding time, gives others an occasion to take sides, or in the example of Michael, tragically choose sides. All of this can leave a climate of revenge more complicated and dangerous.

However, the recruitment of others into the plan is not the only dangerous facet of biding time. People who choose to bide their time and wait to get even, can become *frozen in time*. This was the point James was making when he met with Frank and Martha in his home. James told them, "This has been going on for three years, and I don't see your families moving on. Both families are waiting for some form of retaliation to take place, but this waiting is hurting everyone." Biding time may eventually force people to live in the past, and not move on with important experiences in their lives. Ironically, biding time, in a climate of revenge, ultimately may cause violated people to violate themselves (figure 3.1).

Retaliation

Retaliation becomes the final step in the formation of a climate of revenge. However, revenge rarely ends with someone retaliating against another. What is one person's retaliation can become another's violation, thus escalating the climate to a higher level of intensity. Constant feelings of violation, followed by frequent retaliations, may cause the climate of revenge to grow larger and more destructive. The constant, back and forth, happening between violations and retaliations can eventually develop into a feud, where violations justify people retaliating, and people retaliating cause another round of violations. This ongoing process can keep a climate of revenge alive for many years, as seen in disputes found in Syria and Iraq.

However, feuds surrounding revenge are not only found at the global level. In our case study, Frank and Martha, and their families, were feuding for three years, where either side would retaliate when an occasion presented itself. After three years of retaliation, it became irrelevant who first violated the other. Feuds, sometimes, are ongoing without anyone remembering the origin of the first violation, or grasping the consequences of continued retaliations. James seemed to be the only one involved who was willing to look at the whole picture. He saw that the climate of revenge was bigger than the people in it. He knew that revenge was controlling both families, and they had lost sight of clearing up the violations, or of considering any thoughts of moving on. Later, James successfully directed Frank and Martha to mediation where violations were resolved, and the retaliation stopped, in the creation of an agreement to end the feud. After their discussion with James, neither Frank nor Martha had a desire to be with each other, but at least they were not retaliating in ways that encompassed the entire family (figure 3.1).

Conciliating Revenge

Revenge-oriented conflicts present specific problems for conciliators. The experience of revenge may be perceived by many as a solution to a problem, not necessarily a problem in itself. People who feel violated and decide to get even, may find justification in using revenge as a resolution for their conflicts, and this justification can reinforce their retaliatory behavior. Such justifications make old quotes such as "an eye for an eye" acceptable and understandable to many violated people (Pillutla & Murnighan, 1996). Beyond that, the saying "revenge is sweet" may not be far from the truth, when asking the opinions of certain people who have retaliated against a personal violation. They may tell you that, "It was satisfying to finally get back at the person or persons who caused their pain."

Conciliators might also be careful in what they say to vengeful people. Any form of moralizing that implies they should "forgive and forget" can be contradictory to how some people feel—no matter how much they believe in this common cliché (Smedes, 1985). Keeping this in mind, conciliators need to respect peoples' solutions to problems, be aware that many violated people feel justified in getting even, realize that certain people may feel an immediate satisfaction when retaliating, and that any moralizing may be contradictory to how they feel. The following are skills that take into account characteristics of revenge and the sensitive circumstances surrounding revenge-oriented conflict resolution.

Revenge as a Solution

Revenge-oriented conflict resolution can be difficult. Many vengeful people find retaliation an acceptable solution, no matter how much unrest may occur in its wake. This is especially true in ongoing feuds that have a history with clearly defined boundaries. As an example, the Palestinians and Israelis periodically are immersed in a climate of revenge, ever since the creation of the Israeli state (Jabbour, 1996). Conciliators have attempted, on many occasions, to resolve revenge-oriented conflicts between them, but have run into roadblocks, especially when each violation causes an escalation in violent behavior. To date, their lack of success can be partially understood in that many Palestinians and Israelis see revenge as a justified solution to continued violations from the other side. Violations are the problems, but subsequent retaliations may be viewed as solutions to these violations, and these solutions may feel justified in the hearts and minds of two strong people looking for their autonomy.

Strong beliefs with clearly defined boundaries, (such as having an independent state) can be difficult conflicts to resolve, especially when retaliation becomes a part of everyday culture (Volkan, 1998). Conciliators face the arduous task of changing a climate that accepts revenge as a solution, and includes it in the history and culture of those being violated. With time, people may take for granted that some form of retribution will follow, where retribution is not viewed as a problem but a solution to a problem. Under these circumstances, a climate of revenge becomes embedded into the culture, making reconciliation a difficult and frustrating activity.

However, negotiations with the objective of creating an understanding of each other's violated feelings, and the beliefs supporting them, can foster agreements that end a climate of revenge. This can be effective providing the negotiating process is not sabotaged with further violations from either side. Unfortunately, those who believe revenge is the solution to resolving conflict may increase retaliations, so that such negotiations fail, leaving revenge to continue unabated by less violent forms of conflict resolution. Keeping this in mind, conciliators may consider preparing disputing parties for the possibility of increased retaliations, the moment peaceful negotiations begin.

Understanding Boundaries

For conciliators, the nature of peoples' violations may require an understanding of boundaries that have been either crossed or broken by the behavior of others. We live within boundaries that are constructed by society, families, schools, communities or ourselves. An understanding of these boundaries can create a frame of reference that directly relates to different climates of revenge. For example, if someone assaults another person, most societies have laws that clearly define this behavior as a violation, and it is clear to most people when a violator crosses these boundaries. However, it is less clear when the climate of revenge has boundaries emanating from peoples' personal beliefs and feelings.

In the case study, Frank and Martha's boundaries were very different. Martha felt violated when the comments and behavior of Frank put pressure on her relationship with Michael, and Frank's boundaries were crossed when Martha interfered with his relationships with other women. It was only after talking to James, and going to mediation, that each person's boundaries were clearly understood by the other. Many climates of revenge begin when someone or some group violates another, because they had little understanding of their personal boundaries, and the problem can become more confusing when these violations spread to others who have a different interpretation of boundaries.

For example, both Frank and Martha's families had boundaries that were crossed, and it is a matter of speculation whether these boundaries included any violations of Martha's relationship with Michael or violating Frank's right to date other women. When personal violations begin including other people, violated boundaries may become unclear and violations may capriciously occur. Conciliators, who map out the boundaries of people involved in a climate of revenge, can construct discernable limits to peoples' behavior. James, in our case study, pointed out to Frank and Martha that violations had spread to Michael and both families. He was trying to establish boundaries that were clear to both of them, so that Michael and members of their families were not included in their climate of revenge. He also wanted both of them to be aware of the other's personal boundaries. Through his efforts, and the specific agreement obtained in mediation, he established boundaries that reconciled their climate of revenge.

A Right to Get Even

Jack visited counselors and psychologists for the past month but nothing could change his mind. He was going to kill his stepbrother. Six months ago Jack's stepbrother became drunk, and in a fit of rage hit his mother, killing her. Jack bought a pistol and waited outside the police station for his transfer to a correctional facility in another part of the state. However, the police had changed the time of his departure. Undaunted, Jack contacted prisoners where his stepbrother was being held, and set up a "hit," but he was transferred before the "hit" took place. Obsessed, Jack spent many of his waking hours thinking of retaliatory methods aimed at retribution for his stepbrother's crime. For the past month, his concerned family took him from one professional to another, where they moralized how killing his stepbrother was unwise, and hoped certain anger management techniques could be applied to curb his behavior.

Their advice infuriated him even more. Jack's frustrated family finally introduced him to a counselor who understood conciliation. Jack came storming into the counselor's office and said, "I don't care what you say. My stepbrother's going to die and you are not going to change my mind." The counselor heard him out and said, "I think you have a right to get even but you have a lousy plan." Jack stopped, "You think I have a right to get even?" The counselor said, "Sure I do, but a plan that hurts your wife and children seems foolish to me." This statement caused Jack serious reflection and over the next few months, it gave him time to formulate a plan letting the legal system punish his stepbrother, while Jack slowly removed plans based on retaliation from his thoughts and feelings. In the years that followed, Jack's plan helped him begin a highly productive and successful career in drug and alcohol rehabilitation.

This incident gets to the heart of the problem when resolving revenge-oriented disputes. Trying to convince violated people they have no right to get even, can be confusing, and may contradict how they may naturally feel. People have a right to clear up violations in their lives. In the above example, Jack had a right to get in balance emotionally; however, he was not considering the overall picture. Jack's perspective was narrowly focused on his stepbrother, excluding others affected by his revenge. Conciliators can help justify peoples' right to get even by focusing them on the larger reality namely, the climate of revenge. The counselor helped Jack face his feelings without causing violations to other family members. He acted as a conciliator, accepting Jack's right to get even, but focusing on a plan that did not further violate others within the vengeful climate.

Choosing an Effective Plan

Conciliators can answer a simple question when determining whether plans created in revenge-oriented conflicts lead to clearing up violations, or do they promote more serious retaliations. The question is, "Does the plan reduce the climate of revenge, or does the climate increase through implementation of the plan?" Most formulated plans that are obsessed with getting back at others have a tendency to increase the climate of revenge—no matter how personally satisfying they may feel to vengeful people. Plans that reduce or dissolve the climate may have rewards that go beyond personal gratification. MADD (Mothers against Drunk Driving) is an example. Here is an organization formed on a plan that reduces a climate of revenge through education, awareness and support (MADD, 2002). Parents who felt violated and helpless were looking for some way to get even emotionally after losing their children to drunk drivers. Their efforts helped others who also lost children by creating a climate of justice instead of one based on revenge. Members of MADD clear up their feelings of violation instead of pursuing retaliation, and in doing so, they decrease the possibilities for further violations through spin off organizations such as SADD (Students against Drunk Driving) (SADD, 2004).

Another example can be seen in the story of Jack and his stepbrother. A similar plan emerges from Jack's decision to refocus his energy away from retaliating against his stepbrother, and investing his time and efforts into his family and career. In both examples, violations causing terrible loss and hardship were not resolved through retaliation but by systematically reducing the climate of revenge. They eventually understood that beyond the initial violations, the true dangers lie hidden in the toxic, vengeful climate; a climate willing to violate all those caught within its escalating retaliations.

Conciliators have an opportunity to help people understand these choices. Most violated people can be narrowly focused on their personal experience, and are not aware of the emotional climate surrounding them. Directing these people to plans that reduce a vengeful climate can create choices that might not be considered without the help of someone with conciliation skills.

Rescuing People Frozen in Time

Being violated may be an unsettling experience. Biding time, waiting to retaliate, may be another unsettling experience. People who bide time can find themselves frozen in time, at least when thinking about previous violations. To explain this, let us use a metaphor that compares the difference between a scar and a wound. People who seek emotional stability after being violated may be left with a scar to their psyche, but like any scar it is a reminder of a wound that has healed.

However, when a person bides their time waiting to retaliate, it is like having a wound that will not heal. Previous violations and thoughts of future retaliations keep the wound open, leaving a person vulnerable to the infectious nature of revenge. In a sense, vengeful people remain wounded when they bide their time, and their unhealed wounds keep them frozen in time, unable to move beyond the original violation. The old axiom "forgive and forget" may have validity, especially if forgiving translates into letting go of the violation, and forgetting means accepting the violation as one more scar in living not as an open wound that is remembered from one day to the next (Smedes, 1985). Conciliators have an opportunity to help people accept the scars obtained while experiencing revenge-oriented conflicts, and avoid remaining wounded, frozen in time, and waiting to retaliate.

In the case study, Frank, Martha, Michael and both families were caught within a vengeful climate that kept the wound open for three years, and for three years they were frozen in time, waiting for the retaliatory measure that would end the conflict. James stopped their waiting by instituting measures for healing the wounds, and rescued them from being caught in the past. Another example is when Jack healed the wound that was destroying his family by letting go of his stepbrother. Though he was left with a tremendous scar over the tragic death of his mother, he still remained above the tragedy and let the wound heal. Later, he went on to model success in drug and alcohol rehabilitation, where he helped others, in healing their wounds and moving on, with their lives.

Physical and Psychological Retaliation

Most of us think of retaliation taking place in a climate of revenge as physical. Physical retaliations are the most obvious and dramatic. Go to many action and adventure movies and you may find actors avenging the violations of others, where the expectation of the audience is to view "pay back" in some dramatic way—and occasionally this expectation happens in real life. Certainly, Jack must have felt the pressure to retaliate after the murder of his mother. There are cultural and personal expectations, in corners of society that associate the violation of a loved one with acts of retaliation. When someone is physically violated, the expectations of peer groups, communities or even an entire culture may be to retaliate in some physical way. For example, drive-by shootings in gang-related conflicts have become an all too common display of expected retaliation, in neighborhoods filled with revenge. It becomes a difficult task for conciliators to influence a revenge-oriented conflict when the culture, community or peer group has accepted retaliation as a customary method of conflict resolution.

Yet, retaliation does not have to be physical, especially in everyday conflicts, where people may retaliate in more psychological ways. In our case study, no physical abuse was mentioned, yet Frank and Martha retaliated psychologically by discrediting the other's reputation. In this form of retaliation, the plan does not necessarily call for anyone to physically act out. In place of physical retribution is a psychological plan to degrade the other's character, and let the person's reputation absorb the attack.

Forms of "back biting" can be very common when someone feels violated and wants to retaliate, but does not want to openly demonstrate their vengeful intentions. This less dramatic form of retaliation seems popular with resentful people trying to un-stick themselves from resentment in their family, school, workplace or community. Resentful people, sometimes, use revenge as a solution to their problems. They arrive at the conclusion that retaliation is a far more rewarding experience than the frustration found in resentment.

A conciliator's best opportunity for changing the minds of vengeful people away from both physical and psychological retaliation is still to refocus them back to the climate of revenge. Helping others understand the emotional climate may have a higher probability of shifting behavior away from revenge and on to a more just form of reconciliation.

A Peacemaking Alternative: A Climate of Justice

George was sitting in the reception room of the Cape Charles Correctional Facility waiting to meet the man who robbed him, shot him, beat him and changed his life forever. It all started five years ago when he owned and operated a con-venience store in Queens, New York. Business was booming and George felt that within a few more years, he could slow down and enjoy the company of his family.

Five years ago, life was going the way George planned it when Jerome en-tered the convenience store—packing a club and a pistol. He demanded that George give him all the money in the cash register and get on the floor. Why he didn't lie down and let Jerome take the money haunted him, as he waited to face Jerome for the second time in his life. A man approached and said, "Are you ready for this?" It was Nick, a mediator for the State Victim/Offender Mediation Program (Choi et al., 2013; Christian, 1988). His mandate was to reconcile past violations by having the victim and offender face each other, and look for recon-ciliation and closure for past crimes.

In another room sat Jerome, quietly waiting to meet the man he had attacked in the robbery. For the past five years, there was time to consider the turns his life had taken since he committed the crime. Growing up, Jerome was the type of kid who rarely got into trouble, but that all changed when he tried crack co-caine. From that moment, his life was in a tailspin, spiraling out of control. Now, controlling his feelings may create an opportunity to make a difference for the person he hurt, and for himself. Nick entered the room and said, "Let's go, Jerome, it is time to meet George."

The room was thick with tension when Nick, George and Jerome sat down at a table in a conference room set up for this occasion. Nick started the session saying, "I want to thank you for agreeing to this process of reconciliation. I have talked to both of you many times to evaluate whether this meeting was appropri-ate, and have come to the conclusion that you are entering it in the spirit of good will. Who would like to start?" Jerome said he would and George concurred. Nick said, "All right, Jerome, begin."

Jerome began, "First of all I know there is nothing I can say to make up for the harm I have done to you and your family. I was an arrogant punk, high on drugs, and hurt you for no reason. I didn't even know you. I was looking for money to support my drug habit and lost my temper when you resisted giving me the money. Let me take this opportunity to apologize for all the hurt I have caused."

George replied, "Jerome, you are correct. There is nothing you can say or do to make up for the pain I have suffered for the past five years. First of all, I had to sell the convenience store. It was impossible to stand all day without getting severe headaches. Beyond that, the doctor's bills have made it extremely diffi-cult on my family. I have a wife and three supportive kids who had to alter their lives, in order to help me through this crisis, and still there are questions floating around in my mind, as to why you acted so violently.

Jerome replied, "It had nothing to do with you. I have had plenty of time to think about why I assaulted you, and it came down to retaliating against any authority. For years, I watched my father beat my mother, and the combination of those memories and crack cocaine knocked down all of my boundaries. I was a person looking for revenge and didn't care who got in my way. Now, I am sitting in this prison, realizing that I hurt you and your family, only to get revenge against myself."

George responded, "This may sound cruel to you, but I am not here for you. I am here for my family and myself. We have all suffered enough and it is time to move on. However, I want you to know how important it was to answer that question; it has haunted me all of these years. I will never forget what you did, but it is time to stop thinking about the robbery. You have to live with your feelings the rest of your life, and it seems like you are truly sorry. On the other hand, I have to get on with my life and want this over with."

Jerome replied, "I will live with this for the rest of my life and hopefully it will be a reminder of how easy it is to wreck peoples' lives, when you are only thinking of yourself." He and George went on to describe other examples of how the robbery had affected their lives, and after about thirty minutes George said, "Well, Jerome, you certainly were not thinking of yourself today, and it was helpful to hear your side of the story. I am willing to leave it at that." Jerome responded, "It was important to say what I did. I, also, want to let this go and start helping others not only myself."

Both parties looked at each other, and acknowledged the dispute was over. Nick ended the session by saying, "It took courage from both of you to make this reconciliation work. Do you believe a hand shake is in order?" Jerome put his hand forward and George shook it. Jerome was escorted back to his cellblock and Nick escorted George to the waiting room. Nick said, "George, this process, hopefully, will continue the healing. I want to thank you for participating and showing true courage." George said, "Maybe now we all can move on."

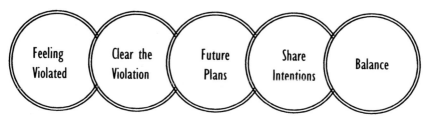

Climate of Justice
Figure 3.2

Feeling Violated

George was violated by Jerome, but the violations did not leave when he was arrested and sent to prison. Justice given by society and one's personal justice may differ in specific ways. With legal justice, some outside authority looks for an appropriate punishment for crimes committed against society. In effect, society finds balance in the system by punishing people for crossing the boundaries from lawful to unlawful behavior. However, these punishments focus on behavior not an emotion. George's feelings of violation remained after Jerome's incarceration. Beyond the justice deemed appropriate by society, was George's sense of personal justice. He was violated, and remained that way for the past five years. The victim/offender mediation program administered in his state recognized a need for personal reconciliation (Hallevy, 2011; Umbreit, 1997). Nick represented this program and spent considerable time making sure that George and Jerome were agreeable, and that neither intended any form of personal revenge (figure 3.2).

Clear the Violation

The program that Nick represented was not connected to legal justice, rather it was charged with upholding personal justice, where George and Jerome were given an opportunity to clear up the lingering emotional baggage connected to the robbery. George wanted to find out information that explained why someone like Jerome would brutally beat him and eventually shoot him. Jerome wanted an opportunity to let George know that his behavior was out of control, and that a life of abuse by his father and later drug abuse was behind his actions. Nick brought George and Jerome together so they both could get even, but not through retaliation. The program he represented was designed to clear up violations, through reconciliation of personal feelings and beliefs, where both faced each other and said what needed saying (figure 3.2).

Future Plans

A climate of personal justice has the intention of forming a plan for the future, where people feel ready to move on with their lives. It is not a plan for retaliating against violators. Nick made sure that before George and Jerome participated in the program, there were no hidden agendas for revenge. Successful reconciliation depended on everyone agreeing to clear up violations without retaliation. Earlier in this chapter, we saw Mothers against Drunk Driving (MADD) form plans to clear up violations associated with tragic auto accidents caused by drunk drivers. In another example, Jack formed a plan to help his family, and move away from thoughts of revenge against his stepbrother. Even in the original case study, Frank and Martha were helped when James referred them to mediation, where they developed a plan to stop the family feud. These were plans based on personal justice that went beyond legal justice. All of these people formed plans not based on violations of the past, but plans for improving the future (figure 3.2).

Share Intentions

Instead of secretly biding time, waiting to retaliate, George shared his feelings with Nick and asked for victim/offender mediation. He openly let others know there was a problem getting over the violation, and that he needed help with his feelings. He was looking for justice, but did not define it on his own terms. He found consensus when Jerome agreed, allowing Nick to set up the proper format for reconciliation. By admitting a problem existed and sharing his intentions with others, George became involved in developing a climate of justice. It was a climate allowing reconciliation for everyone, not only the violated person. Creating a climate of justice can help all those associated with the original violation, and sharing your intentions with others, may give them input into making the plan succeed. Sharing intentions appears important. It allows for checks and balances against developing plans based on retaliation (figure 3. 2).

Getting in Balance

Ultimately a climate of justice is aimed at getting people back in balance emotionally, psychologically and sometimes physically, so life can continue without the weight of previous violations getting in the way of future plans. George wanted to move on from the robbery that threw his life out of balance for five years. He was looking for closure to a traumatic incident in his life that disrupted the balance within himself and his family. The victim/offender mediation helped him find balance lost five years earlier. Legal justice upheld the laws connected to criminal behavior from past behavior, and Jerome was serving time for his crimes. However, legal justice alone was not enough to help George get back in balance emotionally and psychologically for the future. Without establishing a climate of personal justice, memories of the robbery could impair his ability to move beyond this tragic event.

Nick understood the power of reconciliation when he set up the victim/offender mediation. He was aware that retaliation did not have to be the only plan available for resolving the dispute. He knew a fine line separated revenge and justice, and forming the right plan could send the conflict in one direction or the other. He believed that "even truth can have a plan for the future" when he arranged the meeting between George and Jerome. He represented the victim/offender mediation program because he advocated for personal justice when innocent people are victimized in our society (Retzinger & Scheff, 1996) (figure 3.2).

Cultural Implications

In Afghanistan and Northern Pakistan's Pashtun tribal region, the "Pashtunwali" code of conduct calls for *badal,* or revenge, against any person who has maligned someone else's honor—even if the wrong had been committed centuries earlier. In this historic and cultural system of revenge, seeking revenge for perceived wrongs arises out of societal duty rather than an emotional response. Rather than viewed as an act of passion, revenge is perceived as a way to restore social equilibrium in a community that either lacks a formal system of justice or where such a system is considered illegitimate by the population. Therefore, receiving collective punishment in the form of war and drone strikes is not the solution to the ongoing conflict. Moreover, it can escalate the conflict.

In this chapter, you have read about other examples where culture has a major influence on the emotional climate found in conflicts. A culture of racism reinforced an emotional climate of revenge through the rebel flag being used to signify retaliation against southern black church members. Alternately, a climate of justice helped to clear up the same violation, by offering forgiveness to the violator is another example of culture within the Christian black church community. Our emotional stability can be disrupted by violations that may affect us personally but also culturally. From conciliation perspective both may need consideration when resolving revenge oriented disputes.

It appears that a fine line exists between revenge and justice in today's world. What culturally was defined as justice could be viewed by other cultures as revenge, and the opposite also being true. For peacemakers who have to deal with violations and possible retaliations, it may be important to clarify culturally how others view violations to themselves and their community. It may be a better understanding of this phenomenon would help us avoid wars in such places as Syria and Iraq. Without considering culture, one can easily find one defending justice while the other sees it as revenge. Peacemakers have a responsibility in understanding and practicing the difference between the two.

Chapter 4

Jealousy and Conciliation

Jealousy is an escalating emotion that can start with several warnings and end in force, sometimes violence. It is based on a fear of losing something whether it is another person or less tangible characteristics such as control, turf, power or face. In many ways, it is about owning something and not wanting to lose it. In a climate of jealousy, violence can be justified by the person sending out warning signals, putting in claims, and eventually using force. For example, one of the major problems in contemporary society is domestic violence (Trussler, 2009). It may be that jealousy is responsible for this phenomenon more than any other emotion. When someone is faced with a loss of someone they have laid claims to, and whom they have identified and objectified as their own, jealousy can be especially dangerous. It may seem logical to some jealous people that force is acceptable in protecting one's possessions—even if the possession is another person.

Jealousy is often connected to domestic violence, and rightly so, but it can also be seen in the professional world and lead to aggressive means in working towards goals, that is, fighting your way to the top. Being jealous of others who have similar goals, can make the emotional climate of the workplace less about healthy competition, and more about unhealthy claims and counterclaims as to who really deserves credit for achieving success. Combine an emotional climate of jealousy, with personal emotions of ego and greed, and one begins to understand how such a climate can lead to experiences as lateral violence in the workplace, where gossip becomes more important than productivity. The irony in such endeavors as domestic violence or gossip in the workplace is that being afraid of losing something may turn into losing something. An emotional climate of jealousy can lead to both physical violence and emotional violence, both wrecking the very object requiring one's jealous protection.

In this chapter, we point out how a climate of jealousy is connected to violence but also how it can destroy a climate of trust. In a climate of trust, fear of losing something becomes less important. A person respects the boundaries of others and relies on trusting others to find fulfillment in any given situation. In contemporary society, a lack of trust in others makes a complicated world more complicated, where fear slows down conflict resolution, especially in the field of conciliation. It may be that conciliators have to first change a climate of jealousy into, at least, a reasonable climate of trust before any reconciliation can take place.

It also may be that jealousy is one of the most polarizing emotional climates found in human experience. This extends from powerful countries like Russia and the United States to brothers claiming turf in their bedrooms. The basic emotional climate seems the same where someone sends out a warning signal when afraid of losing something, this is quickly followed by claims and counter-claims, and eventually leads to possible violence. Historically, we have seen the pattern so many times that one could make the statement that the emotional climate of jealousy is bigger than the people in it.

Case Study

It would be hard to imagine a more beautiful location to raise a family. The island of Hawaii has majestic views, clear ocean waters and a climate that remains consistent throughout the year. However, for Kim, these attributes were pushed to a back burner of her mind, as she wandered through an inflated social worker's case load, trying to perform a professional service for too many families, in too little time. Kim had seen it all: child abuse, family violence, drug addiction and all those themes that hover over people caught in a tragic cycle of misery.

Lately, she had been speaking on the phone with a mother, who was having problems between her son and a new member of the family—a step-father. It was a phone conversation she heard before, where the mother tries to balance her loyalties between two un-cooperative males, vying for her attention. Here was misfortune waiting to happen, and Kim knew that any intervention to prevent family conflict was a step in the right direction. This opinion was reinforced by case notes, dating back to when the mother and son were a single-parent family. The notes described possible abuse by previous boyfriends, who consistently were in dispute with the teenage boy.

Kim skimmed over the notes, as she walked to the door of this recently created family. Once again, Kim rings their doorbell and is escorted to the living room, only to discover the son and new stepfather huddled around the coffee table—throwing threatening gazes at each other. She at once recognizes the pattern found in her notes, and realizes how important family therapy would be for this struggling family system. However, Kim has a problem of her own. This family is 87 in a case load of 135. Keeping this in mind, she sits down at the coffee table, with intervention strategies for reconciling their dispute, realizing that for now family therapy is logistically impossible and will have to wait.

Kim decides to intervene by using conciliation skills. First, she asks all three of them to describe what happened. The story is not exactly like her case notes but close enough to fit the old pattern. She determines that jealousy is at the heart of their dispute and proceeds with questions that start the process of reconciliation.

She asks them to describe what they are afraid of losing in this family. With some prodding the boy says, "When my mother is with him, I feel there is no time left for me." Kim replies, "So you are afraid of losing time spent with your mother," He replies back, "Yeah, I guess so." Kim then turns to the stepfather and asks, "What are you afraid of losing?" He replies, "It is not that I am afraid of losing anything, but I want him to listen to what I have to say." Kim replies, "So you want to be respected and not 'lose face' in front of your son." He replies, "Yeah, that's probably it." Kim then turns to the mother and asks what she is afraid of losing. She replies, "This family has just come together and I want it to stay together, and it scares me when they fight." Kim says, "So you are afraid the family will break up."

After a lengthy discussion, the family agrees that the breaking point comes when the three of them meet for dinner. Kim asks, "Specifically, what happens at dinner?" The family describes their sarcastic behavior at dinner time and Kim points out how each innuendo causes an escalation in the severity of their disputes. She describes how, at first, they annoy each other by sending subtle warnings. Next, she points out how each person tries to get their way, only to have the other two people reciprocate, by trying to get their way. Finally, she demonstrates how this leads to someone, in the threesome, forcing the other two—to back down by slapping each other.

Kim then asks the question, "By getting your way and having others back down, does that bring anyone closer together, or does it make living with each other more difficult?" They have no difficulty answering the question. The fact that Kim is involved in conciliation with the three of them is an indication of the loss of good will that they are experiencing.

Kim pulls out a piece of paper and maps out five stages found in a climate of jealousy, and for the next half hour, shows how each person can reconcile their disputes, by using skills to short out each stage. She knows that further work through family therapy is recommended, yet she has given them a way to defuse the emotional bomb of jealousy that frequently explodes in this newly established family system.

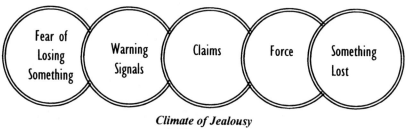

Climate of Jealousy
Figure 4.1

Understanding an Emotional Climate of Jealousy

Fear of Losing Something

A climate of jealousy, more than anything else, can create a fear of losing something in those who experience it. Jealous people believe they possess something of importance and may be afraid others will take it from them. In the case study, the newly formed family demonstrates how a climate of jealousy puts the fear of losing something into a family system. The boy fears that his new stepfather is going to consume all the time with his mother. The stepfather is afraid that he will lose face in front of the boy's mother, if the boy criticizes him. The mother, even though she revealed little jealousy, becomes afraid that the behavior of her son and new husband will eventually break up the family.

In these examples, people feel they possess something and are afraid of losing it to someone else. In the case study, jealousy begins with issues connected to boundaries and "turf." It became an emphatic way of marking possessions by differentiating between one person's territory and that of another. We see a newly formed family where the process of establishing rules, communication patterns, values and emotional bonds are in conflict. The family system is in transition from a single-parent family to a two-parent family system. The dynamics of the family are in flux where old rules, communication patterns, values and emotional bonds are in fear of being lost. This fear of losing something can inadvertently begin a process where the family evolves into a climate of jealousy without knowing it (figure 4.1).

Warning Signals

Within a climate of jealousy, people may send out warning signals, asking others not to interfere with the established boundaries and "turf." The warning signals are sent to maintain the "status quo." In the case study, the son's behavior is an explicit example of a family member not wanting his relationship with his mother to change. He warns the new stepfather about spending too much time with his mother and threatening his personal relationship with her. The annoying behavior he manifests at the dinner table is a statement that says, "You are disrupting the social order in my life and I am warning you."

If the stepfather backs down to the son's warning signals and relinquishes time, then life returns to its previous set of rules, values and communication patterns. However, in the case study, the stepfather begins sending out his own warning signals to the son, causing the problem to escalate. Meanwhile, the mother indirectly sends out her set of anxiety-oriented warning signals, embedded in her non-verbal communication during the annoyances at dinner.

When no one adheres to the warning signals sent by others, a climate of jealousy is born, and it may escalate into more serious warnings and behaviors, where more drastic measures become an acceptable option. Warning signals, within a climate of jealousy, are viewed as indirect gestures for maintaining the status quo, and if not followed can develop into more dramatic and direct methods of behavior (figure 4.1).

Claims

In a climate of jealousy, when warning signals are not followed, jealous people may put in claims to re-establish boundaries and protect their "turf." We see this happening in the case study, when the family goes beyond annoying each other and begins to put in claims for getting their way. The boy puts in a claim for his mother—to get his way. The stepfather counter claims by arguing with the boy over his behavior—to get his way. The mother puts in a claim for the family to settle down and be together—with the hope of getting her way. A climate of jealousy can be notorious for having people lose their sense of common ground, and begin a process of wanting to get their way. Claiming and counter claiming may be at the origin of many jealous conflicts. People are afraid of losing something, and getting one's way, may be a fundamental behavior in a climate, where people are interested in themselves, rather than the common good.

Kim understood this when she began the reconciliation process. She knew the family was headed in the wrong direction. Instead of pulling together, they were claiming personal boundaries and personal "turf." First, she asked the question, "What are you afraid of losing?" as a way of focusing them on their jealousy. Then she pointed out warning signals they were sending to each other. This was followed by a description of how "getting your way" can be detrimental to the family system. As a conciliator, she became both negotiator and teacher in her attempt at bringing the family together (figure 4.1).

Force

What happens in a climate of jealousy when people do not heed the claims and counter claims of others? Many times, force seems a justifiable act that is necessary to maintain old boundaries and protect one's established "turf." In the case study, the family had not reached a stage where force was needed. However, Kim realized that without some form of reconciliation, force could probably be the next step. Unfortunately, for this family and other similar families, a climate of jealousy may be a breeding ground for many forms of abuse. Force might be perceived as a justifiable response and may lead to violence (Holtz-Munroe, Stuart & Hutchinson, 1997). If you ask someone in a family who has physically abused another family member, they may with complete resolve say, "Well! I warned him." In a climate of jealousy, this statement is not uncommon. Many warning signals may lead to putting in claims, and unsuccessful claims may result in using force.

Kim was reconciling an emotional climate of jealousy, but she also was curtailing a cycle of violence developing as a pattern of behavior within the family system. She knew that conciliating the emotional climate of jealousy found in their conflicts, would not replace family therapy, where time was needed to reorganize communication patterns, rules, values and emotional bonds. She also knew that here was a family looking for a chance to lead a productive life, and that a climate of jealousy had become an obstacle in having healthy behavior get under way (figure 4.1).

Something Lost

Ironically, a climate of jealousy may not alleviate people's fear of losing something. Through warning signals, claims and uses of force, frequently something is lost. This describes the irony found in an emotional climate that can produce the very phenomenon it is afraid of losing. A fear of losing something frequently ends in losing something. However, the irony does not stop here. Losing something, as an end product in experiencing a climate of jealousy, may lead people to believe they should be more afraid of losing something in the future. In the case study, one could question why the boy, after having force used against him by his mother's former boyfriends, would start the same jealous behavior with his stepfather? The answer exemplifies how a climate of jealousy can trap those within its borders. The use of force by former boyfriends may make the boy even more afraid of losing his mother, causing him to send out a subtle warning signals and put in more claims. If "other men" counter claim, and then use force, the boy may experience more fear of losing his boundaries and "turf," and may fall into a vicious cycle of physical violence.

Kim had a case load filled with similar experiences, where patterns of jealousy developed as protection from losing something, only to end in violence. It could be argued that a climate of jealousy, and the irony found in it, sheds light on the established phenomenon of multi-generational abuse where, ironically, those who are abused solve their problems by eventually abusing others. Of course, not every dispute where a climate of jealousy is present will end in violence. However, there is a high probability that forceful behavior may emerge when people believe that something is lost and may need force to get it back (figure 4.1).

Conciliating Jealousy

Conciliators may want to consider the irony behind many jealous conflicts, and how quickly jealousy may turn into violence and abuse. When loss occurs in these fragile situations, violence can emerge during later stages of the jealousy process. Jealousy can be an emotion based on justifications for one's behavior where violence, force and destructive actions are believed acceptable.

For the most part, conciliators note that jealous people may primarily be afraid—leading them to reactionary behavior. Changing the reactionary nature of jealousy into feelings and behavior based on action may become the responsibility of anyone who decides to reconcile a jealousy-oriented conflict. The following sheds light on methods for such reconciliation:

Losing Love

Jealous people have many reasons for being afraid of losing something. For many people, jealousy-oriented conflicts are connected to the classic boyfriend/girlfriend nuances of another interested party entering the scene, attempting to sweep a loved one away, only to find their partner putting in a claim to get the loved one back. This remains a common perception of jealous behavior, and it must be admitted that such scenarios are common. They walk a tight rope between jealousy and possessive love, where one may be perceived as gallant behavior, while the other may evolve into forceful behavior, even violence. For example, the woman who had frequent visits to a counselor and on one occasion, came to the office with dark circles around her eyes much like a raccoon, it wasn't long before the obvious news was revealed to the counselor: she had been the victim of frequent abuse. After much discussion, it was obvious to the counselor that her boyfriend had assaulted her, along with committing other forms of violence. However, she did not perceive it in the same way. The woman perceived it as possessive love, where her boyfriend hit her because his undying love could not tolerate her talking to another man. How many significant others stay in relationships because a jealous act of force is interpreted as a form of love? In the above example, when asked by the counselor, "Why do you stay?" She replied that it was better to suffer through love, than to be lonely. Needless to say, the counselor had difficulty helping her when she continued to believe jealousy was an act of possessive love.

In order to successfully conciliate this type of conflict, the counselor needed to help her separate the two phenomena. Possessive love can be perceived as a burning desire to hold someone close, to combat the emotional intimacy lost when they are gone. Jealousy can be perceived as a fear of losing someone to another, where a person has objectified the loved one and perceives that person as property to possess. Actually, forms of jealousy surrounding relationships may have little to do with love. They are primarily about the jealous person being afraid. Conciliators can help people caught in jealous conflicts, based on love, by drawing a clear separation between the two.

What Else Are People Afraid of Losing?

The following is a list of the more frequent themes that make people afraid of losing something. Conciliators take note: These themes are subtler than the classic jealousy seen in relationships, but are no less important in conciliating jealousy-oriented disputes.

Afraid of Losing Time

With the accelerated pace in our dual-income families, time has become an important commodity that is cherished and protected. Time also has become something that people may be afraid of losing. Time with a loved one, time with the children, time to relax, and time to be alone are only a few that can generate jealousy-oriented conflicts. Here is a case where people are not necessarily afraid of losing each other, but may have fear surrounding losing *time* with each other. For example, two commuting parents who spend hours in the car may find when they arrive at home, that a jealous child is sending out warning signals or putting in claims for their attention. Conciliators can help in these disputes by describing how a lack of time can create feelings of jealousy, and how the scheduling of time may be accomplished by asking family members to explain during the day, week, or year, they are afraid of losing something. These subtle adjustments can make dramatic transformations in the emotional climate of a family.

Afraid of Losing "Turf"

Ask teenagers what room in the house they are most afraid of losing and they probably will say their bedroom. For many teenagers their bedrooms are extensions of themselves, with clear boundaries and established identities signifying their "turf." Ask parents who try to re-organize the messy, disorganized bedrooms of their teenage children and you may see teenagers putting in claims for privacy. Or, ask the new employee who is told to share office space with a veteran who has a clear interpretation of office boundaries, and is bothered by the new intruder. In both of these examples, "turf" can become an issue that is disputed by those afraid of losing something. Conciliators may want to take people's turf seriously. What may appear as public space for everyone to use may be perceived differently by someone afraid of losing established "turf." Any conciliator that helps a teenager or veteran employee understand their fear of losing something may be reconciling, possibly, two common jealousy-oriented conflicts.

Afraid of Losing Power and Control

People who are afraid of losing power and control may have subtle warning signals to ward off those who threaten them with some form of loss. For example, "professional jealousy" may arise when established professionals are afraid of talented new-comers who challenge their power and control, in any number of ways. In these cases, jealous "old timers" may send out warning signals that subtly modify the new-comer's behavior to be more compliant and maintain the status quo. They may put in claims or use force when the new-comer's behavior is not modified.

Take the dynamic, new faculty member who has grown in popularity with students enrolled at a college or university, and the warning signals sent out by the old guard. They may subtly threaten the new faculty member's chances at tenure, if he or she does not follow the protocol established by those in power. How many of these bright young minds are denied tenure because their progressive ideas challenged others who were afraid of losing something. One young faculty member once said, about a jealousy-oriented conflict she encountered within her academic department, "There are two ways I can fail in this department—do a poor job or do a great job before I receive tenure." This is one example of how professional jealousy can be perceived as infringing on the boundaries of those holding power and control.

Conciliators may be in a position to help these jealous "veterans" by pointing out the irony connected to jealousy-oriented disputes. People can be taught that sharing power and control may bring more power and control back to those who are afraid of losing it. The connection between being afraid of losing power and control and actually losing power and control, is more common than people think. Conciliators can help people to realize these connections and how unprofessional, professional jealousy, appears to others.

Heeding the Warning in Warning Signals

Conciliators have an opportunity to point out to people involved in jealousy-oriented conflicts warning signals that may be the initial indicators that a climate of jealousy is in its formulation stage. For example, in the case study, Kim, the social worker, might ask the family, "What warning signals do each of you notice in other family members?" The son may point out that he knows when the boyfriend is warning him by the change in the tone of his voice. The mother may tell her son that she knows when he is sending warning signals when he begins to talk in an immature manner. The boyfriend may tell the mother that he knows when warning signals are being sent by the sad look on her face. In all of these examples, jealousy-oriented conflicts can be neutralized before they become more dramatic events. Families that understand each other's warning signals before claims are made or force is used, have a stronger chance for reconciling jealousy-oriented conflicts.

Here is another illustration of knowing warning signals. Take the counselor who was seeing a couple for marital problems but was having difficulty recognizing any real problems between them. They told him their problem was talking to each other, yet they endlessly talked in the counseling sessions and usually in an engaged manner, where both were clearly heard. This was a puzzle to the counselor until he finally asked them if they had any children. They told him that a young daughter named Trish was at home, but they did not believe she caused their problems. In spite of this, the counselor asked them to bring her to counseling. The next counseling session included the couple and their young daughter. Here is what happened:

- The couple would begin a healthy conversation.
- When this happened, Trish would put her hands on her waist and give them a scowling gaze.
- The couple would stop talking.
- The counselor noticed this and got them to continue their conversation.
- When they continued talking, Trish would jump on her mother's lap and stop the conversation.
- The counselor got them talking again.
- Finally, Trish proceeded to disrupt the counselor's office.
- The couple stopped talking.

How did the counselor conciliate this escalating jealousy-oriented conflict? The end result may be a testament to the creativity of the counselor to reconcile the jealousy between the couple and their daughter. Obviously, Trish was ruling this family, by putting her hands on her waist and making a scowling gaze. It was her warning signal to stop talking. The counselor recommended that when Trish sends these warning signals, for the couple to include her in the conversation, until she stops sending warning signals. Later that week, the couple started talking and Trish quickly warned them. However, this time they included her in their conversation, until she became completely bored. Over the weeks, she was included when they wanted to speak to each other, until the day came when Trish had enough of her parents and their conversations, and was more than willing to let them freely talk whenever they wanted to. The couple, by knowing Trish's warning signals, defused them before she put in her claim or used force to disrupt their conversations.

Claiming/Counter Claiming and Common Ground

In the case study, Kim had case notes on the mother and her son that showed a pattern of behavior where the boy puts in a claim for his mother's attention by saying, "Take me to the movies, not him." The stepfather counterclaims by saying, "Don't listen to him. He is just looking for trouble." This leads to the son swearing at the stepfather and the stepfather slapping the son. Conciliators stopping a jealousy-oriented conflict can be far less complicated when jealous parties are still warning each other, but what happens when they go beyond warnings and put in their claims? The back and forth claiming and counter claiming, found in jealousy-oriented conflicts may raise the stakes on what damage will ensue in the final outcome.

The skill of finding common ground can be an effective way to reconcile claiming and counter claiming behavior. When common ground is established between two disputing parties, there remains less to claim. For example, in the case study, if Kim can get the son and the stepfather to agree on the following pieces of common ground, there may be less chance left for claiming:

- So you both agree that you love this woman.
- So you both agree that fighting hurts the family.
- So you both agree that losing your tempers happens when you are afraid of losing something.
- So you both agree that it will take time to know each other.

This list could, actually, be larger than four points of common ground; however, establishing agreement on these four points may go long way to stopping the claiming and counter claiming in the family. Conciliators make note that jealousy-oriented conflicts may benefit from establishing common ground, so the fear of losing something can diminish. It is hard to be jealous when you share common ground with others. Jealousy-oriented conflicts over boundaries and "turf" may disappear when the boundaries and turf are shared. Kim's ability to have the son and the new stepfather understand each other's boundaries in the family, and take ownership of the same turf, may eventually diminish the need for putting in claims and counter claims.

The Irony of Using Force

The goal of any successful conciliator in resolving jealousy-oriented conflicts may be to reconcile the conflict before people use force. When force is used, the chances of losing something may increase, dramatically. Jealousy includes sustaining people's boundaries and "turf," and with the use of force, these boundaries and "turf" may fall into jeopardy. For example, let us look at a story of an old ethnic neighborhood where financially successful immigrant families, from another culture, moved in and started buying homes. At first, long established neighbors sent out warning signals, indicating it was their 'turf' and the new ethnic group should step aside. Unfortunately for the neighbors, the successful immigrants did not step aside but put their claims in for what type of grocery and clothing stores should be available. The older neighbors counter claimed, by teenage boys forcing the new immigrant teenagers to play somewhere else. Finally, gangs were formed and force was used—driving respectable people from both groups out of the neighborhood. Instead of the long-established neighbors finding common ground with the new successful immigrants, they tried to force them out. They were afraid of losing their old cultural traditions. In the end, they lost the very thing they were trying to preserve.

Conciliators may want to point out the dangers of jealousy-oriented conflicts reaching the stage of using force. Usually, when force is continually used as a reaction to jealousy-oriented conflicts, new emotional climates emerge based more on forms of violence including anger, revenge or hatred. When this happens, the fear of losing something has become a reality. People become polarized into groups with little common ground between them. As discovered in the case study, a mother, son and new stepfather have a stronger chance of breaking up, if force is used as a remedy for solving their jealousy-oriented conflicts. Paradoxically, force used through jealousy may be a desperate attempt at holding onto something while forcefully, pushing it away.

A Peacemaking Alternative: A Climate of Trust

George traveled from the Chicago suburbs for an hour each day to reach his place of employment. He owned a convertible and loved flying down the highway at "acceptable" speeds with the wind blowing through his hair. George and his car were inseparable, however George loved the car more than the car loved him. To his wife and family, he had received a "lemon." No matter how meticulously George cared for his car, it frequently had red lights popping on, signaling numerous malfunctions. To make matters worse, he had gone to dealerships, foreign car mechanics and so called "performance experts," with no one being able help him. It was a great car and he defended it against attacks from family and friends, but it was another matter defending the car against mechanics who worked on it. Long ago he stopped trusting these so-called experts to solve his problems.

One day he was getting gas at a local gas station when a young man also getting gas told him, "You do not need to ride around with red lights flashing on your dashboard." He told George that he and his father worked on this type of car and they could fix it in a reasonable amount of time. George thought, "Here we go again, another expert who will cost me time and money." George said, "No, thanks" but the young man insisted he take one of their cards.

That night George thought about what the young man had said. He had tried all other options, so why not. The next day he brought his car to a rundown, two-stall garage with the young man standing outside, next to a crusty-looking character, who turned out to be his father. George said to the older man, "Look, this car means a lot to me and I have taken a lot of grief from family and friends, and have spent tons of money on mechanics I do not trust. If you can't fix it, please let me know." The older man said, "Give me a minute to look at it." Ten minutes later he said, "It will be fixed in an hour. Would you like my son to drop you off at your home?" George said, "No! I'll wait." An hour passed and miraculously the car was finished. George said, "What was wrong with it." The older man replied, "Oh, there was a loose wire to the main computer that was setting off different lights on the dashboard. Quite frankly, this car is in excellent shape."

From that day on, George took his car to the father and son mechanical team for all the car's needs. He knew they would give him an honest estimate, an honest diagnosis and in a reasonable amount of time. As the months passed, George's friends began using them for mechanical repairs. It seemed that having mechanics that could be trusted became more important than the size of the building or the number of tools they possessed. Over the next few years, George developed confidence in them. They had proven their dependability, and he continued using their services. He trusted they would get the job done.

During one particularly gloomy winter day, filled with personal troubles and doubts, George began reflecting on how distrustful he had become with different people his life. For example, he belonged to social organizations but doubted he could depend on colleagues if he needed some form of assistance. There were relatives, on both sides of his family, who constantly asked him for favors, but he distrusted they would come through, if he needed a favor. At work, he was dependable and reliable but noticed how younger employees lacked similar traits, especially when it came to helping others. Fortunately for George, he had faith in the person he married. He felt she could be counted on, no matter what circumstances entered their lives. Over the years they developed a trust in each other that created intimacy and support. However, recently, the focus of the family was diverted to the teenage children, who viewed practicing reliability and dependability as rare behaviors—only performed when you wanted something from your parents.

For some unknown reason, George found himself stopping by the garage owned by the father and son; even though, his car was running perfectly. Later he would admit that he felt comfortable around them and enjoyed their company. He relied on them to tell the truth and was confident they would remain "honest to their words." There was something about these two people that gave George a sense of faith in humanity. Even though their life styles, social class and outside interests were different. With them, he found dependable people who offered him a place to sit and talk, all within a climate of trust.

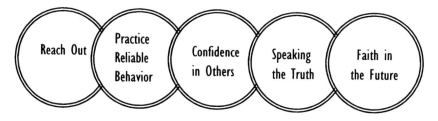

Climate of Trust
Figure 4.2

Reach Out

A climate of trust begins when people reach out and make decisions to rely on others. Such decisions take place every day, when people realize it is impossible to get through life completely alone and make decisions to ask for help. Reaching out starts a climate of trust in motion and the decision to reach out acts as the first step in creating this climate (Butler, 1999; Shea, 1984). However, the opposite can be true when people make decisions *not* to reach out and *not* to seek help. Here are examples from this chapter where people were afraid to reach out. George was cautious reaching out to mechanics because he found them unreliable as a group. In the jealousy case study, the son, the mother, and stepfather needed Kim to help them reach out, because they had not made the decision to rely on each other. The couple with the young daughter, Trish, stopped reaching out through intimate conversation when Trish put her hands on her waist and presented a large scowl.

In all of these examples, no one was willing to make the decision to rely on others. Caution, fear and unreliable behavior caused all the above people to become distrustful. A climate of trust begins by deciding to reach out to others and it can be sustained by perceiving other's behavior as reliable. Trust does not have to be an esoteric phenomenon, but can be a practical method for relying on others, where decisions are made beyond caution and fear (figure 4.2).

Practice Reliable Behavior

Trust may not be a phenomenon that immediately happens. It may require time and practice. Here are some previous examples. George watched the father and son practice reliable behavior not only in fixing his car, but in making estimates, diagnosing the car's problems and consistently telling the truth. Trish eventually gave up trying to disrupt her parent's intimate conversations, after she was included in them and discovered her parents would not desert her. Kim's goal for the son, mother and stepfather was to practice reliable behavior at the dinner table, until they eventually could rely on trusting the behavior of each other. In all of these examples, people's trust levels increased with the practice of reliable behavior. In a climate of trust, people want to believe they can rely on others, and this belief can be actualized through the behavior of others. Telling others to trust someone or some "thing" is rarely enough. People may reach out initially with the belief that others are reliable, but without the practice of reliability, they are likely to withdraw. Trust, rarely is created by only saying, "Trust Me!" People expect others to back that statement with reliable acts. In the case study, George trusted his wife. For years they practiced reliable behavior with each other. Conversely, neither of them completely trusted their teenage children because their behavior lacked reliability. The reliable behavior they demonstrated was in manipulating their parents (figure 4.2).

Confidence in Others

Confidence can be important in developing a climate of trust. People want to feel comfortable when reaching out to others. They may want the confidence that "what was promised will happen, will actually happen." Confidence may be one of the main by-products of trusting others. It can dissolve caution and fear, and can make the statement that others are of good-will. It allows people to talk and act freely and that, what is being experienced is reliable. In the case study, George had little confidence in the colleagues belonging to his social organizations. He experienced less confidence in relationships with his unreliable relatives, and the new employees at work, kept their distance with no intentions of reaching out. For George, confidence came at home from the relationship with his wife, but even at home it was difficult to feel confident. His children consumed their time by not practicing reliable behavior. However, he found comfort with two mechanics who fixed his car. Someone may ask, "How important can that be?" For George it held a great deal of importance. It was a relationship that he could rely on. The mechanics practiced reliable behavior and he felt confident in their presence. He sought after and found a climate of trust that gave him the confidence to speak the truth (figure 4.2).

Speaking the Truth

In a climate of trust, developing confidence in others may open a dialogue for speaking the truth as you see it. Truth can be seen as another pragmatic element of trust, based on reliability and dependability. People speaking the truth do not hold back or camouflage their intentions. For example, the mechanics in George's story had no hidden agendas, nor did they try to con him in order to make money. They told the truth, as they saw it, and by doing this, demonstrated behavior that could be trusted. Their sense of truth was valued by George and his friends, who paid for the truth, as much as, for fixing their cars. Car owners were attracted to both their honesty and their competence.

Most people have had the experience where someone says, "I am telling you the truth." but in reality there are self-centered and self-serving motives behind their behavior (Prater & Kiser, 2002). George wanted to spend time at the mechanic's shop, because they spoke the truth—something he was not getting from others in his life. He balanced his cautious and fearful relationships with visits to their shop. They spoke the truth and he valued and respected them for it. George instinctively knew how important it was to visit the mechanics, regardless of how insignificant it may have appeared to others (figure 4.2).

Faith in the Future

Ultimately, trust and faith seem to be intricately connected; with trust connecting us to the present and faith being our connection to the future (Govier, 1998). Deciding to reach out to others and to have them practice reliable behavior may help us develop a confidence in others, and confidence in others may allow us to speak the truth. Over time, speaking the truth can create a climate of trust based on having faith in the future. Faith in the future may help us trust in ourselves, and in others who tell the truth. Nothing has to be assessed or analyzed when there is trust. For example, the mother, son and step-father in the case study were seeking faith in each other, so they could have a future together as a family. Trish wanted faith in her parents that she would not be abandoned. After they included her in their conversations, she gained faith that her future was secure.

Similarly, George's relationship with the mechanics may be an attempt at discovering faith in his future. A climate of trust seems to create reliability, confidence, truth and faith. All of these are practical phenomena that counteract an emotional climate such as jealousy that may destroy faith, may have little use of truth, may be based on fear not confidence, and may make reliable behavior almost impossible. George found a place to gain these attributes in the company of mechanics. He trusted a father and son to help him keep faith in the future. Though a small gesture in one person's busy schedule, George felt the mechanics helped in balancing his somewhat distrustful life (figure 4.2).

Cultural Implications

When people migrate to a different culture they become more aware of themselves and their own cultural identity. Initially some immigrants resist becoming a part of the host culture because of the differences in cultural values. Therefore, in order to preserve their own cultural and religious identity some immigrant parents think they have the sole responsibility for teaching cultural and religious values to their children. This can result in restrictive cultural behaviors given to children by their parents. Reproducing the traditional culture in their children becomes an important parenting goal for these immigrants (Rahim, 2014). This can lead to intergenerational conflict. Sometimes children of recent immigrants live in two different cultures. They live at home in one culture, while working and attending school in a different culture. Many of the intergenerational conflicts occur due to the children seeking autonomy and wanting to establish their own identity (Shah, 2003).

For example, one cause of intergenerational conflict among South Asian immigrant families in the West comes from the preference for the centuries old tradition of arranged marriages. In South Asian cultures, dating, if allowed, is expected only as a step toward marriage, and premarital sexual relations are generally considered unacceptable (Rahim, 2014). Finally, because religion is a means of transmitting cultural values, immigrant parents usually want their children to marry within their own religion. In those cultures, marriage is meant to strengthen family ties (Shah, 2003). It is not only a union between two individuals, but a union between two families, preferably with a shared ethnicity, faith, caste and/or class (Rahim, 2014).

In this cultural dynamic, conflict caused by arranged marriages can create a climate of jealousy within a family. The children's rejection of the tradition evoke fear of losing cultural and religious values in their parents. The parents send out warning signals to discourage their children. When the signals are ignored parents try to re-establish boundaries to protect their cultural values. When the claims and counter claims are ignored the parents, in some cases, feel justified in using emotional and physical force to stop their children from breaking the cultural norm. There are several incidents where parents took girls to their native country and forced them to marry someone from their culture. By using force, these parents lose the very values they hold dear: familial bond and respect for elders.

In some cultures, "losing face" can be a primary motivation for many jealousy-oriented disputes. We could write an anthology of Hispanic, Native American, Asian and many other cultures where "losing face" is at the heart of disputes. Warning signals are sent and claims are made to regain a lost sense of honor and dignity (Yau-Fai Ho, Fu, & Ng, 2004). Also, "losing face" becomes an issue in many formally negotiated disputes (Hendon, & Herbig, 1997). Sometimes, reconciliation skills are needed to help people regain face before negotiations continue. For example, diplomatic negotiations may take place, where irritating comments by one of the disputing parties causes the other disputing party to lose face. A successful conciliator may separate the parties and discuss what gestures of reconciliation may be needed to restore "face" before negotiations can continue. Successful conciliators frequently spot the warning signals before "losing face" becomes an issue and may caucus with each party to redirect the negotiations, so that face is not lost.

Chapter 5

Hatred and Conciliation

The previous chapters differ, to a certain extent, from the following information on hatred and conciliation. Anger, resentment, revenge, and jealousy came from emotional climates where people were surrounded by an environment of unreasonableness, frustration, insecurity or feelings of violation. In a climate of hatred, the driving force depends on a preconceived ideology that is in search of a conflict to latch on to, or an ideology that seeks out conflict in order to reject and condemn others. For example, terrorists who brought down the World Trade Center in 2001 were driven by an ideology of violence and destruction which was conceived in a climate of hatred against the Western world. They created this devastating event through an emotional climate that justified the deaths of thousands of people

In this chapter, we try to understand a climate of hatred and why hateful people act with impunity against others. In order to comprehend this phenomenon, hatred is broken down into its discernable parts, starting with the rejection of others, leading eventually to some form of justifiable destruction. Ultimately, a hateful climate or environment leads to alienation and condemnation, and in our present world we see social media taking advantage of a worldwide network to promote its violence and destruction—the terror group ISIS being one example of such success.

The case study and other examples in this chapter demonstrate how a climate of hatred can subtly embed itself into any situation where conflicts are taking place, and where reasonable people are tempted to join a climate filled with ulterior motives. For those who are faced with conciliating a climate of hatred, it must be noted how difficult a proposition it becomes to stay on task, and not waver into an ideology that presupposes violence and destruction. Hateful people strive to elevate many conflicts as justification for their dogmatic ideology.

Unfortunately, in this chapter, conciliators who strive to replace a climate of hatred with a more humanistic climate such as compassion may have to wait until the hatred has passed, and compassion becomes a part of the healing process. To make this point, we have included the Sandy Hook Elementary School disaster as one example where reconciliation could only take place after hatred had left its mark. A climate of hatred may be the underlying justification for our anger, resentment, revenge and jealousy. When we look at it through this perspective, hatred may be the "granddaddy" of all emotions that promote violence in our world.

Case Study

The case study is about two groups of teenage boys, one group Native American, the other "mainstream white students" who were fighting with each other in school, where the dispute had now spread to the community. It had escalated to the point where a car was torched on the reservation and another vehicle in the non-Native community was shot full of holes.

The school was asking for Wayne and Sheila, both professional conciliators, (Wayne a White male, Sheila a Native female) to calm the situation down before it became a bigger problem. In the meeting, Wayne said, "Thank you all for coming. Can we begin with an agreement that our main reason for being here is to resolve the dispute that took place in the high school, on Tuesday, September 23?" Immediately, the extremist started their diatribes about prejudice and the evils of opposing cultures. Each time they started on their agenda, either Wayne or Sheila brought them back to agreeing on the reason for the meeting.

Finally, a more moderate member of the Native contingency said, "Look, something terrible is going on and I want to know what happened, so I agree." A member of the white contingency looked at the Native responder and said, "I agree with you. We need to get to the bottom of this and clear the air." With this acknowledgment, other members, on both sides, began to nod their heads in agreement. However, the radical members began lecturing and making judgments across the table—causing an underlying confusion and emotional unrest among everyone present. Instead of trying to stop the attacks of the extremists, Sheila calmly, and in a direct manner, again asked the following question, "Can we agree that our main reason for being here is to resolve the dispute in the high school four days ago on September 23?"

Finally, one of the students told the story while Wayne and Sheila listened and periodically pointed out common ground. The Native students were wearing red bandanas and the white students believed the Native students were in a gang. As it turned out, the incident happened shortly after the tragedy in Ferguson Missouri on August 9, 2014, where a police officer shot and killed Michael Brown.

The white students identified the bandanas as a symbol of defiance against the police, and the Native students felt threatened by the violence directed towards them. Through the conversation, it became clear that the Native students were not being defiant nor were they a gang, but were responding to the red, white and blue being displayed on non-Native student's clothing, throughout the school. The bandanas were a symbol of their culture, as much as, wearing symbols displaying red, white and blue signified being sympathetic with the police.

In the final analysis, Wayne and Sheila felt the group's decision to learn about how Native culture and "mainstream" culture could co-exist was good for the school, community and, especially, for those students who were in dispute. They agreed that both Native and American symbols should be displayed during this time of crisis, and both flags should be represented in front of the school. Shortly thereafter, Wayne and Sheila were invited to a Multi-Cultural Awareness Day where examples of cultural diversity were shared through activities, clothing, family rituals and food.

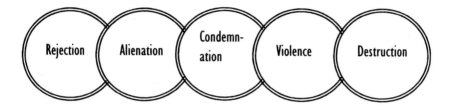

Climate of Hatred
Figure 5.1

Understanding an Emotional Climate of Hatred [4]

Rejection

An emotional climate of hatred forms around the phenomenon of rejection. Whether it is personal rejection or rejection by others, hatred makes the point of drawing the line between those who are acceptable and unacceptable. In the case study, extremists on both sides of the dispute had prior conclusions about the opposing culture. They rejected it and the people who were a part of it. They entered the conciliation meeting, rejecting others with an opposing point of view, long before the actual conflict became an issue—yet where this rejection originated remained unclear. It could have evolved through the racism of their family histories or possibly their personal negative encounters with the opposing culture. What became clear to Wayne and Sheila was their rejection of the opposing side's right to have a point of view.

Hatred often relies on some form of rejection to successfully degrade those caught within its emotional climate (Nancy, 2014; Gaylin, 2003). For example, parents who constantly belittle a child may create a climate where that child eventually accepts degradation. At some intrinsic level of consciousness, the child may reject his or her personal rights as a human being, and this rejection may haunt the child's self-esteem for many years to come (Brockington, 2011: Scharff, 2001). In the case study, we see a similar premise at work. The extremists on both sides wanted to reject the opposing side and degrade the climate, so their fanaticism could prevail. They wanted other members of their faction to reject the opposing culture before discussing the conflict. Their rhetoric was based on convincing others in their group to degrade their opponents and une-quivocally reject them. They were not interested in conflict resolution but in rejecting and degrading the opposing side to enhance their agendas for contin-ued hatred (figure 5.1).

Alienation [5]

There may be a reason that rejection holds such importance within a climate of hatred. Hateful people are now in a position to build walls and become distant from those being rejected. In the case study, the extremists in opposing groups immediately tried to create walls of alienation in the meetings held with Wayne and Sheila. The burning car incident and the shooting of the other car were op-portune moments for dividing the communities. These events were used to fur-ther alienate community members on both sides, and were not used as a premise for discussion or potential reconciliation.

Alienation can gain importance in a climate of hatred. It isolates people from their personal thoughts and feelings, and can start a process where those being rejected can be viewed more as *objects to be hated,* than as people with similar interests, feelings or goals (Kristeva & Herman, 2011; Retzinger, 2001). In the case study, the extremists had an investment in not specifically talking about the dispute that took place or how the teenagers felt about it. They wanted to keep the conversation abstract and general, so they could alienate both parties against each other. Wayne and Sheila recognized their intentions were not based on rec-onciliation but alienation of the groups. Their constant request in the reconcilia-tion to specifically describe the conflict was their way of keeping the process human, not alien, and within a climate of acceptance, not rejection. (Note: This can become a dangerous stage in a climate of hatred. Hateful people may create violence or destruction, if none is present, to encourage others to reject and al-ienate themselves from an opposing side. Though never proven, many believed that extremists were responsible for the destruction of both cars) (figure 5.1).

Condemnation

A climate of hatred that has successfully convinced people to build walls that alienate and objectify outsiders is now in a position to condemn these people as inferior, unacceptably different, evil or inhuman, the rationale being, "we must condemn these outsiders and defend ourselves from their continued threat." In the case study, the extremists had an investment in the condemnation of the oth-er side. If they were successful in having one side condemn the other, then their agenda of rejection and alienation would have been effective. However, Wayne and Sheila kept the reconciliation descriptive, not judgmental. They looked for common ground and for different points of view. Without having dramatic rhet-oric filled with condemnation, the extremists were neutralized to a minor role in the reconciliation.

Yet, another part of this story does point out the danger misunderstanding can produce in forming a climate of hatred. The symbols that were displayed by the students after the incident in Ferguson, Missouri, on August 9, 2014, show how fragile people's beliefs can be within a major emotional crisis. Some "white" students rejected and alienated themselves from Native students. They believed their culture threatened the authority of the police. The Native students retaliated by wearing red headbands, depicting pride in their culture. Here we see a conflict based on a misunderstanding leading to people feeling violated and wanting to retaliate. Without a successful reconciliation of this conflict, extremists who have already rejected and alienated themselves from their neighbors could use the incident as another opportunity to condemn them. Under these circumstances, the initial conflict could go unresolved and an overriding climate of hatred could prevail.

Wayne and Sheila understood an emotional climate of hatred, and focused on the student's feelings of being a symbol of hatred. They avoided the rejection, alienation and condemnation advocated by the extremists, and demonstrated that pride in one's culture does not have to result in the condemnation of another culture. Without this understanding, the conflict could have escalated into rejecting, alienating and eventually condemning each other as cultural enemies. This would be to the benefit of extremists, promoting an emotional climate of hatred, but would appear to have little benefit to students trying to reconcile a conflict (figure 5.1).

Violence

A climate of hatred may condone violence whether physical or psychological. Violence helps hateful people reject, alienate and condemn others (Egerton, 2011; Jorisch, 2004). Unfortunately, a climate of hatred may be more concerned with hating others than in protecting its own. In the case study, the extremists were more than willing to sacrifice the students in the conflict to further their cause. They seemed obsessed with rejecting, alienating and condemning another culture, and gave little intention to reconciling the conflict or protecting the rights of students.

A climate of hatred can use violence as a way of promoting itself, and violence seems the most effective tool hateful people can use in recruiting others into the climate (Gaylin, 2009; Gaylin, 2003). Once people have committed themselves to violence, they now have solidified their behaviors and beliefs, and have made a commitment that is difficult to unravel. In the case study, the extremists were at the reconciliation not to resolve a conflict, but to have a forum for promoting hatred through the use of violence. Unchecked, they would have polarized the communities and sacrificed the relationship between the students to obtain their goals.

A climate of hatred depends on violence to force its will on others. If the extremists could have sabotaged the reconciliation, then violence becomes an option even for more moderate members of the opposing sides. If extremists could have brought both groups to violence, then rejection, alienation and condemnation may become more justifiable beliefs. Violence can be the turning point between having thoughts of hatred, and acting on them. It appears to be the primary activity of those who want to spread hatred throughout our world (figure 5.1).

Destruction

The final stage in a climate of hatred is a need to destroy something. Hatred begins with rejection, alienation and condemnation with all three stages leading to violence. Violence can emerge as the primary activity of hatred. However, violence seems important but not the ultimate goal for those within a climate of hatred. Violence may remain meaningless unless something is destroyed. Destruction makes violence justifiable based on a climate of hatred's need for rejection, alienation, and condemnation.

In the case study, the extremists were at the reconciliation meeting to destroy it, not to reconcile a conflict. Destruction became a mandatory goal in their efforts to reject, alienate and condemn the other side. Without something being destroyed, their efforts would seem unfulfilled. To put it another way, destruction can become the final goal that hateful people pursue, in order to find meaning in their lives. It can justify the rejection, alienation, condemnation and violence. Without destruction, a climate of hatred may remain an unfulfilled phenomenon. In the case study, it was no surprise to Wayne and Sheila that the reconciliation attracted extremists. What a better place to fulfill one's destructive goals than in a reconciliation meeting. On a larger scale, it is no wonder that professional conciliators and mediators on the world stage, expect potential violence any time "peace talks" or "negotiations" are about to take place. Such activities can be a direct threat to maintaining a climate of hatred. As much as, compassionate people seem to have a goal of creating good will, hateful people's goal may be to destroy it. Coming together, to reconcile conflicts, seems a direct threat to people who find destruction a meaningful goal in their lives (figure 5.1).

Conciliating Hatred

Conciliating hatred-oriented conflicts may require an understanding of the "mind set" of hateful people entering into conflict resolution. The psychologist Rollo May once said, "Commitment without doubt is the sign of a fanatic and requires little courage. True courage requires commitment but with doubt" (May, Angel & Ellenberger, 1958). The "mind set" of many hateful people seems more along the lines of commitment without any doubts. Rejection, alienation and condemnation may lead these people to embrace violence and destruction—leaving little room in their ideology for reconciliation. Any attempts by conciliators to reverse the climate of hatred that forms their beliefs, may be considered a daunting task.

Fortunately, hateful people are usually not the primary participants in different forms of conflict resolution. Such people may have little use for reconciliation, and for the most part, may see it as a threat. The danger conciliators face can be their impact on the majority of moderate people who may be convinced by extremists that violence is the only successful method for resolving disputes (Madonna, 2011; Lindsey, 2002). For conciliators, acts of violence may be a reasonable expectation, any time hateful people feel threatened by the conflict resolution process. The following are methods that can be used to counteract the efforts of hateful people in sabotaging valid attempts at reconciliation:

Hatred as a Form of Conflict Resolution

People who feel hatred rarely conclude they have a problem, unless it is some form of self-hatred. People who hate others have made a decision to reject, alienate and condemn, where violence and destruction seem reasonable alternatives. The danger in hatred-oriented disputes may be that hateful people have already decided on a resolution to their problems, and they may be unwilling to consider alternative dispute resolution methods. It becomes important for conciliators to understand what hateful people do with their pain, and *not* to spend countless hours trying to change the hearts and minds of people practicing hatred. Any experienced conciliator may tell you that hateful people appear more willing to transfer their hate to others, than reconcile it within themselves. The famous author and poet James Baldwin once said that, "The reason people hate is because once they stop hating they will have to feel the pain" (Newman, 1998). Many hateful people see their hatred as *a final solution* to avoid emotion-oriented conflicts such as; anger, revenge, resentment and others. The ability of conciliators to re-direct the destructive ideology connected to hatred and to refocus disputes to more manageable forms of conflict resolution may go a long way to reconciling hatred-oriented conflicts.

The Revenge/Hatred Difference

From a reconciliation point of view, many hatred-oriented conflicts begin as revenge-oriented disputes that go beyond retaliation and become an ideology of rejection, alienation and condemnation against anyone opposing the ideology. Revenge has its base in violation, and being emotionally thrown out of balance, with retaliation being vengeful people's answer to getting even.

Hatred may have different motives. It does not necessarily begin with violation, though violation may be one of many starting points. Hatred forms through embracing an ideology that rejects, alienates and condemns others as evil, with few redeeming qualities. Hatred can become an uncompromising point of view that draws the line between good and evil, black and white, us against them, the righteous against the infidel. It can portray itself as a phenomenon that survives on derision and divisiveness, and has difficulty making sense out of any form of reconciliation.

Ironically, conciliators may have a higher probability of helping violated people reconcile their revenge then letting it evolve into a hatred-oriented conflict. In the case study, the true battle was not between the opposing students but between Wayne, Sheila and the extremists. The students felt violated and needed to get emotionally back in balance, a symptom of a revenge-oriented conflict. The extremists wanted to use the conflict as a symbol to exercise violence and destruction on the opposing community—a symptom of a hatred-oriented conflict. From the point of view of a conciliator, Wayne and Sheila's most important success was in diverting a hatred-oriented conflict into a conflict based on revenge, and the extremist's most important failure was their inability to change a revenge-oriented conflict into their ultimate goal of invoking violence and destruction.

If the extremists had provoked the disputing parties to storm the community barricades manned by the state police, then they would have succeeded in their ultimate goal. As described in chapter three, revenge-oriented conflict resolution is based on creating a constructive plan based on justice, and we have an example of this taking place in the current case study when the school developed a Multi-Cultural Awareness Day. Hatred-oriented conflicts may have little investment in plans for reconciliation. Their goal appears to be violence and destruction toward an enemy, as any true fanatic will tell you (Newman, 1986).

The Trap of Hatred-Oriented Conflicts

The entire conflict had blown up in everyone's face. Recently, a medical doctor who practiced legal abortions was shot and killed by someone advocating a Right to Life position on abortion. Certain Pro-Choice advocates were condemning all Right to Life advocates as hypocrites who were willing to take a life, in order to protect life, and extremists on both sides were looking for a forum to condemn the "enemy." These were examples of the climate surrounding the protest at the Mid-State Planned Parenthood Clinic, when Linda was called to reconcile "bad blood" on both sides.

Resentment appeared everywhere. The doctors and nurses at the clinic felt resentful of the protestors who harassed patients entering the building. Protestors resented the disruption of their right to peaceful protest by the constant intrusions from police, and other officials trying to keep a semblance of order. Both groups resented the extremists using the conflict as a media event for violence and destruction toward their enemies. As a conciliator, Linda decided she must separate the fanatics from the legitimate advocates. She brought together leaders from both sides of the dispute and made this statement, "Before we go any further, can we agree that our reconciliation meeting is not a forum to determine when life begins?" After thoughtful discussion both sides acknowledged that such a polarizing issue was un-reconcilable, at this time, and agreed to mediate only those issues causing resentment.

Linda had reconciled the hatred-oriented conflict that was about to consume the Mid-State Planned Parenthood Clinic and shifted to mediating issues surrounding the growing resentment, on both sides. By the end of the mediation, all parties agreed to proper procedures for a legitimate protest. One doctor actually helped the protestors by pointing out medically incorrect information displayed on all of their signs. Linda, having reconciled a hatred-oriented conflict, found herself in a position to mediate issues surrounding a resentment-oriented conflict, in order to finalize an agreement.

In this example, we see hatred being used more as a *trap* than as a problem to be reconciled (Yanay, 2012; Bader & Baird-Windle, 2001). Linda conciliated the Mid-State Planned Parenthood Clinic dispute by redefining it as a conflict based on resentment, not hatred. She avoided the *trap* of reconciling a conflict where violence and destruction were the pre-determined goals of extremists. She acknowledged the relationship between resentment and hatred, making sure that hatred did not dictate the outcome of the conflict resolution process.

Prejudice, Racism and Terrorism

Conciliators who find themselves in the middle of hatred-oriented conflicts most likely could benefit from a perspective on the connection between, prejudice, racism and terrorism. All three appear intrinsically connected with deep roots embedded in the phenomenon of hatred. What differs may be the degree of involvement (Jones et al. 2013; Volkan, 1997, Volkan, 1998).

Prejudice

Prejudice remains the most common, and possibly the most misunderstood of the three, because for many, it lies hidden inside our feelings and beliefs. We experience prejudice when consciously, or unconsciously, we reject others who are different, even though we may vow to effectively practice diversity. For example, teachers who believe all students should have equal rights but treat students from poverty differently than middle-class students are subtly practicing prejudice. Parents who accept their sons and daughters playing soccer but subtly disapprove of a child who dislikes sports is another example of prejudice. Employers that have every intention of including women in their workforce, but hire men because they are more comfortable with the "good old boy network" are practicing prejudice. Members of a community that believe heterogeneous communities are healthy until a person from another race begins dating someone's son or daughter are practicing prejudice.

In all of these examples, consciously or unconsciously, feelings of rejection may be felt within the emotional climate, and a person or a group of people may experience the phenomenon of prejudice. Fortunately for conciliators, prejudice can be the result of ignorance and fear, as much as, any ideology of rejection (Lakritz, 2007; Zanna & Olson, 1994). In the case study, certain students demonstrated prejudice by rejecting the red bandanas of the Native students. Their prejudice was not based on a premeditated ideology but on their ignorance and fear surrounding the events following August 9, 2014. The reconciliation meeting became beneficial for them. They were able to gain an understanding of the Native student's point of view. Conversely, the Native students relieved any harbored prejudice they may have experienced by realizing the common ground both groups possessed.

Conciliators may want to assume, in hatred-oriented conflicts, that the potential for prejudice can be a threat, whenever ignorance and fear are part of a dispute. Experience tells us that many of us harbor prejudice, and on occasion, we find ourselves rejecting people through our ignorance and fear over differences we do not completely understand. Keeping this in mind, it may be essential for conciliators to understand their personal prejudices before reconciling the prejudice of others. In understanding one's ignorance and fear, conciliators can better understand the common ground in those who exemplify a different, race, gender or socio-economic background.

Racism

Racism from the perspective of hatred-oriented conflicts can be defined as prejudice that has gone beyond the experience of rejection to include alienation and condemnation. Not all prejudiced people can be called racists, but all racists harbor some prejudice, through their rejection of others. However, what makes people racists may be their unwillingness to reconcile the ignorance and fear caused by their hatred-oriented conflicts. Instead, racists form an ideology that may include alienation and condemnation of their enemies. For example, in the early 1960s in the United States, students were isolated and condemned for trying to integrate southern universities by an ideology of racism. In South Africa blacks suffered under the rules of "apartheid" and were condemned to an inferior level of society. In the United States, and abroad, Neo-Nazi groups still alienate and condemn blacks, Jews, and other non-Arian groups as a danger to the existence of the Arian race.

These examples of racism go beyond any form of ignorance and fear. People, in these examples, may remain ignorant and afraid, but their rejection has created an ideology that condones alienation and condemnation of their enemies. Alienation and condemnation may be perceived as solutions in establishing hateful feelings against others.

Conciliators note the giant step taken between those who unconsciously practice prejudice and those who avow racism. Beyond attempts to reconcile the rejection formed through ignorance and fear, is the resistance to change that appears at the heart of a dogmatic ideology that thrives on alienation and condemnation (Adamczyk et al. 2014; Fedrickson, 2002). Conciliators might consider that, trying to change racist views of the world may be a direct threat to how these people resolve their conflicts. They may need some "one" or some "thing" to hate in order to avoid doubts about their ideology having flaws, or being faulty in any other way. Alienation may be a place to hide from many complex conflicts facing racists, and condemning others may serve as an ideological solution to many of their problems.

However, conciliators can reconcile conflicts focusing on racism, especially when interventions attack ignorance and fear. For example, there are common methods for the reconciliation of teenagers, who join hateful groups and are swept away by racist ideology (Singh & Aspy, 1997). Their success depends on the conciliator's ability to demonstrate flaws in the ideology, by showing compassion and by creating a dialogue where other viewpoints become acceptable. Though such interventions may be forceful, they are considered legitimate approaches for reconciliation, demonstrating how conciliators can be forceful without using force.

Terrorism

Conciliators may have a better opportunity to experience a complete understanding of hatred-oriented conflicts, when they look through the eyes of a terrorist and realize their prejudice and racism stand as pre-requisites for violence and destruction. Prejudice may be understood, as only the first step, leading to the practice of violence, and racist condemnation of others, may be perceived as— not enough. Terrorists define themselves through their ability to practice violence and inflict some form of destruction on their enemies (Toros, 2008; Moore, 2002). For example, terrorists destroy the World Trade Center and a video tape shows their jubilance and satisfaction in killing thousands of "infidels." A terrorist blows up a building in Oklahoma City and goes to his death unrepentant—finding meaning in his destruction, soldiers practice ethnic cleansing, killing thousands of people with the belief that destroying an entire race is the solution to living in peace. In all of these examples, violence is regarded as mandatory and destruction is perceived as the final solution.

For conciliators, negotiation may not make sense as a form of reconciliation when involving terrorists, and other forms of conflict resolution seems questionable when facing hateful people who practice violence to achieve an ultimate goal of destruction. Negotiating with terrorists, on the world stage, has been such an abysmal failure, for these reasons (Zartman, 2003). A more effective approach may be to isolate terrorists from more moderate factions who *will* negotiate, and are open to reconciliation. However, the influences of terrorist groups such as ISIS are becoming a real threat to the compassionate people of the world. This can be understood in their use of violence; even though, their weakness may lie in the number of people they represent (Corn, 2001). Unfortunately, the Internet gives them power they do not deserve. For conciliators, winning the hearts and minds of moderate people caught within a climate of hatred seems one of the most effective remedies to hatred-oriented conflicts based on terrorism. Like any extremist, terrorists can lose power when they are isolated, and are considered a fringe element of society.

They can gain power, not through their violence, but through convincing others that violence seems justified. Terrorists appear to have an investment in forcing their enemies to use violence. Through retaliatory violence, they can seek the support of moderates caught in the middle of violence emanating from both sides. For example, in the case study, the extremists wanted to convince the Native and "white" communities to join them so they could gain legitimate power for their violence and destruction. Wayne and Sheila's ability to win the hearts and minds of moderates, on both sides, probably saved the community from further violence and destruction. The terrorists' "Achilles' heel" might be found in the ability of conciliators to present a perception of terrorism as an extremist activity that serves as an ineffective form of conflict resolution. Yet, the "Achilles heel" for conciliators may be the influence of the internet and other media devices that help terrorists appear more powerful than they are in physical reality.

Psychological Tough Mindedness (Facing the Fear)

Reconciling hatred-oriented disputes that involve violence and destruction may not be for the timid at heart. They may require a certain tough mindedness on the part of conciliators to sustain the fallout of violence and the loss experienced by witnessing constant moments of destruction. Some people say that fear is a great "motivator." It may be the opposite where fear is a great "destabilizer." For example, the famous conciliator, Jimmy Carter, has reconciled disputes where continued violence and destruction prevail. It is his psychological tough mindedness that helped him remain non-judgmental when trying to reconcile hatred-oriented conflicts in hot spots around the world. His ability to face the fear and uncertainty in the presence of overwhelming conflict is a part of what has made him an effective conciliator. (Toros, 2008; Troester, 1996). We can see the same tough mindedness demonstrated in other examples from this chapter. Wayne and Sheila did not back down to threats of violence and destruction, nor did they try to avoid them. In the two meetings preceding the reconciliation meeting, they allowed extremists to vent their feelings, knowing their survival as effective conciliators depended on being perceived as fair while not backing down from the fear generated by the extremists. They absorbed the abuse of extremists and remained above retaliation or negative judgments, in order to reconcile the conflict at the final meeting. Their tough mindedness gave the reconciliation a chance to run its course, and let moderate people state their points of view.

Linda, at the Mid-State Planned Parenthood Clinic, is another example of a conciliator demonstrating tough mindedness in her ability to face the fear of the abortion dispute. Instead of becoming trapped in the extreme rhetoric of hatred-filled protestors and clinic personnel, she held her ground and stated there would be no reconciliation meeting until opposing sides agreed the meeting was not a forum for determining when life began. She remained the constant figure in the reconciliation. She allowed both sides to resolve their resentment and frustration while limiting the fear both sides demonstrated for each other's positions.

In all of these examples, the conciliators act as models for successful reconciliation. They face fear-producing people without becoming fearful themselves. Their tough mindedness demonstrates power without having to use force. They model a form of reconciliation based on power—the power of not being afraid. In the course of world events, not all disputes are resolved through peaceful negotiations. Countries have entered countless wars where negotiations have broken down and violence and destruction prevail. However, when the wars have ended and the violence and destruction subside, it may require tough minded people to pick up the pieces. In this regard, conciliators may find themselves preventing hatred-oriented conflicts from engulfing the climate of a school, an abortion clinic or a country. They become the tough minded people who are not afraid, and remain committed to avoiding violence and destruction, when hateful people try to inflict it on others. They hold their ground unafraid when violence and destruction make their mark on the psychological landscape of our society.

A Peacemaking Alternative: A Climate of Compassion

It was December 14, 2012, and the country remained in shock after a lone gunman crashed into the Sandy Hook Elementary School killing twenty children and six staff members. The media ran images of the unspeakable tragedy, while the country was waiting for an appropriate response. There were few people around the world who did not believe a response was justified. The climate was changing and America had lost its innocence with the death of innocent children. However, a remarkable phenomenon had taken place shortly after the incident that showed a side of human behavior—most notably recorded during times of crisis. There were countless examples of total strangers reaching out to family and friends in the community. People wanted to help in some way—no matter the time or money needed to accomplish this goal.

Joan was a concerned neighbor in Newtown, Connecticut, where the tragedy was felt by many families, with one or more children being among the victims. These were families she recognized but beyond that, had little contact with them. It was not that she disliked or rejected them in any way. She *was* a busy person with a demanding job and spent most of his waking hours on work related issues. On December 14 that changed for Joan. She found herself reaching out to people she hardly knew.

One evening shortly after the tragedy, she attended a meeting at the Town Hall in Newtown. She noticed an overall acceptance between the participants. She became involved in the lives of strangers, and she was discussing intimate thoughts and feelings with them. Two weeks prior to this meeting, she could not imagine sharing such matters with total strangers, but now she was confirming their right to grieve. Joan wanted to be a part of her community's healing process and she went out of her way to offer support.

After the meeting Joan made a point to call certain people she met at the Town Hall, and continued support by listening to their problems. She started a financial relief fund for the victims she met at the meeting, to guarantee their lives did not spiral into deeper tragedy. She noticed her efforts were matched by others who were doing their part to keep the community together. From December to May the level of compassion among the Connecticut community was matched by other examples of compassion throughout the country. The United States was in a climate of compassion and Joan became a willing participant in supporting and maintaining that climate.

In May 2013 the climate began to change. The gunman that performed this tragedy was dead and the media focus had shifted to other shootings and conflicts that took up a new focus and new interest with the general public. From

December 2012 through May 2013, efforts were still being made to help families of this tragedy, yet the climate of good will that enveloped Joan's community had changed. Special funds created for victims and ongoing connections to prior strangers were still a part of people's everyday pattern of existence, but the unity and spirit that rallied them together slowly disappeared when legislation to help prevent such tragedies died and was forgotten in the Congress of the United States.

Upon reflection, Joan concluded that enough people had committed themselves to seeing the crisis through, even though, the climate of good will that dominated people's behavior was gone. She realized that an old Chinese proverb was accurate, namely, "Overwhelming crisis can bring opportunity." The events of December 14 had thrown the Newtown community out of balance and compassion was needed to reconcile the overwhelming violence and destruction it had suffered. She realized that it was possible for strangers to work together, with the primary goal being the creation of good will, and she knew that such a climate could produce remarkable behavior in people, who normally were focused on more mundane feelings and behaviors. She was proud of her country for showing compassion but wished that such compassion could be maintained over a longer period of time.

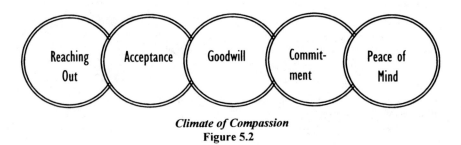

Climate of Compassion
Figure 5.2

Reaching Out

The first stage in a climate of compassion, we see people reaching out to others with the intention to help them in some way. In the case study, Joan and members of her community reached out to those affected by the tragedies of December 14, 2012. The country experienced shock and feeling out of balance, and was reaching out to bring balance back into people's lives. Reaching out can become our first gesture of compassion when others are in need. Whether the gesture is on a grand scale as during December 14, or reaching out to a colleague at work who is going through troubled times, the gesture remains the same. It is the recognition that someone needs your help and you are willing to help them.

Ironically, the gesture of reaching out seems to be made easier by the magnitude of the crisis. Joan and members of her community began reaching out at the Town Hall. The immense shock of Sandy Hook compelled them to help in some way. Their willingness to help seemed measured by the magnitude of the event.

In times of crisis, reaching out can be our way of offering our humanity to others who are in trouble, and during a major crisis compassion seems an appropriate priority for those who are affected by the suffering and pain of others.

However, reaching out to others may not require a major crisis for a climate of compassion to exist. A climate of compassion can begin by reaching out regardless of the crisis's magnitude, and from a conciliation stand point reaching out can be the activity that helps people, in dispute, avoid crisis. Many hatred-oriented disputes are neutralized by one person reaching out with compassion, where others are creating a climate of rejection and alienation. Sometimes we overlook countless examples of people showing compassion. The crisis seems mundane and un-dramatic, and sometimes we forget to reach out for the same reasons (figure 5.2).

Acceptance

Acceptance of others appears less difficult to achieve during a major crisis. The crisis supplies all involved with ample common ground. During December 14 people from different walks of life, with little in common, were bound together by the tragedies of that day. In a sense, the walls between them were dropped and acceptance of others became their way of stating, "We are in this together." What can make this possible is the common ground created by the crisis. The more people experience similar feelings and beliefs the more the concept of acceptance seems possible.

However, acceptance may not need a major crisis to establish common ground (Gaylin, 2009; Gaylin, 1989). Those who reach out can find common ground if they are willing to accept the differences in others. By accepting differences, what remains *is* the common ground. In a multi-cultural society, reaching out and accepting cultural differences may go a long way in establishing common ground, and lessen the chance that we find acceptance only in crisis. Effective conciliators seem to understand this phenomenon. Their ability to reach out and accept differences in people, demonstrates their understanding of a climate of compassion. Having compassion for others may require acceptance, and acceptance of others may become one more step to successful reconciliation. Acceptance of others, also can be a major hurdle in reconciling the rejection found in hatred-oriented conflicts (figure 5.2).

Goodwill

In the case study, Joan found herself missing a certain feeling generated during the time period between December 2012 and May, 2013. She missed the good will found in the climate of compassion surrounding the Sandy Hook tragedy, when people reached out and accepted each other. She realized how such a grand demonstration of compassion can be contagious—the more good–will shared during tragic moments, the more good–will created. She also realized how good will can act as an expression of power in a climate of compassion in soothing people's pain, and how it can be that element that drives people to make commitments to others. She recalled that after the tragedy, many people in her community reached out and accepted others, and many were proud of the good will such behavior generated.

For most of us, good will seems easier to sustain during a crisis than in everyday living. In a crisis, our individual differences usually are put aside in order to successfully resolve problems (Lanceley, 2002). In everyday living, we may become more discriminating. We may find ourselves involved in separate lives, with separate routines. The ability of people to maintain goodwill in everyday living may determine the strength and durability found in any climate of compassion. It is during these moments when reaching out and accepting others are put to the test. Keeping this in mind, conciliators should consider how fragile good will can be, and how it should not be discredited no matter where it comes from.

The events of Sandy Hook showed a community practicing its humanity, and the good will generated during this tragic period created bonds between people that are still functioning over time. However, in spite of its power to influence people over time, good will still appears the most fragile element in a climate of compassion, and it rarely continues without people making a commitment for its survival (figure 5.2).

Commitment

In a climate of compassion people's good will can survive, by making a commitment. For example, Joan made a commitment to call her neighbors from the Town Hall meeting and she further committed herself to creating financial support for families of those affected by the tragedy in her community. Goodwill can be a magnanimous gesture, but without commitment, such a gesture may have a remarkably short "shelf life." Commitment can become the element in a climate of compassion that remains long after an open outpouring of goodwill has lost its popularity.

Joan wished the level of goodwill experienced in her community, between December and May, could have lasted longer. However, she was proud of her commitment to others, while at the same time showing disappointment in the government's commitment to facing such problems. She realized that good people had committed themselves to seeing the tragedy through, and she believed higher levels of support could be created if those in power showed a similar commitment long after the emotional climate had changed.

A climate of compassion can begin with reaching out and accepting others and seems most recognized through its goodwill, but becomes sustained through its commitment to others. Therefore, commitment to reaching out and accepting others and a continuance of goodwill when such practices have lost their popularity, may determine a far deeper understanding of compassion (Theresa & Lovett, 1993). For example, the climate of compassion surrounding Nelson Mandela during his many years of incarceration was based on his continued commitment to all races even though a climate of goodwill returned only after his release from prison. (Nwagbara, 2013; Sampson, 2000) On a smaller scale, conciliators working behind the scenes to create goodwill during a conflict, show their commitment to reconciliation; even when, the intentions of others may be questionable (figure 5.2).

Peace of Mind

The person who coined the phrase "it is better to give than receive" was on to something. The final stage in a climate of compassion might be the peace of mind people feel when they have done all that is possible to help others. Unlike the instability found in a climate of hatred, a climate of compassion can create stability and can give purpose to our human condition. Compassion can develop into a commitment that may take us outside ourselves, in search of common ground, and it may create peace of mind within ourselves, after finding it. In a world filled with conflict, a climate of compassion may help people to reach out and accept others, while demonstrating a commitment to the practice of good-will, and peace of mind may become life's reward for our involvement in compassionate behavior.

Joan was shaken by the tragedy at Sandy Hook. She needed an outlet for her feelings. She reached out to members of her community and accepted them unconditionally. Through her efforts, and the efforts of others, she created good-will and participated in the climate of goodwill, until the emotional climate changed, but for Joan it did not end there. She extended good will by making commitments to follow through on activities in her community. Upon reflection, she acknowledged the importance of her efforts but also realized the lack of effort from her political leaders. She recognized the compassion shared by many people throughout the world in response to the tragedy, and such thoughts gave her peace of mind. She knew that the tragic deaths of the children from Sandy Hook Elementary School would not be forgotten, but also she knew that compassion had not helped to stabilize her country's response to violence. She realized that not all weapons to combat hatred were delivered through the use of force (figure 5.2).

Cultural Implications

Prejudice and hatred exist all over the world. To threaten, injure, or kill innocent bystanders because of political, religious, ethnical, racial or ideological conflict is an ancient form of human behavior. We humans are social beings and from an early age we become influenced by the hatred and prejudices of the members of the group we belong to and we view certain groups accordingly. Globally, the climate of hatred is formed through peoples' allegiance to a common cause against a common enemy (Hamburg & Hamburg, 2004). If we look back at the last hundred years we will find examples where atrocities were done in the name of race, ideology, politics and religion. Here are some examples. The first one is the holocaust during the Second World War in which mostly Jews along with various other ethnic and political groups were murdered by the Nazi regime.

Another is when one million people perished, and as many as 250,000 women were raped in the ethnic and politically motivated genocide of the mostly Tutsi population in Rwanda in 1994. Then there is the massacre of the Muslim population in Bosnia in the 1990s.

When a population experiences such atrocities, the victims in a climate of hatred will keep alive feelings of condemnation toward the perpetrating group from one generation to another. For instance, even six decades after the Indian partition, India and Pakistan have still not healed from its wounds. Nearly one million people were killed and 14 million Muslims, Hindus, and Sikhs were uprooted and displaced in the largest and most terrible exchange of population known to history. The partition continues to influence how the peoples and states of postcolonial South Asia see their past, present and future. India and Pakistan have been at war twice since the partition and are still arguing over the landlocked region of Kashmir. Both countries have nuclear weapons. A large portion of their budgets goes to defense and the military. Many believe that partition not only broke the unity of India, but also took away the sense of belonging for many people who were torn apart from their native regions. The generation which had been through the partition is still alive and the politicians on both sides are maintaining the climate of hatred in their respective countries.

The conciliators must seek ways to expand favorable contacts between people from both groups and nations to break the climate of hatred because without positive interaction the stories of horrifying mass violence will pass on from generation to generation and will keep the cycle of hatred going on through numerous generations.

Notes

4. Information on hatred from a mental health perspective can be found in the following book. Ladd, P. D. & Churchill, A. (2012). *Person-Centered diagnosis and treatment: A model for empowering clients.* London: Jessica Kingsley Publishers. 304–321.

5. Also in Ladd, P. D. (2009). *Emotional addictions: A reference book for addictions and mental health counselors.* Lanham, MD: University Press of America. 217–238.

Part II:
Emotional Climates That Promote
Mental Illness

Chapter 6

Apathy and Conciliation

Apathy may be considered by some as a mental disorder, or a lack of emotion by those experiencing it. Professionals may confuse apathy with depression where in depression people care too much, while in apathy they care too little, even though, people show similar behavior. For others, the experience of apathy resembles post-traumatic stress, only presenting with many small traumas as opposed to one or two large traumas. Exposure to trauma and violence through the media, personal experiences, and chronic trauma may numb our senses and question the meaning in our lives. Yet, apathy does not only happen within people. We experience apathy as a backdrop to our social interactions. A climate of apathy may have as much influence on us as the experience of chronic trauma, and occasionally chronic trauma is responsible for an apathetic environment.

In this chapter, we are considering apathy as an emotional climate that happens to people when they experience too much trauma. Apathy is best described as a series of losses. Loss of other emotions by feeling numb, begins this downward spiral. This is followed by a loss of meaning, where not only are you feeling numb to the world, but you also do not care one way or the other. Not caring over time leads to a loss of respect in yourself and the environment around you. Ultimately, people experience a loss of hope and settle into a way of life with little positive feelings for the future.

Being in a climate of apathy can be a dangerous place for those looking to improve their present life. This may be why addiction and mental illness can be associated with a pattern of apathy—where some addicts become suicidal while others act out acute bouts of violence. Furthermore, a climate of apathy can be the breeding ground for depression, and other mood disorders where the environment in which you live may have a strong impact on your mental health. A climate of apathy may be fertile ground for many emotional conflicts and disputes. Conciliators may need to understand an apathetic climate if they want to be successful in helping others in gaining meaning, respect and hope. It may be that conciliating a climate of apathy requires fundamental human skills and not complex formulas for reconciliation. Love, caring, listening and creating a climate of hope may be the skills necessary in overcoming a climate of apathy.

In the case study, you will learn about a cosmetologist who acted as a conciliator in order the change the apathetic climate surrounding her mother and her friends into one of hope. It may be in certain situations that changing the climate is easier than changing an individual in that climate. This became the case for Darlene who paid back the people who raised her by changing a climate of apathy into a climate of hope.

Case Study

"Lincoln Street" was the term commonly used in describing a neighborhood in a rundown section of a struggling city in the Midwest. At one time, families took pride in the name but that was many years ago. There was little to be proud of on a street filled with crack houses, garbage, gutted buildings and drug addiction. Lincoln Street had gone through a series of declines, and the people who stayed had declined with it. No one understood this better than Darlene who grew up there, and through the help of a scholarship, moved on to a professional life in cosmetology. Now, she stood looking down the street of her youth, wondering what the future held for her neighborhood.

Darlene had come home to take care of her widowed mother and to start work as an instructor at the city's community college. Moving in with her mother seemed like an obvious place to regroup. Her career at the community college was flourishing, and students found her skillful and approachable. Yet, something was wrong. Every evening she returned to Lincoln Street and felt a wall of despair hit her, as she walked from the bus to her mother's rundown duplex. Many times, she would think, "What if I didn't have my work? How would I survive these stifling living conditions?" Adding to these feelings was the attitude of her mother and her friends. The women she most admired, when growing up, now seemed lost and out of touch with their place in life. Darlene thought, "Here are women who encouraged me to better myself, and now they keep slipping further into neglect."

It took time but Darlene finally reached the conclusion that starting a new life was not going to be successful unless something dramatic was done to the emotional climate surrounding the women she admired. She was committed to her work and her mother, and now she decided to make a commitment to the neighborhood. She invited her mother and all her friends to be subjects in her cosmetology class. They were going to get a makeover. At first, none of them wanted to go. They were ashamed of their appearance. Darlene told them, "You would be helping some dedicated students learn about bettering themselves— just like you helped me." This statement worked. Even though these elderly women were numb to self-improvement, they would not deny younger people an opportunity to improve their lives.

On a Tuesday morning, Darlene led a group of eight frightened women into her class of fifteen young cosmetology students. They were going to spend the morning getting a complete treatment from head to toe. The students were excited, and especially kind and thoughtful. Laughter, joking, storytelling and huge expressions of feelings and opinions filled the room. Darlene thought, "Now these are more like the ladies I remember." By the end of the morning, eight elderly women emerged from the classroom transformed both physically and emotionally. It was hard to recognize them in both behavior and appearance.

In the weeks that followed, you could observe any one of these elderly women walking up and down Lincoln Street where people commented on how beautiful they looked. Something different was in their eyes. They were beginning a transformation that was filled with hope. Lincoln Street still had problems, but for these women respect was no longer a cynical memory.

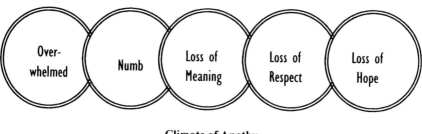

Climate of Apathy
Figure 6.1

Understanding an Emotional Climate of Apathy

Overwhelmed

There may be a certain irony in calling a climate of apathy emotional. In many respects, it is the absence of emotion that makes it different than, for example, a climate of anger or revenge. People, in a climate of apathy, find themselves traumatized by everyday experiences, until the trauma becomes overwhelming, and they begin to shut down emotionally. This process of being overwhelmed is not an experience that can be attributed to one traumatic event, but is a series of small traumas that eventually accumulates—causing people to feel empty and devoid of feeling (Cunningham, 2003). In the case study, the elderly women of Lincoln Street had experienced too many traumas over the years and were in decline, along with the decaying buildings. They had pulled back within themselves, in order to survive the overwhelming trauma in their lives, but the cost of surviving in this manner was extremely high. The trauma chipped away at meaningful experiences—leaving them with a sense of being numb and out of touch.

They tried to be gracious to Darlene, when being with her and her mother, but their hospitality was forced with little emotional substance behind it. They had become overwhelmed with trauma, and it was showing up in subtle, half-hearted gestures of an era that had passed. Their emotions had retreated to a supposedly safer place within themselves, where they feigned protection from the next round of subtle trauma. However, by individually pulling back, they added trauma to the overall climate of the community, causing the neighborhood further decline, and the decline in the emotional climate of their neighborhood, became their demise. Subtly and indirectly, the climate of their surroundings added trauma to their lives, causing them to retreat further into themselves (figure 6.1).

Numb

In a climate of apathy, people overwhelmed by trauma may withdraw into themselves by becoming numb to their surroundings. In the case study, the hardship of living on Lincoln Street became an ongoing trauma for those who remained in the neighborhood. They had to "tough out" the hard times and endure the declining conditions. They survived by becoming numb to the hardships surrounding them. However, the price for becoming emotionally numb had its side effects. Darlene recognized that the women she admired no longer had the passion she remembered in her youth. Being numb helped them through the hard times, but deterred their desire for new experiences. They had lost the sensitivity and energy for recognizing life's positive and peaceful moments.

Unfortunately, people who become numb may not realize their loss. A climate of apathy can be fed by too many traumas, where becoming numb eventually becomes its own trauma namely, the trauma of missed opportunities (Wentzel & Brysiewicz, 2014; Herman, 1997). Under such conditions, significant moments can be lost, because they are not recognized as important. It is highly doubtful that Darlene's mother and her friends would get a "makeover" on their own. Hard times made them numb to such opportunities, and their numbness seemed stronger than their desire to experience something new and exciting. They were coping the best way they could under, what were perceived as, deteriorating circumstances. They had given up emotionally, and were only going through the motions of being with each other; even though, the energy for true involvement was not there. In a climate of apathy, becoming numb can emerge as a common reaction to, too much trauma. It can become a way of protecting oneself from constant hurt and pain. It may allow people to continue existing in a climate filled with trauma, but at the expense of emotional involvement and personal energy (figure 6.1).

Loss of Meaning

People going through the motions of being involved in a climate of apathy may eventually lose meaning in their everyday lives. They may practice the same routines as before, but the meaning in their behavior may be absent. The experience of constant trauma and numbed feelings can leave little room for personal meaning. When people lose what is meaningful to them, a threshold can be crossed from feeling numb and experiencing physical and emotional exhaustion, to not caring anymore, and becoming exhausted spiritually. Many residents of

Lincoln Street had crossed that threshold, and stopped caring about the community. Not only were they numb and exhausted, but they also showed signs of being spiritually bankrupt. Beyond anything else, Darlene found this phenomenon the most disturbing. She understood the physical decline of the neighborhood, but was unsettled with its spiritual decline. All of her role models had lost the spirit she most admired while growing up. The spirit that helped her obtain a scholarship, and become a successful teacher originated in these people, and now that spirit was gone.

One of the dangers found in a climate of apathy is that trauma may lead to being numb, and being numb may lead to losing meaning, even in the most dedicated and idealistic people. Sometimes those who are the most involved can suffer the bigger losses in meaning. They are willing to constantly endure trauma in order to meet their goals. It is not uncommon for dedicated people to become numb and spiritually exhausted, especially when meaningful experiences are exposed to constant trauma. Apathy has a way of negatively affecting those who care the most (Thomas et al. 2013; Maryhen, Kreider & Zupnanicic, 2000). Darlene understood this, and tried to put meaning back into the lives of her mother and her friends with the "makeover." She was hoping for a spiritual makeover, as much as, a physical one. She challenged her mentors to become spiritually renewed and start showing the same qualities that inspired her while growing up in the community (figure 6.1).

Loss of Respect

A climate of apathy can feel like a downward spiral that begins when trauma after trauma makes people numb to their surroundings, until they eventually lose meaning in their lives. Without meaning, they lose respect for themselves or others. In the case study, Lincoln Street was filled with people who fit this description. Darlene's mother and her friends were embarrassed when offered a "makeover" because respect was taken from them, and it was hard for meaning or respect to be associated with their deteriorating life styles. This can be one of the serious dangers associated with an apathetic climate. Apathy can become a method of survival and may leave little meaning for the experience of respect. When people stop believing in their surroundings, it may not be long before they start acting in disrespectful ways. Darlene's mentors behaved more honorably than many apathetic people. They limited the lack of respect to themselves.

However, Lincoln Street was filled with others who demonstrated their disrespect by approaching everyday living with an attitude of cynicism—making them capable of negating any growth or positive change. To a certain degree, cynicism is the language of choice for people caught within a climate of apathy. A cynical attitude allows an apathetic person to remain numb, find little meaning in life, and disrespect others who are in search of meaning. If left unchecked, cynicism may develop into a lifestyle where peoples' cynical behavior seems justifiable. This can make positive change appear as a meaningless exercise. Helping apathetic people make positive changes becomes difficult. They are numb, lack meaning and have little respect for it. It is also why Darlene's make-over experiment was so successful. The makeover was about regaining respect and making positive change meaningful once more (figure 6.1).

Loss of Hope

Darlene understood that offering a "makeover" to her mother and her friends might improve their self-image, giving them hope for the future. The "makeover" was all about hope, and not only for her mother and her friends. When they walked down Lincoln Street it generated a climate of hope in others. Here we see how a climate of apathy and hopelessness may be intricately connected, and how an apathetic climate can dissolve, when hope is entered back into the equation. Apathy is based on surviving the present, where hope is directed toward having a future. The "makeover" addressed both and gave Darlene hope that her mentors were not in permanent decline. A climate of apathy ultimately cannot survive when hope is accepted as an alternative.

In a climate of apathy, feeling hopeless can be the ultimate form of despair. It can increase trauma, leave people numb, wreck meaning in their lives and cause them to disrespect others. In an emotional climate where hope is considered important, trauma seems more manageable, people are less likely to be numb, meaning is sustained and respect can be found in peoples' behavior. This case study shows an example of an apathetic climate reconciled by the power of hope (figure 6.1).

Conciliating Apathy

Several themes come to the surface when thinking about apathy-oriented conflicts. The most obvious being, the experience of apathy seems more like an affliction than a solvable conflict (Green, 2004; Goodwin & Attias, 1999). Apathy-oriented conflicts are similar to resentment-oriented conflicts. Both are subtle and happen over a period of time, with resentment being frustrating over time and apathy being traumatic over time, and neither having the immediacy of anger-oriented conflict. Under these circumstances, problems in a climate of apathy can easily be embraced as a part of a life style, not as conflicts. However, life styles and conflicts differ, and how they are perceived, can have an impact on peoples' behavior. Life styles are perceived as ongoing, with no intended end in sight. Conflicts are different. They have a beginning, middle and are intended to end at some point in time. Conciliators first may need to demonstrate, to apathetic people, that apathy is more than an affliction. It can be perceived as a series of conflicts with a beginning, middle and an end.

The second observation is that people come from different orientations, when considering the most appropriate group to manage apathy-oriented conflicts. Religious and spiritual leaders come to mind, especially when people enter the later stages of apathy. Loss of meaning, respect and hope are common themes in religious and spiritual doctrine (Becvar, 1997). Counselors, psychologists and psychiatrists also appear in a position to treat apathy. It can be seen as a subtle form of post-traumatic stress, and in some cases, depression (Agibalova et al. 2014; Terr, 1990).

However, in our case study, a cosmetologist treated apathy by acting as a conciliator, where she saw her mentors suffering from apathy-oriented conflicts, found in the emotional climate of their community. She specifically focused on what she saw in the community's *climate of apathy,* and made no reference to anyone's psychological or emotional problems. Her purpose was not directed toward seeking any higher power. That does not mean the people of Lincoln Street would not benefit from psychological or spiritual leadership, but in this case, Darlene was practicing conflict resolution, where being a conciliator does not supplant more comprehensive interventions found in psychology or spirituality, but compliments them.

The Anger, Resentment, Apathy Connection

Conciliators should be aware that some conflicts are the end product of a pattern of substitutions, where the original conflict is resolved by substituting another conflict in its place, and by substituting one emotional conflict for another, people indirectly practice an ineffective form of conflict resolution. This phenomenon is clearly evident in many apathy-oriented conflicts. For example, a wife may get angry at her husband for going out at night and not informing her of his activities. If the conflict is not resolved, she may, over a period of time, begin feeling resentment in place of her anger. She has resolved her anger-oriented conflicts by feeling resentful. Over time, if her husband does not change, then she may resolve her resentment by becoming apathetic. Now she feels numb but less frustrated with her husband's behavior. However, conflicts surrounding her husband may not be over.

At some point her relationship with him may lose its meaning, and self-respect and lack of respect for him may bring her to the conclusion that the marriage offers little hope. At this point, she may solve her apathy-oriented conflicts by getting a divorce. Unfortunately, in this example, what may appear as two people falling out of love can be understood as a series of unresolved emotions-oriented conflicts. Where one disputed situation, unfortunately became automatically *substituted* for another. In this particular pattern, apathy becomes the final destination in conflicts containing too much anger and resentment. That is why the popular term "burn out" or "being burned out" seems so descriptive. Certain apathy-oriented conflicts are at the end of anger and resentment oriented conflicts that went unresolved (Ashanasy, Hartel & Zerbe, 2000). For conciliators, making people aware of this substitution process may give apathetic people an understanding of their trauma. With understanding comes meaning, and loss of meaning can be at the center of apathy-oriented conflicts. When conciliators bring meaning back into apathy-oriented conflicts, they can create hope, and people with hope may feel less apathetic.

Apathy and Its Relationship to Post-Traumatic Stress

Post-traumatic stress is caused by serious trauma that leaves an emotional mark, where peoples' personal existence seems threatened by their experience. For example, a war veteran has post-traumatic stress symptoms from the experience of battle, or someone survives an accident where others were killed and has symptoms following their recovery (Armstrong & Rose, 1997). In both cases flash backs, anxiety and loss of sleep are common. If left untreated, these symptoms go underground and resurface when triggered by cues that remind people of the incident. In most cases, post-traumatic stress victims cope with their trauma by becoming numb to their feelings—as a way of protection against recurring traumatic episodes (Gibson, 2000). However, traumatic events can overwhelm a person or group of people, making the trauma difficult to forget, and becoming numb to these feelings can result in an unsuccessful attempt at coping with the trauma.

A climate of apathy is not caused by a large trauma as in post-traumatic stress, but a series of small apathy-oriented disputes that accumulate over time in the emotional climate of the group, and they leave a traumatic emotional mark on the people within the climate. Apathy does not contain obvious trauma that appears to threaten one's existence. It can be a series of small, subtle traumas that add up over time, eventually making people feel overwhelmed and numb to their feelings. In this way, apathy has a connection to post-traumatic stress in that both begin with trauma and both use becoming numb to feelings as a coping mechanism. Professionals trained in recognizing post-traumatic stress know that a post-traumatic stress debriefing can be a common method used in treating this phenomenon.

During a debriefing, people are asked to describe the trauma, while expressing their deepest feelings for each event that took place. In this way, post-traumatic stress victims are debriefed by getting feelings out before they go underground. If a debriefing does not take place, people suffering from post-traumatic stress may develop post-traumatic stress disorder, and eventually may need psychological help at a future point in their lives (Regel, 2009; Williams & Sommer, 1994). Conciliators can borrow from procedures used in post-traumatic stress debriefings by helping apathetic people debrief in more symbolic ways. In the case study, Darlene took her mentors for a "makeover" and the student cosmetologists helped them face years of trauma and subtle degradation, by letting them tell their stories and share their opinions. In an indirect way, they allowed the women of Lincoln Street to debrief the subtle trauma that had accumulated over time. In doing this, new meaning was restored and self-respect became a meaningful experience.

The Power of Active Listening

Active listening is a skill, where one person puts his or her feelings and opinions to the side, and focuses on what another person is saying and feeling, followed by giving a brief synopsis of what was said. In this way, the person listening gives feedback to the other, that he or she was heard and understood (Moss, 1999). When this skill is practiced with a genuine desire to listen to another, the message is sent to the speaker that what they are saying means something and is important. This is why active listening can be such an important skill in the helping professions. Listening to others, can give meaning to the thoughts and feelings of people who share their problems (Curtis, 1998). This can be true in helping people suffering from apathy-oriented disputes. People in a climate of apathy have experienced too much trauma, are numb to their feelings, and are susceptible to losing meaning in their lives. Conciliators who actively listen to apathetic people send a message that what is being said has meaning, and that their lives are meaningful—no matter how much they have lost over time. For example, the teacher with high ideals who experiences constant trauma from students, administrators and parents may need an ally who will actively listen, in order to restore or keep alive important ideals and values. Unfortunately, without someone to actively listen, an idealistic teacher may become apathetic and close down emotionally, leading to loss of meaning for these ideals.

Becoming apathetic to one's ideals does not come from a change in philosophy but from experiencing too much trauma. Some of our best teachers may leave the profession, each year. They may become exhausted from the stress of living up to their ideals, while experiencing overwhelming trauma. Under these circumstances, allies make excellent conciliators, if they are willing to actively listen. However, this phenomenon does not only apply to teachers. People in many walks of life have an opportunity to "play it safe" or to risk their ideals in professions or avocations filled with stress. The choice to continue risking one's beliefs, even when feeling traumatized and numb, can be reinforced by an ally who actively listens to what is important and meaningful to that person. The power of active listening is that it can restore meaning to ideals that have been battered and torn, and it allows an idealistic person to continue practicing these ideals, in spite of their stress (McGuire, 2001; DeCarvalho, 1991). Listening becomes the glue that holds people together, regardless of the stress associated with many traumatic experiences in our jobs, families, schools or communities.

Cynicism: The Language of Apathy

We have talked about how in a climate of apathy, too much trauma can lead to being numb, and numbed feelings can eventually lead to meaning disappearing in people's lives. Until now, these symptoms could easily be explained as existential problems. Losing meaning in life seems a highly personal undertaking, and that may be why so many people, living in a climate of apathy, seem so lonely. However, an apathetic climate has an interpersonal side, especially at the point where apathetic people lose respect for others. The loss of respect for one's self can leave people vulnerable to also losing respect for others, and it often manifests itself through cynical language and behavior. If trauma becomes a constantly overwhelming experience, and people become numb to their feelings, and meaning has left their everyday living, it seems a small leap to visualize a world from a disrespectful point of view, and begin behaving in cynical ways.

It may be important for conciliators to realize that, in a climate of apathy, cynical behavior can be symptomatic of being overwhelmed by trauma and loss of meaning, and being overly critical of cynical behavior, misses an opportunity to help people with their apathy. For example, nurses who work with terminally ill patients understand the cynical behavior of patients questioning meaning in the last moments of their lives. They are trained to listen and respect their condition—no matter how disrespectful their behavior may appear. They listen, because they understand their disrespect emanates from the trauma of coping with a terminal illness (Cole, 2001). In the same regard, people in a climate of apathy who have become cynical may not be physically at the end of their lives but they may still find little respect for their surroundings. For these people, cynical language and behavior seems appropriate. It becomes the culmination of traumas causing them to feel devoid of feelings. Unfortunately, it may be the cynicism that is heard by others and not the emotional climate behind it.

Conciliators have an opportunity to go beyond the language of cynicism and hear the underlying message that may speak to a loss of meaning and respect. In the case study, Darlene's great dilemma was in watching her mentors, the women from her childhood, deteriorate. The gift they gave her was a sense of purpose to further her education, and become a success. The apathy-oriented conflicts they experienced, over the years, took that away from them, leaving in its place a climate of apathy with little purpose and direction. To use a metaphor, they were a ship without a rudder. They were too traumatized and numb to take charge of their future, leaving them little purpose or direction to begin again. Darlene changed that when her "makeover" gave purpose to something far deeper than their appearance. She gave them hope for the future, by rekindling their purpose in the community—a purpose they had lost years before.

A Peacemaking Alternative: A Climate of Hope

They were from the upper reaches of the Canadian wilderness—seven aboriginal adolescents who sniffed glue, smoked marijuana, and were dropouts from the Canadian public school system. To the elders of the local tribe, they were "loafers around the fort"—a saying that depicted Native people in a most derogatory manner. Counselors, psychologists, and social workers had taken their turns trying to reach them, with little success. Here were seven boys who had given up. They didn't care about themselves and had little use for others. These were the conditions described to Shane, an aboriginal healer, who was approached by the elders of the tribe, to make a difference in their lives. It was a big responsibility and he did not take it lightly, but what could he accomplish where others had failed?

He met the boys one afternoon in a group home that was located on their reservation, and where all seven stayed as a last resort from years of rejection by parents and relatives. His first impression was that each boy seemed empty, lacking little energy for even discussion. He decided to take time, over the next few weeks, and get to know them. He was looking for any spark of life that he could use to make a connection. As he observed them, it became obvious that beyond the use of drugs, music seemed one of the few experiences that roused their interest. One day he asked them, "Would you mind if I brought in some Native music? It is unlike your music but it is music just the same." They passively nodded their heads and cynically said, "Go for it!"

The next day Shane started with a recording of a chant that was used at certain feast days during the year. One boy said, "What the hell is that all about?" Shane said, "It is your ancestors coming alive and speaking to you." The boy cynically replied, "What do you mean? I don't see any ancestors coming alive." Shane said, "Just watch me for a moment." Now all the boys were circling him—waiting for something to happen. Shane looked to the sky and spread his arms out straight. He closed his eyes and appeared to be meditating on some unknown source. All the while, a constant chant was emanating from the tape recorder that he brought with him. Suddenly he broke into song while he wildly danced inside the circle they had formed around him. He seemed to be from another world, as he made sounds they had never heard before. Sometimes his movements were aggressive and direct, and then he would slow to an almost meditative state. To the boys, he acted as if he really wasn't there, or possibly someone had possessed him. Finally, the music ended and Shane's eyes opened and a big grin covered his face.

Some of the boys asked him, "Why are you smiling?" Shane replied, "It is always a meaningful and exciting experience for me to visit with my ancestors. They are my protection in the present and my guide to the future." One boy replied, "Good for you—at least you have a future." Shane answered him by saying, "So do you. Maybe you are looking for it in the wrong places?" The boys looked at him with a cautious curiosity, and then went about their everyday routine.

A week passed, when some of the boys approached Shane and asked him, "Could you teach us that dance?" Shane hesitated and told them the dance was sacred, and held great value in the tribe, and should not be learned for the wrong reasons. He told them to ask their ancestors in their dreams for a reason to learn, and then he would teach them. The next day, a few of the boys approached him, and they had a soul-searching discussion about what their ancestors said to them. Shane smiled and began a long process of explaining the music, and the significance of each movement in the dance. Later, the other boys joined in, and the training went on for many months, and during this time he told them no illegal drugs were allowed, in respect for the sacred ceremony. He showed them how to burn tobacco as a sign of respect to their ancestors, and modeled respect by treating them as dancers of the tribe, an honor they achieved through their hard work.

As time went on, the boys became dancers at powwows and other Native events (Brown, 1992). Shane helped them get back in school, where they performed their repertoire of dances for their peers and curious adults. They gained a reputation for their excellence, and looked forward to spiritual feasts and tribal events, where they could honor their ancestors with their performances. Shane helped them find a purpose, and in doing this, he brought hope back into their lives.

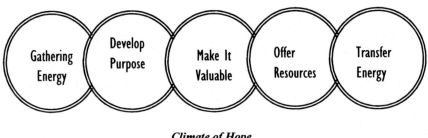

Climate of Hope
Figure 6.2

Gathering Energy

It is understandable for apathetic people to assume that constant trauma leaves them without the energy to continue with purpose in their lives, and it is easy to assume energy will not return. When we look more closely at this phenomenon, it becomes evident that the energy has not left, but has pulled back to a safer place, where it can survive life's traumas without risking future traumatic events. The native boys seemed empty to life. They had left school, did not have employment, and spent most of their time taking drugs and listening to music. Shane accepted that they were apathetic, but did not accept that energy was lost and would not return. His first encounter with them showed an enthusiasm for drugs and music. He made the decision to gather energy around musical interests and approach the emotional climate—not each boy's individual problems. He gathered their energy by accepting the energy that was available, and adding new energy of his own. Shane shared Native music and performed a Native dance, in an effort to engage them in using their energy in new ways. In a sense, he gathered energy to plant the seeds of hope. He felt trauma had robbed their meaningful energy, and he was determined to bring it back (figure 6.2).

Develop a Purpose

Conciliators who gather energy for apathetic people may need to connect this energy to some purpose that is meaningful and valuable to them. Having a purpose can take many forms such as future dreams, goals, aspirations, projects, activities and desires, to name a few. The point is to give the energy a direction that excites and improves a person's outlook on the future. A climate of hope begins to take shape when human energy is connected to meaningful purposes.

In our case study, Shane understood this and connected Native music and dance to his ancestors. He told the boys that his future was connected to their wisdom, and he found purpose while communicating with them during Native dancing. He did not begin moralizing that they should be educated on Native culture, nor did he tell them what their purpose should be. He gathered his energy and modeled his purpose through music and dance. He demonstrated what gave him hope and purpose, and let them make purposeful decisions on their own. Creating a climate of energy and purpose is more effective than direct intervention, especially when people feel apathetic. The difficulty lies in convincing traumatized people, who have lost meaning in their lives, to invest in the future. Sometimes it appears more beneficial to *model* investment, than to talk about it (figure 6.2).

Make It Valuable

In our case study, Shane understood that a purpose also must be something of value, or ironically, it may lose purpose. He would not let the boys practice Native dancing without giving up their use of illegal drugs. They had to value the dancing over their drug abuse, and show their purpose in dancing was not a waste of gathered energy. He reinforced the value in Native dancing by introducing them to Native tobacco rituals that gave honor to their ancestors and to themselves. He made the purpose valuable by making it sacred.

Not all conciliators are Native healers and, in a climate of hope, not all purposes become valuable by making them sacred or spiritual, but there may be something to be learned from Shane's example. In a climate of hope, gathered energy that is given a purpose, might be made "special" in some way. Purpose can gain value when it is not taken for granted and is not a matter of routine behavior. This explains why those who are given material riches in life may still lose hope. Constantly being given valuable things, does not guarantee you have gathered any energy, or found any purpose in these things. Their value may only be experienced on the surface, and have yet to reach the inner workings of hope. A climate of hope can make dreams, goals and desires meaningful when people find value in them. Gathering energy and connecting it to a purpose can become just as valuable as obtaining any given goal, dream or desire (figure 6.2).

Offer Resources

Gathering energy and connecting it to a meaningful purpose that has found value can be a fragile enterprise. In our case study, Shane understood that the seven boys were attempting to rise above a climate of apathy and invest in a climate of hope. He believed that someone needed to clear a path for their journey, and he accomplished this by becoming their mentor. By doing this, he created a resource for their dancing and got them back in school. People stepping out of a climate of apathy may be cautious and fragile. They may have been numb for quite some time and they certainly have experienced previous trauma. Sometimes, it may require clearing a path and allowing people space to grow. Concil-iators can supply that space by offering resources along the way, for a purpose-ful future. Offering resources for others to grow, takes on many forms and can be accomplished in many ways, and an understanding of its importance can be as necessary as the methods used. If we take the time to think about it, all of us have needed resources at moments in our lives, and conciliators can offer these resources to people who have lost hope for a meaningful future (figure 6.2).

Transfer Energy

In our case study, Shane helped seven boys gather energy, find a purpose, and make the purpose valuable, while offering resources along the way. The story ends before the final stage in creating a climate of hope unfolds. Shane helped the boys create a climate of hope, but *sustaining* that climate is another matter. The old saying, "Don't put all your eggs into one basket" holds true when con-sidering a climate of hope. Creating hope, and keeping it alive, can be different activities. Conciliators can help sustain a climate of hope in others, by helping them transfer their energy into many different purposes—making their life valu-able in many different ways.

For example, in our case study, if some of the boys can take their energy and apply it to school, then school will sustain their dancing and dancing will sustain their work in school. If others can transfer their energy into meaningful relation-ships, the relationships will sustain their dancing and their dancing will gain momentum in their relationships—making them stronger and more meaningful. The transfer of energy into other valuable purposes can make a climate of hope more resilient and more self-sustaining. People who lose hope in one portion of their lives can transfer energy into another. This allows a climate of hope to be transferable when trauma strikes. Instead of retreating into an apathetic climate filled with feeling numb and a loss of meaning, traumatized people can transfer their energy to other hopeful experiences where the energy is not wasted, and purpose is allowed to flourish (figure 6.2).

Cultural Implications

Cultures where apathy is more prevalent and buried in conditions of poverty and negative surroundings can make apathy more difficult to alleviate. Therapists should be mindful of resources in these types of communities and cultures so they can provide hope to the members. For example, the wars in Afghanistan, Iraq and Syria have created a toxic climate of apathy for the people who are di-rectly affected by them. Many displaced people are forced to live in horrific conditions in refugee camps. The misery of those displaced by the conflict is evidence of a major humanitarian crisis. The climate of apathy and despair in those refugee camp could provide a breeding ground for more troubles. For in-stance, after the first Afghan war in the 80s, the Taliban were born out of Af-ghan refugee camps in Pakistan. When western countries walked away from

Afghanistan after the fall of the Soviet Union, Pakistan was left to deal with the largest population of refugees in the world. Many children who grew up in those camps were caught in a web of apathy and despair and became vulnerable to religious fanaticism. Therefore, giving hope to the people affected by war is vital to avoid future conflicts. Rebuilding is critical to reviving local communities. A military victory will mean little to the local population if it means leaving behind more destruction and dispossession.

In the case study on apathy, a similar war was going on, only under the surface. Darlene's mother and her friends were the by-products of the community's war between the former culture of the community, and the drug culture that had taken over the beliefs and behavior of the people in the community. The similarities between wars in Afghanistan and refugees in Pakistan and Darlene's community, surrounds the marginal focus on reconciliation of the people affected by a culture of war. In other words, more time is spent on creating war than cleaning up the mess left behind. Instead, reconciling the outcome of the cultural war in Darlene's community between the drug culture and the former culture, the community fell into a climate of apathy. Similarly, the Afghan War breeds the hallmarks of a climate of apathy with the experiences of feeling numb, loss of meaning, respect and hope. All of these being the breeding ground for future wars both within people and the communities they represent. Conciliation may be a starting point when trying to restore hope in a community and in a war torn country.

Chapter 7

Guilt and Conciliation

In this chapter, we explore the phenomenon of guilt, and how it can become an identity problem for those who accept the shame associated with feeling guilty. Guilt also can turn into a mental health problem especially when guilt is confused with sadness. This happens when it becomes a negative emotional reaction instead of an emotion that is a natural part of healing. For example, when a loved one dies, the attachment to that person may cause others to experience acute sadness. Sadness becomes a part of healing, and is beneficial with people who grieve. However, when sadness turns to guilt, the grieving process is interrupted. A person or the climate surrounding grieving people is filled with making judgments and placing blame. From a conciliation point of view, it may take a conciliator to help grieving people understand the difference between guilt and sadness. Clarification of this difference can be an effective resolution by those who experience grief. However, if left alone guilt may turn to depression—causing mental health problems.

Another example of the phenomenon of guilt comes from numerous religions around the world. For example, the Catholic Church has the experience of guilt within its core beliefs. From Original Sin to not following the New Testament, the church deals with unacceptable behavior through guilt, when practitioners do not follow the laws of Jesus. However, the Catholic Church also practices reconciliation through the rituals of Confession and saying the Rosary. For many, this experience with guilt does not rise to the level of a conflict. Guilt becomes fallout from not practicing spiritual beliefs based on faith.

Some people in our society use guilt as a form of victimization—not by others but by one's self. In addiction recovery, guilt can be used to justify avoiding growth and change. Some may say, "I cannot risk changing my life because I am an alcoholic." "I never do anything right." In these statements, we see people who are not afraid of failure but fear success. Unfortunately for the people surrounding a guilty person, a climate of guilt may form where others begin lacking motivation for growth and change.

In our case study, we start the chapter with alcoholics who are practicing self-victimization. This is followed by alcoholic mentors who practice the art of "guilt tripping" in order to control an Alcohol Anonymous support group. The case study requires a conciliator to create a climate of respect to counteract guilt. When guilt is used against others it walks a fine line between emotion and judgment. "Guilt tripping" others, forms a judgment that others are doing something wrong. An emotional climate of guilt is filled with strong emotions but also a myriad of judgments and peer pressure. Personal guilt is a subtle emotion that can be devastating anytime a climate of guilt fills the air.

Case Study

Michael moved to Boston only a short while ago and was already searching for a group meeting that would address his alcohol problem. He had been a recovering alcoholic for eleven years and had a keen realization of how important these meetings were in turning his life around. Though a successful businessman, Michael found alcohol was his drug of choice, following his divorce. These were memories from the past and he wanted to assure himself that nothing equivalent in his life would return.

After considerable searching, he discovered a quiet and what he believed to be low-key meeting in the Boston suburbs. He looked forward to making new connections both professionally and personally, and his past experience demonstrated the effectiveness of these meetings in helping him connect in many areas of his life. Michael entered the first night with enthusiasm and the promise of goodwill. As he sat quietly listening to others speak, something was subtly different about the atmosphere surrounding the conversation. In the past, alcoholic group meetings were highly supportive events where people honestly shared their stories about their struggles with alcohol, and from this self-disclosure, came the confidence to tackle another day with the hope of remaining, drug free. However, this particular alcohol program seemed different, though he could not specifically figure out the subtleties he experienced in that initial night.

In subsequent meetings, Michael took note of the dynamics taking place among group members. It was apparent that several long-standing people in the group had cleverly and forcefully taken charge of the meetings, while the rest of the group consisted of younger and more passive members who quietly listened without any attempt to initiate the conversation. Secondly, he noticed these older members acted as judges or arbitrators whenever younger members told their stories. They would point out each person's indiscretions and lecture them on their previous wrong doings.

As time passed, Michael's observations were confirmed that not all participants were treated equally. The meetings were controlled by the three or four power brokers who determined the value of each persons' story. As a result of the self-righteous indignation that seemed to follow each self-disclosure the accused feared persecution and the self-righteous indignation that followed and wanted to share less about their past.

Michael decided he had to personally address the climate of the group and see if change was a viable option. The next meeting turned out to be a pivotal moment for many group members. The difference was Michael would intervene when elder group members judged the behavior of the younger members. When they made negative generalizations about how they should be ashamed of past behavior, Michael would ask them to be specific. He would say, "Just how would you recommend these young people be ashamed?" When elder judges made reference to how younger members must change their ways, Michael would ask, "What specifically do you recommend they do to change?" Michael then proceeded to tell the group that he did not have the answers to these questions, but was willing to work on finding answers—with the group's help.

In the meetings that followed, the climate of the group slowly shifted. Group members were not judged but supported, and the self-esteem of younger members was enhanced. A couple of the group elders decided not to continue with the meetings but for the others who stayed—they were welcomed as contributing members. The guilt that surrounded the climate of the group was gone. Many members remained concerned about their futures, but the acute feelings of shame they were experiencing had disappeared from the conversations.

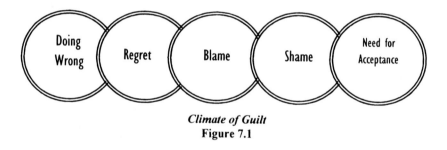

Climate of Guilt
Figure 7.1

Understanding an Emotional Climate of Guilt

Doing Wrong

A climate of guilt develops when people are constantly judged by others or when people experience wrongdoing for behavior that seems unacceptable to themselves or others. In some cases, it appears in the form of social pressure from the group itself. Other times, guilt may be created by the judgments of those in a position of authority. In the case study, Michael noticed that the elders in the group had established a climate, where they acted as judges and jury, and the younger members passively accepted their judgments, and returned each week to accept a renewed version of the elder's retribution.

The beginning stage in a climate of guilt can be unsettling, when judgments are made that disrupt the feelings of the accused. These disrupted feelings have been described as "walking on eggshells" where peoples' beliefs are controlled by cautious feelings and behaviors, that have a subtle, yet profound effect on the emotional climate. In the case study, Michael felt it the first night he attended the alcoholic support group. He witnessed older group members creating a climate, where everyone else was struck with a sense that something was wrong, and that younger members were at the heart of the wrongdoing. The more the younger members allowed the judgments to continue, the more cautious they became, and the more cautious they became, the more these judgments controlled their behavior.

This example is an indication of the power guilt has on people who confuse needing support with some form of acceptance by others. The younger members were attending the group in order to experience a climate of support for their alcohol problems, but were forced into proving their worth to elder group members. They were not given support but had to earn group acceptance. In this example, group support would have made each person feel stronger emotionally, but group acceptance gave the power to the elders, at the expense of younger group members. Powerlessness and a need for acceptance, contributed to younger group members' sense that something was wrong, and unfortunately, the emotional climate was amenable to placing the wrong doing in their hands (figure 7.1).

Feeling Regret

Once a climate of wrongdoing is established, guilt can create feelings of regret in those who accept they have done something wrong. It is this stage of guilt where people may *dwell* on their wrongdoings and decide to have regrets. They now sense wrongdoing and begin to consciously regret it. In the case study, we see this progression in newer group members, from sensing something is wrong to regretting their past lives. Every time they tell their stories, elder members condemn their behavior. The judgments made by elders forces them to look at past moments in their lives and knowingly regret their abuse of alcohol. The elders send a message to younger members that they did something wrong and their behavior can be judged as unacceptable. The emphasis on the message "you did something wrong" sets the stage for these younger group members to progress into vaguer and damaging self-judgments.

Guilt creates a sense that you have done something wrong and need to regret your behavior, regardless of an understanding of the wrongdoing. How many times has someone, in a climate of guilt, felt overwhelming regret and has said to themselves, "I did something wrong," yet if questioned, they are unable to identify the specifics of their wrongdoing? A climate of guilt has a tendency to avoid specifics when establishing feelings of regret, and seems more concerned with making wrongdoing into vague, generalized events.

We all have experienced moments of concern when we have done something wrong, and if we specifically identify what happened in these moments, we probably are in an improved position to change our behavior. However, in a climate of guilt, there may be nothing specific or clear about the way we regret.

In the case study, elder group members were not pointing out wrongdoing to help younger members, or to solve disputes. Their intentions were to plant the seeds of regret so that younger members could be controlled by feelings of doing something wrong (figure 7.1).

Blame

With regretting firmly in place, a climate of guilt encourages people to blame themselves for their perceived wrongdoing. The blame stage can be critical. It takes guilty people out of the realm of feelings and places them in the realm of judgments. The judgments of others are now no longer necessary to sustain the guilty climate. Constant judgments tend to shift guilty peoples' perceptions from *we did something wrong,* where they feel regret to *we do things wrong,* where they judge themselves and accept blame. This subtle shift from regret to blame can lead guilty people away from resolving any specific disputes. In the case study, the newer group members went beyond regretting past behavior. They went from, *we did something wrong* to, *we do things wrong,* making their present day behavior just as culpable as any behavior from the past. Michael realized they were generalizing more than their abuse of alcohol. They were making a general statement of how they perceived themselves as human beings, and they found blame in their conclusions.

The only people benefiting from the blame were the elder group members, who held a tight grasp on the climate of the group, and found power and control in their constant judgments of other people. Generalization becomes a key word in this stage of a guilty climate. People often lose the specifics needed to solve conflicts, and begin to generalize, by making statements such as "We never do anything right." or "We are always messing things up." Michael saw this happening with younger members of the support group, and realized he needed to intervene. He came to the conclusion that the alcohol support group was overgeneralizing the lives of its members by placing blame on their past and present behavior (figure 7.1).

Shame

Guilty people who accept blame through generalizations by saying *we do things wrong* may eventually arrive at the experience of shame. Constant reinforcement of the message *we do things wrong* has a high probability of having a new message appear in the beliefs of people, caught within a climate of guilt. *We do things wrong* can be replaced with *we are wrong as people* and should feel ashamed. The experience of shame can create a sense of worthlessness that is highly controllable by others casting blame in a guilty climate, and can lead the accused to fall into a state of vulnerability, where it becomes difficult to defend one's point of view (Kapur & Rai, 2013; Williams, 1993). In the case study, it was Michael that realized the defenseless position newer group members were experiencing, through their acceptance of shame. He knew that their *feeling ashamed* allowed the elder members to control the group, and he knew that unless he intervened, these young members would become a self-fulfilling prophecy. They could feel ashamed of their drinking, and may consider drinking again, because of their shame (Konstan et al. 2001). Shame can be an encompassing phenomenon that fundamentally sends a message to guilty people that they are of lesser worth. These worthless feelings can make the experience of shame devastating to people looking for some form of acceptance. Even when people act in ways that are acceptable to others, ashamed people may find methods to sabotage this acceptance (Aledort, 2014; Moore, 1996). In the case study, newer group members were on the verge of accepting the shame of the group when Michael intervened and challenged elder members, and their judgmental behavior. Without this intervention, newer group members could easily bog down in a need for acceptance, and be consumed by the elder's version of experiencing shame (figure 7.1).

Need for Acceptance [6]

People in a climate of guilt experience a subtle sense that something is wrong. With time, these subtleties may turn to feelings of regret, as people begin to say, *we did things wrong*. Constant regretting may lead to blaming, where people now say, *we do things wrong*. Unchecked blaming can have a devastating impact on guilty people when they experience shame and shift their views to *we are wrong as people*. Finally, the experience of shame may increase their need for acceptance, by placing power in the hands of those who judge them. In the case study, the younger members were looking for acceptance from group elders, who had no investment in seeing them as acceptable. As long as they remained unacceptable, group elders remained in power. Thus, we see the reasoning associated with the lack of any specific information shared with newer group members for changing their lives.

A climate of guilt can be filled with generalizations that lead people to some form of shame, and shame can create a need for acceptance—making the guilty climate vague and mystifying. Michael's actions were effective, because he specifically talked to the elder group members and asked them for specific answers to his questions. It becomes difficult for a climate of guilt to survive specific, direct action. It feeds on generalizations that lead to the experience of shame, and a need for acceptance by others. The vague and mystifying judgments found in a climate of guilt can have serious implications for people looking for self-acceptance. A guilty climate directs people away from self-acceptance and towards looking for acceptance from others. Michael made a concerted effort to stop the need for acceptance found in the newer group members. He specifically and directly confronted the old members with questions that were designed to eliminate guilt—not reinforce it. Without making any judgments of his own, he reconciled the guilty climate, allowing for each continuing member to experience direction and support (figure 7.1).

Conciliating Guilt

Guilt can be a tactical tool in many forms of conflict resolution. Guilty people seem less defiant and more amenable to being controlled, yet guilt may offer compliance more than reconciliation for resolving emotion-oriented conflicts (Kornelsen, 2013; Jenkins, 1950). Those who are the receivers of guilt in a dispute may comply, but it rarely means the conflict is over. Caution, blame and worthless feelings of shame may still continue. Forms of conflict resolution that rely on guilt tend to have distinct winners and losers, where someone may be sacrificed in order to resolve the problem. In spite of this, guilt is commonly used to resolve conflicts. It can create, for the accusers, a sense of order and control. Constant judging has a tendency either to keep guilty people in their place, as they eventually seek some form of acceptance, or to redirect their feelings into other emotions such as resentment or revenge. In this regard, guilt-oriented conflict resolution rarely considers people's feelings. More frequently, emotions in a climate of guilt become covered up, so the so-called accused lose a sense of self-worth and the accusers can continue to remain in power.

It may be important for conciliators to understand the autocratic nature of this form of conflict resolution. Democratic methods, where both sides emerge winners in a conflict, do not seem realistic when guilt is involved in the process (Konstan, Chernoff & Deveney, 2001). Guilt-oriented conflict resolution may require conciliators to understand the effect that constant judging and blaming have on people caught within a climate of guilt, before any fair and balanced reconciliation can take place. The following are some of the dynamics to consider when reconciling guilt-oriented conflict.

"Walking on Eggshells"

In reconciling a guilt-oriented conflict, conciliators may want to consider the atmosphere surrounding the conflict's guilty parties, where constant judging and blaming may create caution in those receiving the guilt. For example, parents who repeatedly blame their children may discover how cautious these children can become, when asked to share their feelings or points of view. The children have learned to "walk on eggshells" in order to avoid blame, and may be less likely to be forthcoming when a dispute arises. Parents may believe the constant judging shows the direction their children should take in order to comply with family rules; however, constant judgments can create a climate of caution and insecurity when family rules take precedents over family unity. Children may follow the rules, as they cautiously gain emotional distance from interactions with their parents. In this example, parents have won the battle over the rules at the expense of close family relationships. The children have learned to "walk on eggshells" in order to avoid constant judgments and blaming.

As a point of clarification, it is not being suggested that conciliators should disregard rules. Social institutions do not function without rules, but the enforcement of rules seems an ineffective rationale for constant blaming and judging. Effective rules can improve peoples' emotional surroundings by creating reasonable boundaries. However, constant blaming and judging might make what is inside these boundaries more cautious and less direct (Freedman, 1998). Conciliators have an opportunity to change a cautious climate of guilt by becoming more descriptive and less judgmental. In the case study, Michael never judged other group members but asked for specific problems to be solved. He conciliated the group by asking group members to be less cautious and more specific with their answers. The more descriptive the group became, the less group members relied on cautious behavior, and the less reliance on cautious behavior, the more group dynamics improved.

Social Pressure

Not all guilt-oriented conflicts begin with constant blaming and judgments by those in charge. The group itself may develop strong beliefs and behaviors, causing a sense that something is wrong for anyone who chooses to act differently. Religious organizations, families, clubs, peer groups, workplace cliques and any number of other groups may put pressure on its members to act according to certain criteria, and a sense of "wrong doing" may emerge when someone acts against the wishes of the group.

This is not to say that people in the above examples cause guilt-oriented conflicts. People with strong beliefs may perceive social pressure positively as a part of their commitment to the group, and openly seek direction from others to do the "right thing." However, it is when groups leave little room for dissent that problems may arise. Without an opportunity for reasonable dissent, social pressure may cause regret, blame and feelings of shame in the dissenters. For example, if someone wants to marry a person outside their ethnic group, a conflict may develop based on the social pressure of the community surrounding the couple. Social pressure may create a sense of shame based on the disapproving perceptions of neighbors—and other strangers who have little investment in the couple or their marriage.

In this example, a conciliator may not be in a position to judge the correct point of view, but may help all parties accept each person's *right to a different point of view*. People in conflict can agree to disagree. However, the difficulty for any conciliator is that social pressure may hold tremendous power, even when people know someone's disagreements are accurate. Take for example, the competent workplace employee, who becomes ostracized by other employees for "making waves." Others know she is right for pointing out ineffective workplace procedures, but social pressure deems this behavior wrong for calling attention to workplace problems.

In extreme cases, such an employee may be designated as a "loose cannon" for doing the right thing, and may be shamed into leaving the organization under social pressure from peers. Some guilt-oriented conflicts may be filled with such ironies, and conciliators have an opportunity to point out the negative aspects of social pressure when it adversely affects productive conflict resolution. However, making people aware of the power social pressure holds on solving everyday problems can be a step in the right direction. Many of us make important decisions in our lives with little awareness of how social pressure molds our decisions, or how guilt may enter our lives, when we accept the social pressure of others.

The Problem with Labeling

We use labels in everyday living to keep our lives organized, and it may not be difficult to imagine embarrassing moments developing if we stopped using them. Imagine walking into a supermarket looking for a can of peas and not having labels on any of the cans, or needing to use the restroom only to find two doors with no labels above them. Labels, when used correctly, can give us direction and clarity in everyday living, but the misuse of labels can cause serious problems. For example, in guilt-oriented conflicts, labels are primarily used to identify those who have done something wrong. Terms such as dummy, klutz, stupid or any other disparaging remark are labels for blaming people and making them feel ashamed. An example of this can be seen in an ineffective school system, where damaging labels determine peoples' worth.

How many students actually learn at their full potential after a judgmental teacher labels them as stupid? Most likely the word *stupid* may be one of the last words that is completely learned and understood. Yet, numerous public school students can attest to the tragedy of being unfairly labeled only to find out later in life that the label had little connection with their full potential. Unfortunately, the misuse of labels, in public and private schools, is still a phenomenon to be reckoned with (Cook-Sather, 2003).

It may not be only ineffective schools that use labels to categorize people and create a sense that something is wrong. Families, workplaces, communities, and many other groups have used labels to blame and shame people into being subservient. It becomes a difficult task for some of these people to rid themselves of a label that was acquired through guilt ridden judgments and social pressure. Unfair labeling may dictate shame and worthless feelings for the rest of their lives.

Conciliators have an opportunity to help those damaged by the labels of guilt, and can also give guidance to those doing the damage. Helping guilty people work through damaging labels can be a primary concern in resolving guilt-oriented conflicts. Negative labels have a tendency to rob people of their confidence when engaged in a disagreement, where guilt is used in the argument. Helping people to put their labels aside and specifically face the conflict goes a long way to reconciling the guilty feelings encountered in this type of conflict resolution. Conciliators, also, can help those who use unfair labeling to win arguments, by pointing out the benefits in using more specific and descriptive terms to resolve guilt-oriented conflicts. Calling people names or labeling them into some category can create added problems in the future—when all that is remembered from a past conflict is that label or name.

Guilt Survives on Generalizations

Guilt survives on generalizations, especially in the language used when guilty people are shamed into submission during a conflict by vague, inaccurate statements. The following are supplied as a short list of examples:

You *never* do anything right!
You are *always* making things worse!
You *should* see things my way!
You *must* do this my way!
Nobody will *ever* trust you!
Nothing you say will make *any* difference!

The more generalizations used in a guilt-oriented conflict, the higher probability of winning the argument. If you look at how a climate of guilt is formed, the reasons may become clear. When people are told they *did something wrong* and have regrets, they are still in a position to specifically argue what they did right and what was wrong. However, if they are forced to go beyond their regrets and have to constantly accept blame, they may switch from *I did something wrong* to *I do things wrong,* and if the blame affects them personally, they eventually may find themselves feeling ashamed and say, *I am wrong as a person.* At this point, guilt has made them ashamed but controllable. Statements such as "You never do anything right!" Or "You are always making things worse!" may mystify guilty people into feeling ashamed, eventually giving control to their accusers.

As stated previously, this form of conflict resolution may create winners and losers with no guarantees that any *specific* resolution to the problem will take place. What remains may be a sense that certain guilty people are doing things wrong—no matter what validity is found in their accusers' points of view. Conciliators can help guilty people become more specific in their questions and answers, when involved in guilt-oriented conflicts. Guilt cannot tolerate specificity of expression, and the more specific the dialogue, the less chance guilt will dominate or influence conflicts, when constant judging or social pressure help to generalize any given set of circumstances.

The Safe Rut

Experiencing regret, followed by constant blaming, and feelings of worthlessness and shame may be debilitating, but for some guilty people, these feelings become predictable over time, requiring little risk or change. People who are the constant losers in guilt-oriented disputes may be faced with a secondary problem beyond the potential for inherent shame. Guilty people who accept their shame have a tendency to play it safe when disputes arise. For example, employees who are not given credit for their exemplary work, but are constantly criticized when things go wrong, may accomplish enough to fulfill their job description, but not much more. They may work in a climate where their activities are neither unsatisfactory nor dynamic. In other words, they will play it safe to avoid constant criticism.

The down side of this behavior is that over time, their careers may lack noticeable growth and systematically fall into a rut. One morning they may wake up blaming themselves, and wonder how they wasted all their time in such a dead end career. In reality, there appears to be little safety in remaining in a rut to avoid the criticisms of others. Safe ruts may be anything but safe. They may inhibit confidence and eventually deter people's ability to grow and change. The safe rut can protect people from the judgments of others, but may do little in protecting people from any form of negative self-evaluation.

Conciliators have an opportunity to point out to guilty people the dangers of falling into a rut, and can help them gain confidence in viewing their behavior as anything but safe. In the case study, Michael saw the alcohol support group falling into a rut, where certain people were the judges and others were the ones being judged. Each week, the group demonstrated this predictable pattern of behavior—with its predictable results. He realized that support groups were designed to offer safety and support, but this particular group offered only a "safe rut" that seemed heavy on judgments and light on support. He conciliated the group by forcing people out of the rut they had devised, and reconciled with other group members by creating an emotional climate that demonstrated successful support and growth.

Center of Control

Control becomes a major theme in many guilt-oriented conflicts and, for the most part, guilty people will relinquish control to their accusers. Through regret, blame, and shame, guilty people may succumb to those passing judgment and become co-dependent on their judges for acceptance. It is the need for acceptance that may make guilt-oriented conflicts so one-sided, and it is also what can make guilt a powerful force in conflict resolution. For the winners of these conflicts, it means the center of control can be firmly in their grasp and if the losers want acceptance, they must give in to this control. For example, in an abusive family, a father may abuse his children by making them feel worthless and ashamed, yet the children may spend large portions of their lives seeking the father's acceptance. These children may be clearly aware of the father's abuse, but still seek his approval, because the center of control resides in the judgments of the father.

To outsiders, the obvious solution is to get away from the abuser, but for those who have been shamed, there may be a strong need to seek some form of acceptance. Here in lies the danger of guilt being used in conflict resolution. Reconciliation of conflicts can become secondary to who maintains the center of control. In the above example, the father's abuse was not reconciled, yet he remained in control of his children, solving the problem for himself and no one else. This is why we hear of examples where everyone in the group knows they are doing something wrong—yet no one changes. They may be seeking the acceptance of the person or persons who maintain the center of control over the group (Cummins, 1996).

Conciliators have an opportunity to refocus the center of control away from those controlling a conflict by developing ground rules, where everyone shares the power and control for solving problems. The center of control for solving conflicts is not placed with any specific person, but is found in the conflict resolution process. With everyone treated equally, it becomes difficult to shame anyone into a specific point of view. Needing acceptance is replaced by what seems acceptable to those involved in the process. In the case study, Michael shifted the center of control away from the group elders and placed it in the procedures everyone would use to sustain a successful support group. He did not emerge as the leader of the group, but created a process where each person developed a center of control for combating their alcohol problems. The blame and shame previously controlled by a select few was replaced with a democratic process, where the center of control was in the hands of all participants.

A Peacemaking Alternative: A Climate of Respect

Alice entered the special education resource room of Franklin High School on the first day of her new job, and was struck with the sullen faces of ten students who made every attempt possible not to make eye contact with their new teacher. During her job interview, it became obvious that special education was not the premier activity in this particular school's objectives. This observation was reinforced when speaking to teachers and students at the school's opening orientation. The subtle judgments of the students, staff and administrators were at best condescending. All the right words were used to describe her new class assignment; however, the underlying message was the special education resource room was "trouble," and no one seemed supportive of her unenviable position.

The students in the resource room had similar beliefs about themselves. The term "loser" emerged as a common theme when she asked her students to share personal information about how, teachers, classmates, and others perceived them. Reluctantly, they described a climate of shame where they judged themselves as retards that occupied the lower strata of the school system. As Alice listened, she realized that more than learning disabilities were being discussed in their remarks. They pictured themselves as bad people who were the brunt of many comments and jokes. In a sense, they accepted the labels doled out by their peers, and lived up to their reputations as trouble-makers and dummies. In an age of political correctness, no person in the school used trouble-makers, losers, retards or dummies to talk about Alice's students, but it really did not matter. Her students had done the translations of other people's behavior towards them, and had given themselves the labels without the help of others.

Alice found the climate of the school unacceptable in the treatment of her students, and she was determined to treat them with dignity, and demonstrate how they could respect themselves. Her first step was to develop an understanding of the unique skills each of them possessed, and acknowledge these skills as worthwhile and important. For example, one student had difficulty with writing but was an excellent cello player. She made him the musician of the group, and he would play the cello each morning for the class. Another student had reading difficulties but was a competent artist. She was the artist of the group, and was responsible for all art in the room. A child with attention deficit hyperactive disorder was put in charge of handing out papers, making announcements and reporting on school events. As she got to know each student, they were given a specific role in the classroom, where others could appreciate their unique talents regardless of their performance in the mainstream classrooms.

To her peers, all of this so-called "extracurricular activity" seemed a harmless distraction, even though her students' academic grade performance improved dramatically. For example, there was artwork everywhere and music filled the halls. When asked why she focused on these secondary activities, she would defend them as basic skills that helped her students experience, respect. This answer seemed irrelevant to others who were only concerned with student performance, and mandates from the state's department of education. It appeared that respect was only given to those who *performed* according to certain rules and procedures. Individual differences were not acknowledged, and had little influence in the school, and in some cases, caused negative judgments and retribution.

This was most evident outside the resource room where others judged her behavior as intrusive and threatening to many school functions. For example, her students were excluded from social activities. Their grades were not high enough. The school had a long-standing policy that if your grade point average fell under a certain number, then you were excluded from social activities. She lobbied for one of her students to be on the student council, only to be told the student's grade point average was unacceptable. She tried to get another student on the school yearbook committee, but was told only honor students were allowed. When she asked if some of her students could participate in numerous clubs and activities, she was informed that no room was available.

Her problems were not related to her effectiveness as a special education teacher, but were connected to the disruption she was causing in the culture of the school. The unspoken rule was that learning-disabled students were not acceptable models for others to follow. Her crime was that Alice had broken from the attitudes held by the school's mainstream culture—by treating each learning-disabled child with honor and dignity. She described them as contributing members of the school regardless of their grade point average, and discussed the importance of their unique contributions—no matter how different they appeared to others. Her students loved her and respected her, and she treated them in the same way.

When she was fired, five of her students followed her to a neighboring school district, where she continues to treat the learning disabled with respect.

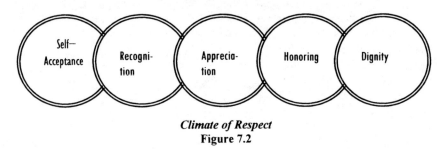

Climate of Respect
Figure 7.2

Self–Acceptance

Self–acceptance can be a crucial component in developing a climate of respect, whether it is acceptance by others, or begins with self-acceptance. In the case study, Alice was aware that the attitudes and behaviors of school personnel perceived the resource room as less acceptable than other factions in the school. She experienced a school climate that had obvious hierarchies of who was acceptable and unacceptable. Her students were intelligent members of the school—some of them were more intelligent than the high achievers. However, they had learning disabilities that inhibited them from high performance in the school's mainstream culture. They were included "physically" in the mainstream classrooms, but were less acceptable in everyday behavior demonstrated by administrators, teachers and students.

Regardless of federal laws on inclusion in the mainstream classroom, the special education students had not changed the beliefs and behaviors of a faculty and administration that accepted students only on their achievement (Damer, 2001). Alice understood her students' dilemma, and accepted them regardless of the dynamics found in the school culture. She accepted each student as a unique human being, and went out of her way to discover their uniqueness, and by doing this, students began learning self-acceptance (figure 7.2).

Recognition

Respect becomes noticeable to others when some form of recognition takes place within the emotional climate. Such acknowledgment can bring self-acceptance to the surface, and can recognize admirable characteristics of a person or group of people. In the case study, Alice recognized her students in spite of their disabilities, and devoted time to discovering characteristics about them she could openly acknowledge to others. She created a venue for a musically gifted boy to play the cello. She recognized the artistic abilities of another student, and made her the class artist. A boy with ADHD became the spokesperson for the class. Instead of simply helping her students with their disabilities, she recognized them at a more fundamental level, as human beings.

The school had not developed procedures to recognize these students, so Alice created ways to acknowledge them, in spite of the rules. In a climate of respect, the recognition of others may be more than accepting and recognizing only those who meet the criteria of the stated rules. It can be the art of finding others acceptable and acknowledging their unique contributions. Alice understood this and recognized her students, who in turn, improved their learning through these recognitions (figure 7.2).

Appreciation

Over time, the recognition experienced in a climate of respect can change to appreciation for those who have been accepted by others. Appreciation goes beyond recognition. People may develop strong emotional ties that bind people together. In the case study, faculty and staff did not appreciate what Alice was doing for her students. The climate of the school appreciated success, as determined by grade point average. They did not appreciate her disruption of the school's rules because they found her intrusions unacceptable. However, the students appreciated her efforts, and showed respect by following her to another school when she was asked to leave. In a climate of respect, appreciation becomes the act of valuing the accomplishments of people in the group and developing strong emotional connections to these people. When people appreciate each other, there can be a stronger desire not to let them down. Such established bonds can influence relationships, learning and self-esteem (figure 7.2).

Honoring

Honoring people you appreciate may not be a difficult concept to understand. At some point, if you appreciate a person or a group of people, the emotional bonds developed can make honoring them a natural phenomenon. Honoring becomes our way of symbolically, accepting, recognizing and appreciating people for their unique contributions to others (Bishai et al. 2015; Augsburger, 1992). In the case study, five of the ten students (with the support of their parents) leave their former high school and follow Alice to her new employment in a neighboring school district. Their leaving is a symbolic gesture in honor of her achievements, and a symbolic way of showing that her efforts were appreciated. However, honoring and *rewarding* someone still remain different phenomena. Honor is based on appreciation. Rewards are based on giving someone privileges for following basic guidelines or rules (Skinner, 1953). Alice honored her students, even though their disabilities inhibited them from receiving rewards or performing well under the basic guidelines and rules of the school (figure 7.2).

Dignity

Being treated with dignity, seems crucial in sustaining a climate of respect. Honoring each other in such a climate may dignify the expectations of people's behavior. People who honor others may begin to treat them with dignity by speaking and acting differently in their presence. Sometimes this switch in language and behavior is identified as, having "good manners" or is seen as, "being polite." When this happens, the entire emotional climate can be elevated to a more dignified level of interaction. In the case study, Alice understood that, if she honored her students and treated them with dignity, they would show her respect and, more importantly, begin to feel self-respect. It can be said that in developing a climate of respect, "The process can be as important as the final product." Schools that lose sight of the learning process and focus on the final product, not only stop treating students with dignity, but stop treating learning with dignity (figure 7.2).

Cultural Implications

In some collectivistic cultures, honor and shame are inherently public. Members of such cultures are expected to maintain the status of the group. The community is more important than the individual. In some of these cultures, a climate of guilt is used positively to resolve conflicts. For instance, in numerous African tribes, if a theft is discovered in the community and the identity of the thief is unknown, the public shaming process is carried out as a part of normal conversation. People sitting in common meeting places speak about the evils of stealing in general and the recent one in particular. People express their sadness over what had happened and express their hope that such incidents never happen again. By doing this, they create a climate of guilt around the thief. The impact of the climate of shame and guilt is so intense for the wrongdoer that he restrains himself from such behavior in the future (Augsburger, 1992).

The tradition of the hunger strike in Ireland goes back to medieval times. The idea was to appeal to the consciences of the violators, and to create a climate of guilt and shame to elicit justice. Traditionally the aggrieved person would fast at the door steps of the offender. If the person died, the offender was held responsible and forced to pay compensation to the deceased family (Augsburger, 1992).

Both of these examples show historical connections to using guilt in order to shame others into doing the "right thing." This may bring up more than cultural implications. The conflict resolution found in more long-standing societies may differ greatly from conflict resolution in more democratic societies. Our beliefs lead to our behavior. Even though this chapter proposes ideas for conciliation in democratic societies, it must be noted that using guilt still remains a popular conflict resolution style in other parts of the world. In the case study, Michael may have found little wrong in the blame and shame assigned by elders to new and younger members of a prominent African tribe. He may have viewed it as the right thing to do based on his cultural beliefs. Conciliators should be aware of how guilt is used to resolve conflict in both democratic and more traditional societies.

Guilt seems to be a remnant from conflict resolution that took place in many ancient cultures. In our present-day society, guilt is less a part of the culture and more based on emotions taking place in actual disputes. However, those ancient cultures tend to seep through and guilt becomes a collective part of our society through judgments from media, families and communities.

Notes

6. Information on a need for acceptance from a family systems perspective can be found in the following book. Ladd, P. D. (2007). *Relationships and patterns of conflict resolution: A reference book for couples counseling.* Lanham, MD: Rowman & Littlefield. 203−218.

Chapter 8

Egotism and Conciliation

A climate of egotism can be identified as insecurity or exaggeration being masked with confidence. On occasions this takes place in a competitive environment where the perception of confidence may be as important as actual feelings of confidence. In such a climate, "putting your guard down" may signal weakness or vulnerability. On other occasions, a climate of egotism is generated by an egotist who solely changes the emotional climate with a need to be right along with forms of condescending behavior. Here we see someone who tries to take over the narrative of a group by using force. Furthermore, an egotistical leader in a position of power may create a climate of resentment, where the more egotistical the leader becomes, those under the leader become more resentful. Sometimes this will polarize a group of people into camps—one camp devoted to acting egotistically, while the other acts out their resentment.

An emotional climate based on these experiences is subtly different than a climate of healthy dialogue, where people collaborate based on their expertise—not on a need to be right. Take, for example, the politicians who believe their policies will be beneficial to others, and authentically back them with historical facts and effective results, as compared to the politicians who form bombastic rhetoric and false promises to win the confidence of others, while inside lack the confidence or exaggerate their convictions. Even if both groups of politicians agree on the issues, one group may be perceived as authentic while the other is perceived as inauthentic.

Another point to consider is how egotistical people seem similar to people with the mental disorder of narcissism. Narcissistic people need to be the center of attention as a way of controlling others. Egotistical people need to be right as their way of controlling others. However, both phenomena are based on a level of insecurity and exaggeration that needs to be covered up with a sense of false confidence.

In today's modern world, we may see a rise in the number of people who take on these two positions in society. Are we living in an "Age of Entitlement," where insecure people feel entitled to being the center of attention or believe their entitlement allows them to be right? It may be that egotistical people can be right and wrong at the same time. Society may tell these people that they are entitled, and therefore right, while at the same time they wrongly believe they earned that right by just saying they are right. Feeling secure may take more than entitlement to actually be right. It may require suffering through the pain of one's convictions to earn such a right.

The case study in this chapter talks about such a person who believes he is entitled to the accomplishments of others, and continues his need to be right by condescending to others. The fallacies of his convictions turn out to be found in the lack of respect given him by those who have earned this right through their efforts and competence.

Case Study

Dorian moved to the Northwest to pursue his career in technology. The area surrounding Seattle was perfect for his needs: reasonable weather, advancements in computer technology, and an opportunity to work with some very smart people. For the last year, he had a job at a well-known computer company working with ten other highly skilled analysts in the research and development area. Many times, he would marvel at his good fortune, "Just think I get paid all this money for simply thinking," and it was obvious that others in research and development felt the same way.

In spite of this, tension and distance existed between the workers and their boss. Unlike the workers, George was hired as an administrator, not an analyst. His technical skills were limited, but administratively he was responsible for the success or failure of the research and development department. In many ways, he seemed threatened and insecure about his position, but made a point to remind everyone that he was in charge. This was obvious by the constant barrage of memos he sent to his research analysts demanding they keep him informed of every new idea. They were required to give him written reports anytime a breakthrough was about to take place.

If this was the department's only problem, Dorian and his colleagues might have found George at most annoying but tolerable. However, their concern went far beyond the memos. Anytime a breakthrough took place, George called the analyst or team of analysts, into his office and proceeded to "punch holes" in their theories, and find fault with their conclusions. His words were consistently condescending and his mannerisms were smug and self-righteous. He invariably changed little in the ideas but took credit for their creation. George needed to be right and he was not going to let anyone else prove him wrong, and this is how he gained a reputation for being the "daily topic of conversation."

One day Dorian confronted George when he made a breakthrough on a new computer chip design. As expected, George wanted a full report followed by a meeting with him the next day. The next day Dorian described to George their new computer chip design, and informed him that it was fully tested, and he would like credit for the breakthrough. George began his common litany of punching holes in his request, by hitting him with a barrage of questions in a highly judgmental and emotional manner. Instead of explaining himself, Dorian repeated a description of the computer chip, followed by a comprehensive description of the tests run on it, and again asked for credit for the invention. George continued to analyze and find problems with his statements. Instead of defending himself through explanations or emotional outbursts, Dorian repeated his request, only this time, asking if he would support going to a higher authority to obtain credit for the design.

Their statements dumbfounded George. If he did not support Dorian, he was sure Dorian would go to a higher authority without his support. His bullying and judging seemed to have no effect. He recognized Dorian had a well thought out plan for how he was going to proceed. After moments of silence, George smiled, "Of course I support you and if the tests hold true, I will make sure you get credit for the new chip. Both of us will present the new discovery to higher management."

After leaving George's office, Dorian thought to himself. "George is an egotist but he is not stupid. He would have taken complete credit for it if I had fallen into one, or more, of his old traps. George is insecure and threatened by my expertise, and needs to be right, and so I let him be right. I came up with the plan that the both of us get credit. I know he doesn't deserve it, but my plan was to make sure I received credit. He joined me and did not dismiss me. He wanted to be a part of my success."

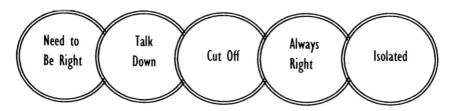

Climate of Egotism
Figure 8.1

Understanding an Emotional Climate of Egotism

Need to Be Right

Egotism develops, as a phenomenon, based on a person or a group of people needing to be right. The need to be right describes an image of self that originates from an inward insecurity, while demonstrating an outward appearance of competence and confidence. In the case study, George took every opportunity to remind his staff that he was in charge. He demanded credit for all of their accomplishments, and would argue with them in order to keep up the appearance of being right. He worked from the assumption, "Looking right will indicate confidence and control over others." His need to be right was more important than a need to be understanding, magnanimous, or fair. It wasn't that George *wanted* to be right, demonstrating a sense of confidence found in many competent people. He *needed* to be right. It was his way of controlling an underlying insecurity over the expertise of his staff.

The first stage in a climate of egotism may be in establishing a need to be right. It seems easy to imagine how difficult it must be for egotists to listen and actually hear other people's points of view. Their "false front" becomes filled with bravado and strong judgments toward others. However, egotists rarely see any of this as a problem. They perceive life from a frame of reference where others around them have the problem. George had no problem with his behavior, and made a point in giving all of his staff a sense that they had the problems— by frequently talking down to them. His need to be right created an emotional climate that kept the focus on him, while lessening the accomplishments of others (figure 8.1).

Talk Down

Egotists, with a fully developed need to be right, usually have perfected their methods for establishing "being right" around others. Some egotists will use patronizing behavior as a method of condescension, and others exhibit obnoxious behavior or bullying, as proof of being wiser and smarter than the people around them. While others become unbearable, by walking into a room and immediately taking control. Regardless of the specific method, egotists have the intention of talking down to others to control their behavior. The rationale is, "If I control the emotional climate, then I can be right, and since I have a need to be right, my condescending behavior is justified."

In the case study, George had many methods of showing egotism toward his staff. He would send them condescending memos, ordering them to report all activities. When they reported their work, he would find fault and make changes, even when no changes were needed. When he reported the work to higher management, he would solely take credit, giving those who actually did the work a sense of being cut off. His insecurity over not being as qualified as the technical analysts caused him to establish methods for being right, regardless of his shortcomings. He made condescension acceptable and necessary. George needed to prove something to himself and his staff that he was competent and in charge; thus, reinforcing a climate of egotism, where he becomes the main topic in everyday conversation (figure 8.1).

Cut Off

Egotists, who need to be right and practice condescending attitudes have a tendency to cut themselves off from others in the emotional climate, and others reciprocate by avoiding their condescending behavior. For obvious reasons, not many people prefer to be around egotists for any significant period of time, unless they are also insecure or prone to exaggeration and practice their personal brand of condescension. Actually, egotists may have little trouble cutting themselves off from others. It may help them justify their overbearing behavior. They may cut themselves off from others because they have no investment in becoming close, and possibly altering their points of view. Their insecurity has brought them to a point where they need to be right, negating any reason to welcome alternatives. By cutting themselves off, they can maintain their game plan and fulfill their need to be right.

In the case study, Dorian understood the emotional climate George had created. He refused to get in an argument with George or explain his position, making it far more difficult for George to condescend. He described how to solve the problem but did not look for George's approval, and he included George in the final plan of sharing credit for the technological breakthrough. Dorian knew that George would condescend if he argued with him, and if he cut him out of the credit, George would again win by stealing all the credit. In a climate of egotism, it becomes difficult to argue with egotists and just as difficult to be cut off from them. Dorian's plan was to assertively state his position and not argue, but also not back down (figure 8.1).

Always Right

In the case study, Dorian's approach was very different that possibly other members of George's staff. It may be simple to visualize others trying to please him, or talking about him behind his back, or looking for revenge, or openly arguing with him. None of these positions would stop George from accepting credit for their accomplishments. These methods actually may cause more insecurity in George; justifying his need to be right, practice of condescending behavior, and reinforce cutting himself off from them. The climate depicted "George against them," and George was determined to defend his position at all costs.

In a climate of egotism, egotistical people may defend their positions at all costs. They seem convinced that by giving into other positions, they may lose their power and control. Any form of collaborative effort seems threatening. It might nullify the egotist's need to be right. Egotists would rather be right, even at the expense of successful problem solving. Power and control can be bigger issues for egotists. They defend their position at all costs where appearing wrong may be too threatening a position to hold. Unfortunately, egotists may defend their positions, even when it is clear that their positions are wrong (figure 8.1).

Isolated

If there is an "Achilles heel" in a climate of egotism, it might be that egotists ultimately may end up isolated and alone. Their need to be right, combined with condescending behavior, and being cut off from others, and their overwhelming need to defend their position at all costs, may leave them outside the circle of others in the climate. Unfortunately, feeling isolated and alone may do little to improve one's sense of security. Isolation may lead to insecurity and insecurity may lead to a further reinforcement of a need to be right—thus justifying more egotistical behavior. In the case study, Dorian saw that George was outside the circle. He was isolated and alone. In his plan, Dorian included him in the credit for the new discovery. The question may arise, "Was that manipulative?" The answer is yes, but it was not dishonest. The ultimate goal was for Dorian to get credit for his discovery. He accomplished his goal by giving George partial credit. Dorian's need to solve the dispute was bigger than his need to be right. This allowed George to save face with his superiors, and lessened his need to be right and feel insecure.

The obvious difficulty, in a climate of egotism, is that including egotistical people, who are condescending, prone to exaggeration and insecure, may not be an easy task. Their condescending behavior may warrant an opposite response. However, understanding isolation, sometimes may be the key to resolving an egotistical climate. People who feel safe and secure may be more amenable to working and living with others, and may not need to be right, in order to obtain these goals (figure 8.1).

Conciliating Egotism

The place that egotism holds in resolving emotion-oriented conflicts seems a dubious one. Egotists can act in such overbearing and condescending ways that others find themselves reacting emotionally through anger, resentment, revenge, apathy, or guilt. Many of the emotional conflicts discussed in prior chapters may have had an association with someone acting in an egotistical manner. Another way of putting this is, "Egotists have a way of creating emotional conflict in others without admitting they personally have any problems." Thus, we find the difficulty in conciliating egotism-oriented conflicts. Egotists tend to believe they have few problems. Everyone else has the problems. Their beliefs and behavior can put an extra burden on conciliators to help egotists with their problems when they are, most likely, in denial.

In the case study, Dorian had the "Machiavellian" task of working through George's egotism, in order to receive credit for his discovery. Yet, George sees no problem in his behavior. His need to be right is all the rationalization needed to take credit for the work of his employees. Dorian must come up with a plan to resolve a dispute with someone who denies a conflict exists. Since George holds the power, Dorian's methods are planned carefully to usurp George's hold on credit for other's achievements. The positive outcome for conciliators is that, "even good–will can have a plan." There are methods that limit the negative impact egotists have on the emotional climate of a workplace, family, class-room, or community. The following are methods that can be used in conflicts where egotism is involved.

The Futility of Arguing with an Egotist

Egotists argue to uphold a particular point of view, and to guarantee the point of view prevails by the end of the argument. Egotists are people who may do al-most anything to win arguments, and control the outcomes of these arguments. They fundamentally work from a sense of insecurity or over-exaggeration and need to compensate by being right. Their need to be right can be more important than a need to be competent, productive, collaborative, sincere, or fair. Herein, we see the futility for all of those who argue with egotists. For example, egotis-tical people can be extremely frustrating for highly competent people who be-lieve their knowledge and expertise should have an impact on the resolution of a conflict. Knowledgeable people may suffer at the hands of egotists. Egotistical people are more influenced by their need to be right, than the knowledge others bring to an argument.

Another example can be seen in many workplace settings, where some unin-formed people assume that egotistical people value productivity as much as their colleagues. Again, arguments over productivity can be secondary to egotists remaining right and in charge. This was evident in the case study where Dorian had produced an innovative computer chip, but George was far more concerned with who deserved rightful credit for it. Finally, some people enter arguments with egotists assuming all involved are of good–will and the disagreement will be collaborative, sincere and fair, only to find out that being right outweighs any attempt at using democratic principles.

The futility of arguing with egotists can be understood in the term *kitchen sink fighters*. Metaphorically speaking, they may throw everything at you during an argument—even the kitchen sink. In order to be right, they can be compas-sionate, obnoxious, vague, loving, boisterous, ruthless, or whatever else it takes to win the argument (Brinkman & Kirchner, 1994). For example, we can see this happening in politics where to politicians are in dispute and one of them needs to dominate the other by being right, no matter what argument arises.

In a dispute with another politician, an egotist might start out by being ruth-less and try to dominate the discussion. If the other politician counteracts this, they may switch to being compassionate and complimentary to get their way. If that does not work, they may become obnoxious or vague until they win the argument. They may throw everything at the other politician, even the "kitchen sink." The point is that it may be futile to argue with someone who has a need to be right, and will do what it takes to win an argument. If you are arguing to accomplish a goal or solve a problem, arguing with egotists can be an exercise in futility.

Conciliators go a long way in helping others caught in such fights by pointing out that the behaviors of egotists, no matter what form they take, may be intended as acts of condescending behavior, in order to win arguments. People in a climate of egotism, should be aware that no matter what emotion is expressed or what behavior is manifested, egotists usually intend to be right at the end of the dispute. By keeping this in mind, people should be careful in accepting what egotists say, literally. There may be an underlying hidden agenda of needing to be right, influencing even the calmest arguments. Pointing out to others that egotists use many ways to win arguments may clarify that no matter what egotists say, their need to be right may be at the foundation of each argument, and winning the argument may be their primary motivation. With this awareness, people can determine whether what egotists openly say matches what they internally mean, and what they usually mean may focus on being right and winning the argument.

The Broken Record Technique

If people cannot argue with egotists, then what can they do? Before answering this question, let us first understand what can happen when people argue with someone who has a need to be right. First of all, most egotists may welcome anyone who becomes emotional, in any way, during an argument. They simply can nullify the other's position, and say the matter is now *personal*. They win the argument by making others emotional, in some way, and then judge the emotion as though it were a flaw in their argument. Actually, it is no wonder that egotists use condescending behavior. The bigger the emotional reaction to their condescension, the more they can dismiss other opinions and remain in control.

For example, this can happen in a family where a father and his teenage son constantly argue, and the father wins each argument by making his son angry. If the boy explodes with anger, the father is now in a position to reprimand him for his disrespectful behavior. He condescends in order to make him angry, and by doing so, wins arguments. Over time, the boy may decide to stay clear of such arguments and resent his father from a distance. At face value, we might say that a tragedy has taken place. A father and son have lost contact with each other, but that is not how egotists think. Egotists may intentionally condescend in order to cut people off. As long as the father is cut off from the son, he can remain in control, and meet the criteria for his underlying insecurity.

So, it seems difficult to argue with egotists, and it may accomplish little when you avoid them. Becoming emotional may justify their condescending behavior, and avoiding them may justify cutting themselves off from others. Conciliators can use a technique euphemistically called the "broken record technique" to counteract egotistical behavior. In the case study, Dorian used it to discuss his new discovery with George. He did not argue with him or avoid him.

He confronted him with a plan for getting credit for his discovery, and objectively and unemotionally described what he was going to do to get credit.

He was not trying to convince George to go along with the plan. He simply described it to him. When George condescended, he continued describing his plan by adding the next step. Like a broken record, Dorian assertively held to his plan, without explaining himself or trying to convince George to accept it. He remained unemotional and objective, and spent time rehearsing and fine tuning the approach before he met with him. He faced George by holding his ground, and not falling into the trap of explaining his behavior or becoming emotionally involved.

Self-Centered and Self-Serving

Frances dominated every holiday, birthday, and special event. She was the third child of Barbara and Tom, who raised four children (two boys and two girls), all now in their thirties. For whatever reasons, Fran's insecurity made her the dominant influence in how the family interacted with each other. When everyone was together, she would incessantly talk about herself and the problems facing her life. For the most part, she felt misunderstood by her family. She criticized her brothers and sister, and took every opportunity to criticize her parents. Her behavior created extreme caution in all the family members. Frances was continuously looking for ways to keep the focus on herself when the family gathered together. Since her parents were committed to family unity, Frances constantly got away with her negative behavior that was outrageous and self-serving.

For example, one winter she had to go on a business trip for two weeks, and left her children with her sister, without informing her of the length of time she would be gone. Even Barbara, her sister, found this behavior shocking and vowed not to let her needs dominate the needs of other family members. However, when she returned, Barbara gave in to her demands. This caused anger and resentment in other members of the family, and especially upset her brother Billy, who refused to tolerate her self-serving behavior. However, by arguing with Frances, Billy was criticized for making waves, and in family discussions that followed, it was Frances, not Billy, who remained the center of everyone's attention. Frances was an egotist who coped with her insecurity by devising ways of staying in the spotlight, while condescending to others. She was not afraid of being cut off and she was willing to defend her self-centered and self-serving behavior at all costs—even at the cost of fragmenting her family.

Conciliators take note that egotists may have a habit of dominating situations with their self-centered and self-serving behavior. Their need to be right seems to focus on themselves, and a commitment to intentions that benefit themselves. They may be constantly pushing a self-centered and self-serving agenda of their needs. For example, Frances was always at the center of discussions concerning her family. When she was with family members, she talked about herself, and when she was not present, the family spent most of their time talking about the impact she had on them. She had found a way of getting what she wanted and remaining the center of conversation.

The key for conciliators in unlocking problems with egotism, where the egotist acts in self-centered and self-serving ways, may be to focus on the other parties—not the egotist. People who allow egotists to practice self-centered and self-serving behavior can easily find themselves constantly thinking about them, and trying to meet their needs. Unfortunately, it may be a losing battle trying to meet the needs of people who have a need to be right. Even when you meet their needs, they may be reluctant to give you credit. Their self-centered and self-serving needs may be greater than a need to be magnanimous and other directed. Thus, we see why it seems so difficult living, working, dating, and in general, being with egotists. Reconciliation of any kind might not take place until an effective conciliator can help egotists begin to focus on others. However, reconciliation may happen when egotists begin to feel connected to a group and feel secure within the group.

Explaining vs. Describing a Point of View

Simply put, "Do not explain your point of view when interacting with egotistical people. Describe your point of view." When you explain yourself, power may be lost (Betz, 2015; Carol, Diesel & Weber, 1994). The primary intention of an explanation is to *convince* someone that a point of view is valid. Egotists have little reason in making valid your point of view, when their goal is to alleviate their insecurity or to promote their exaggerations. When you explain yourself to egotists, you are put in the position of having them judge a point of view that they did not conceive. You now may be in a weaker and less defendable position—even if your explanation is more accurate and knowledgeable. Your explanation runs the risk of being wasted on people who are concerned with power, control and being right. Under these terms, no amount of convincing makes your explanation any more palatable.

On the other hand, describing a point of view has the purpose of *mapping out* one's intentions, and does not have a main focus of convincing anyone whether the map is valid. It can be a way of taking a stand and assertively expressing a point of view. It does not require others to be convinced as to the accuracy of your perception, nor does it ask for any form of judgment from others. It becomes a map of your point of view that does not ask others to accept or reject it. In describing a point of view, conciliators put themselves on equal footing with egotists. They avoid the dangers associated with convincing them of an argument's validity. It becomes one opinion being expressed among other differing opinions.

Keeping this in mind, it may be important to do your "homework." An effective conciliator may need to collect accurate facts, develop an objective plan that gives direction, and remain unemotional in the presentation of the plan. This combination avoids arguments and explanations that may derail the plan's success. In the case study, Dorian did his homework. He made judgment calls, in anticipation of George's outbursts, and he remained objective and assertive throughout George's direct questioning and subtle attacks. He described his position—he did not explain it. He stuck by his position without arguing, and knew where he was heading with his strategy to get credit for his accomplishments.

The Insecurity of Being Alone

There exists a certain irony in being egotistical. Much time can be spent in condescending and isolating oneself from others. Yet it may be isolation from others that allows for more insecurity, resulting in more egotistical behavior. Granted, it feels more comfortable to establish relationships with individuals who listen, respect your opinion, and are interested in what you are saying, but we are not always in a position to pick our partners, colleagues or relatives. Reconciling with egotists may require being cordial to someone who you really do not like. Conciliators who want to influence egotists might keep in mind that the last stage in a climate of egotism may be in feeling lonely and alone, followed by more insecurity. Trying to include someone who is fighting to be excluded may not be an easy task. However, when egotists are included it becomes difficult for them to uphold a need to be right at all costs.

For example, an egotist can constantly brag in the presence of others. Insecurity may drive this person to impress people with exaggerated stories about past accomplishments. However, the bragging may actually drive others away, at least emotionally (Bazerman, Curhan, Moore & Valley, 2000). Even if, what is related to people is accurate and true, the condescension in the form of bragging can create emotional divisions, making it difficult for the egotist to become a trusted member of a group. Not many people are emotionally comfortable with the constant bragging and self-gratification, except possibly other egotists. Most people figure out that bragging, and other forms of condescension, can make it difficult to share intimate and personal information. Even when "charismatic egotists" are not alone and have a following of admirers (followers or "groupies"), their need to be right may make it difficult for them to venture into intimate relationships with others—where being vulnerable becomes a pre-requisite for personal intimacy.

Keeping this in mind, what conciliators can do to include egotists in any given group may appear a bit masochistic. Conciliators may want to connect with egotistical people, and model behavior that is "other directed." In the case study, Dorian included George, even though it may have been painful in sharing credit with someone who was extremely condescending. In the story of Frances and her family, she remained the center of attention but in reality, family members talked *about* her but did not seriously include her in the dialogue of the family. Reconciliation might take place, if someone helped Frances sincerely share her feelings of insecurity, while family members remain non-judgmental during her attempt at vulnerability. As stated in the example above, people who brag can become wrapped in their personal aggrandizement and may constantly focus on themselves. Conciliators can direct their attention to the needs of others, and learn humility in the face of personal gratification. For the most part, egotistical people can and probably will join in, if people are willing to tolerate and work through their condescending behavior.

Loneliness and insecurity are often connected, and that an egotist's need to be right, may isolate him or her from others, and ironically, may create more insecurity (Bell, et al. 1990; Symonds, 1968). Their inflexibility and inability to collaborate may make them less likely to try new ideas or behave in dramatically different ways. They can be, truly, creatures of habit, using a very similar pattern of condescending behavior on all those they meet. Their insecurity foreshadows problems emerging in friendships, working relationships and family affairs. They may become lonely and insecure, but may have a pattern of behavior that masks it with a condescending need to be right.

A Peacemaking Alternative: A Climate of Humility

The Chesapeake Bay stands out as an ecological masterpiece skirting the shores of Maryland and Virginia, and early in the 1970s concerned residents around the "Bay" founded an environmental organization to protect its natural habitat from polluters and other forms of ecological destruction. For many years, this organization was run by an egotistical, self-centered director who was concerned more with photo opportunities in the newspapers than involving volunteers, or raising the public's awareness to the myriad of problems facing the Chesapeake Bay's future. Many would say that a lack of commitment by volunteers and the general public had slowly made the organization fragmented into groups more consumed with self-interest, than saving one of the natural wonders of the Eastern Seaboard.

These were the thoughts and reflections running through Clara, the organizations present director, who sat silently waiting for an award for her meritorious efforts over the past ten years, for re-energizing the organization, and refocusing its mission statement back to the environment. Ten years ago, Clara entered the Chesapeake Bay area with a passion for ecology and a true sense of what could be accomplished, if people worked together. She remembered how fragmented the group had become and how countless hours were spent listening to others, in order to redirect activities back to the environment—with the ultimate goal of protecting this important body of water. She reflected on how overwhelming the task felt to her as she discussed their strengths and weaknesses with disgruntled volunteers, who were waiting to see if it was worth re-investing in an organization that previously seemed dominated by one person. With a faint smile on her face, she recalled the early days of admitting to volunteers her limitations, and her skepticism in making the organization work.

However, she also recalled the inner struggle she had with moving beyond her personal needs and refocusing her attention outside herself, and the day she finally came to the conclusion that nothing would change until all involved were again perceiving the Chesapeake Bay as their primary focus. Those were the days when getting people to stop talking about prior organization politics and begin talking about environmental changes. She remembered the countless hours of informing and educating volunteers on what they could do to make an environmental difference, and the constant struggle with clashing personalities in the organization to look beyond themselves to a higher calling.

As the presenter was introducing her, going through the list of her accomplishments, Clara sat silently remembering those dedicated individuals who reached out to help. These were the people who answered her call for unity. They had little concern for organizational politics or any personal rewards they would receive for their efforts. She thought of how much she appreciated their efforts, and their dedication to working with her, and helping the Chesapeake Bay return to its natural beauty.

She also remembered their selfless attitudes and dedication to working for the common good. In her moment of reflection, she realized the importance of being involved in projects that transcended any one person. She realized the power and strength that is achieved in creating activities for the common good, and how being a volunteer was a way of strengthening yourself, by focusing outside one's self. She became lost in the realization that true humility can be paradoxical, where focusing outside yourself, in effect, may bring you closer to your true identity. These were her thoughts as the speaker called her name to come to the podium and accept an award for her public service.

The next day, Clara began a new campaign to reduce the mercury amounts found in an isolated bay along the Chesapeake's eastern shore. As she called volunteers and asked for their help, she quickly refocused the conversations away from praise for the former night's award ceremony, back to the environment and the importance of preserving the future. Clara had transcended her personal interests and was again fighting an ecological battle for the common good.

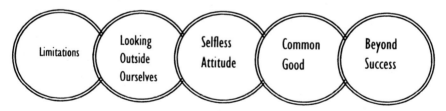

Climate of Humility **Figure 8.2**

Limitations

Sometimes understanding personal limitations can be just as valuable as understanding personal strengths. We live in a world filled with diversity where knowing our limitations can give us a base line to focus outside ourselves. Humility begins with recognizing, that assessing both our strengths and weaknesses may lead us to others who can help us (Sandage & Wiens, 2001). For example, Clara knew that re-generating the Chesapeake Bay environmental program would require many volunteers, with differing areas of expertise. Her recognition of this reality sets the tone for a different emotional climate in the organization. This seems quite different than egotists who set a tone of needing to be right, and far different than her predecessor who was more self-centered and self-serving. The emotional climate being started by Clara was based more on wanting to be realistic and accurate. She only achieved these goals by assessing her strengths and limitations, from the very beginning, and asking others to join her in doing the same. A climate of humility begins when people honestly evaluate their limitations—leaving more quality time for engaging their strengths (figure 8.2).

Looking Outside Ourselves

We have all had moments of insecurity, where we become completely self-absorbed and find that humility is not even a remote possibility. Insecurity, sometimes forces us to make choices, and one of these choices can be defending our point of view, and needing to be right. Paradoxically, a climate of humility can guard against personal insecurities by helping people focus outside themselves. Looking outside personal concerns can broaden the perspective of anyone who feels personally insecure. It can create an opportunity to see the whole picture, and to gain knowledge of what may be workable and what is not. For example, Clara took the time to call volunteers and let them provide input into reforming the organization, and by doing this, she strengthened her base of volunteers, while feeling more secure in her personal time and effort. She did not condescend to them or cut them off, but let them know that they were a part of a project that had importance, beyond any one person's needs and desires. She stayed outside herself, and let the needs of the institution be the primary focus. This allowed her insecurity level to drop, as her volunteer participation increased. Focusing outside oneself, paradoxically, can strengthen self-confidence, while allowing insecurities to be transformed into productive behavior (figure 8.2).

Selfless Attitude

Modeling a selfless attitude can add another layer to the benefits of looking outside one's self. Not only are you putting energy into self-confidence and productive behavior, but an unspoken rule of selfless behavior may develop for others to follow. In a climate of humility, modeling a selfless attitude tends to reproduce that model in the behavior of others (Bransen, 2006; Johnston, 1995). In a sense, it may set the tone for the group to have a common voice and purpose. Clara was the person who modeled a selfless attitude for others to follow, and she was the person who set the tone for the environmental organization. Her predecessor set a different tone in establishing a climate of egotism. Here we see how modeling a selfless attitude can have a major impact on the emotional climate of any group of people. So much so, that Clara became a person to be honored and received an award for her selfless activity. Clara's true security did not come from gathering the power and control of the environmental organization, in order to feel more secure. True power and control came to her by creating a climate of humility, where others were more than willing to give her the power and control needed for running the organization successfully (figure 8.2).

Common Good

The old saying "Whatever goes around comes around" can apply directly to both egotists and to humble people. For example, egotists who isolate themselves from others many times become self-fulfilling prophecies, where others find reasons to hold back support, money, expertise and other forms of help. People practicing humility for the common good have a similar dynamic at work, but only in a more positive way. Humble people who make efforts to achieve activities for the common good may attract others who will give support, money, expertise and other forms of help. Creating efforts for the common good can create an attitude of "good will" and good will may be the reward for those who have accepted their limitations and have focused outside themselves (Schweigert, 1999). Clara received an important environmental award not only for her activities in protecting the Chesapeake Bay. She, also, was rewarded for her good will, and creating efforts for the common good. Her predecessor might have had a history of protecting the "Bay" but his egotism and the lack of good will, among volunteers, in no way put him in line for any award. Focusing outside one's self and modeling a selfless attitude can lead to efforts for the common good, with an end product of good-will (figure 8.2).

Beyond Success

Clara's behavior the next day after her award acts as poignant examples of how a climate of humility can be sustained. Instead of reveling in her award and promoting herself, through it, she moved on to the continued work of the environmental organization. The organization had gained momentum, and her focus was outside herself in attempts at keeping the momentum going. In a climate of humility, the purpose of a person or a group is not to be self-centered or self-serving, even when it comes to receiving an award. The main intention may be to continue efforts for the common good. That does not mean that humble people should not celebrate, when they have received an award. What it does mean is that awards exist as benchmarks of achievement that may create future possibilities for looking beyond any personal accomplishment. Clara's award became a gesture of appreciation and respect that honored a moment in the life of an environmental organization. Her humility helped in looking beyond that celebrated moment to the accomplishment of other future goals that were other directed, for the common good (figure 8.2).

Cultural Implications

Leaders of some countries have a clear need for egotism in creating order, making clear definitions of roles where nationally egotism is accepted and revered. For example, under a dictatorship a leader exercises unrestricted control over the government. The way dictators maintain their power is by brainwashing, isolation, controlling access to resources, and creating fear through elaborate political persecution. In some cases, the people are brainwashed to believe that they live in paradise and are far better off than the rest of the world. Isolation and censored media plays a central role in keeping the population in the dark about the outside world and also from the negative aspect of the regime. By doing so, dictators create a climate of egotism. They may believe they are right and they know what is good for their people. Anyone who questions the ruler becomes a target of political persecution and is treated as a traitor. Dictators rule with an iron fist and isolate their own country and its people to gain control. North Korea is a prime example of a climate of egotism where the leader's need to be right is more important than his need to be, just, fair, competent or understanding.

In this chapter, Dorian experienced a similar phenomenon with his boss, even though there were no cultural implications involved. However, in some working environments employers and employees can continue to act in egotistical ways and call it one of the premises of participating in today's workforce. Unfortunately, for those who have a need to be right, this premise may have a negative effect on them. They may miss out on new and creative products because they were unable to practice generosity in the workplace. It may be important to note that in the chapter on greed, you will find a dangerous combination when a climate of egotism joins with a climate of greed. Such events can change the climate of any workforce, and eventually change the culture of the people working in it. This also can be applied to those emotional climates found in Part 1 where violence can be the outcome. However, the type of violence in the workforce is called lateral violence, where workers subtly attack each other.

Chapter 9

Greed and Conciliation

It may be that a climate of greed does not engender any form of conflict or dispute in some people. We look at the word "greed" and it brings up visions of selfishness, self-interest, and even egotism. Yet, the actual practice of it seems rooted in some of our most social behaviors. Phrases such as "Those who end up with the most toys, wins" or "The ends justify the means" permeate our society yet hold a negative stigma when talking about it. With greed, there seems to be a constant battle between what we believe and how we act. Most people applaud the virtues of generosity, but some act in ways that discredits our use of it.

Conflicts may erupt when our beliefs about the negative nature of greed are in conflict with how we act in greedy ways. We may need to make justifications for our behavior by suspending our negative beliefs about greed and make justifications that satisfy our behavior. In the case study, you will see that certain accounting professionals suspend their negative beliefs about greed with justifications that "Everyone else is doing it" and "Business is business." Such justifications merge from a climate of greed where the climate itself may be stronger than the people in it.

Another aspect in a climate of greed may be the influence it has on the mental health of people in the climate. For example, a climate of generosity encourages mental health, while a climate of greed may do the opposite. Certain anxiety-oriented disorders are based on obsessive and compulsive behavior—a phenomenon we find in a greedy climate. Hoarding behavior is another crossover between mental health and a climate of greed. In both cases, a certain level of anxiety and uncertainty emanate from both phenomena. Hoarders are immersed in anxiety with the thought of giving up their possessions. In a climate of greed, there is a tendency to hoard one's possessions with the belief that some person will enact the same greedy behavior as was practiced by the initial greedy person. Sometimes people, places and things are not beneficial for your mental health.

In the last chapter on egotism, one finds a similar climate, with greed focusing obsessively on goals while in a climate of egotism focusing on a need to be right. The combination of a climate of egotism and greed may be a formula for some of the unhealthy work environments, where resentment and revenge take root in the minds of oppressed workers. Here we see the possibility of mental problems with workers turning into potential violence. A climate of egotism and greed exacerbates resentment and revenge in others. In these types of situations, the emotional climate is a key player in people's emotions. Both violence and mental illness can flourish in an obsessive climate where people need to be right at the expense of others.

Case Study

"Cooking the books" remained a dangerous practice after the indictments of several key business people, but these were troubled times and the market breathed competition. The "Ajax" accounting firm was going to compete regardless of the pressure on companies by federal prosecutors. Ajax was a firm that viewed success as making a profit, and had indirectly teamed up with "Technext"—a company that it was supposed to maintain as an independent, professional accounting relationship. However, a small number of people representing both companies were determined to succeed, and do it better than anyone else. A clear an unspoken rule existed between them. They would appear, on the surface, independent of each other but underneath would share information that made the annual report more positive than what was actually on the books. Under these conditions, cutting corners or illegally getting the jump on competitors became a part of the game, and exaggerating earned profits was a reality considered a sign of the times.

This ended when federal prosecutors indicted Technext for unscrupulous practices. Ajax administrators were stunned by the news and became noticeably frightened by their connection with Technext. Tension reached its peak when certain administrators at Ajax were indicted and were forced to resign. The remaining administrators needed to save the firm, and changes were expected before public opinion closed the doors. Call it fear or a true sense of wanting to do the right thing, that prompted Ajax in the hiring of Samuel to re-organize the firm's policies and procedures, but regardless of the intent Samuel's job would be difficult and time consuming. He would have to meet with groups of employees who were in a climate that practiced dubious accounting methods and find out those beliefs and behaviors that might cause future problems. He knew that remaining independent of Technext, their biggest client was questionable and, if nothing else, he wanted a re-establishment of Ajax's independence and objectivity.

When he met with each group of accountants, it became clear that a certain pattern dominated their responses to questions surrounding, "What exactly were you thinking and doing at work and what procedures came out of this?" Remarkably, most of them believed their practices were acceptable, or at least, indirectly condoned by industry standards. They all admitted that independence and objectivity were two axioms taught at business school, but it seemed that actual accounting practices had found ways to bend work to a more collaborative level with companies such as Technext and others. Almost every accountant, in each group, found rationalizations to justify their behavior. On the whole, they thought of themselves as honest people, who learned to play the game in order to succeed, and where success was measured by the bottom line.

When Samuel began to press them on how they felt about their behavior, a certain reticence came over the groups to actually describe specifically their activities. With coaxing, they told a story of employees insensitive to the needs of their fellow employees, and in some cases, the competition for success that caused them to obsessively focus on succeeding, no matter who was left behind or professionally hurt. The common phrase to rationalize this behavior was "business is business," as though that phrase made their insensitivity understandable and acceptable.

Samuel believed the methods used to succeed seemed unethical, if not immoral. It appeared that certain accountants would do anything necessary to win, and justified their behavior by saying, "The ends justify the means." Their behavior was like drawing a straight line from point "A" to point "B" and staying on that line was the strategy for achieving their goals. They were not proud of this behavior, but could justify it by practicing rules found in their field of business. The most remarkable of all was how unhappy and fearful many were that success would not last. They were distrustful of colleagues taking away what they had gained, and hoard their accomplishments.

At first, it was hard for Samuel to convince the accountants that some of their assumptions might be false. Sometimes the shortest distance between two points is not a straight line. Secondly, it may be more productive to be sensitive to others. It could create emotional alliances where others will support you during difficult times. Thirdly, there is little reason to do anything necessary to succeed, especially if the behavior hurts the company and other employees. Finally, people who hoard their successes may spend their time worrying that someone just like them will do anything necessary to take success from them. For the next few months, Samuel spent his time trying to instill these assumptions into the climate at Ajax, one where working together and being successful went hand in hand.

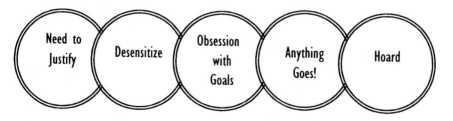

Climate of Greed
Figure 9.1

Understanding an Emotional Climate of Greed

Need to Justify

A climate of greed begins with people discovering ways to justify their actions and behavior. Our beliefs have a tremendous impact on our behavior, and this seems nowhere clearer than in a climate of greed. For example, some of the accountants, in the case study, had created reasons to justify their illegal and unethical actions. Even though they were taught to remain independent and objective when working with client companies, they found ways of collaborating with these companies. Their behavior was justified by the rationale that everyone else was practicing the same procedures. A climate of greed can flourish when strong justifications are made in allowing what is normally unacceptable behavior, now be acceptable. Another example of this can be seen during the fighting of a war. People who would never think of killing anyone will accept killing as reasonable, according to the justifications made for going to war. When people accept reasons for justifying their behavior, they are capable of almost anything. It becomes the beliefs found in the emotional climate of any given set of circumstances that allows for people's actions to become justifiable. In the case study, the accountants worked from the belief that "business is business." This vague cliché acted as a justification for action regardless of what they were taught in graduate school. They had established reasons for their behavior, and could justify these reasons in the emotional climate by saying, everyone else was doing it (figure 9.1).

Desensitize

In a climate of greed, establishing reasons for justifying certain behavior now puts greedy people in the position to act on their justifications. The old cliché "The ends justify the means" may be one more justification found in a climate of greed that says certain behaviors are possible. This may lead greedy people to the next step of de-sensitizing themselves from others who would object or question their justifications (Schumaker, 2004). In the case study, many of the accountants admitted they were insensitive, and behaved in a manner that would have been unacceptable if they remained sensitive to each other's needs. They did not reach out and work together, but remained behind a series of justifications, allowing them to act in underhanded and aberrant ways. Whether it was for profit or simply people following the lead of others was not clear. People are influenced by different personal motivations. What remains clear is that the accountants found reasons for de-sensitizing their behavior, allowing for a climate of greed to take hold among the administration and staff at the Ajax accounting firm. Their insensitive behavior found a way to be justified, and the emotional climate of greed at Ajax became bigger than the people in it. They were now in a position to give up their independence and objectivity because highly sensitive issues were now de-sensitized. They could focus on their goals without worrying how others felt (figure 9.1).

Obsession with Goals

When the reasons are established for justifying certain behavior, and the climate of greed has de-sensitized people from worrying about sensitive issues such as loyalty, friendship or professionalism, greedy people are in a position to focus obsessively on their goals. It is greed's way of saying, it is "ok" to put on "blinders" and disregard other areas of living. In the case study, some of the accountants elevated their jobs to *the* most important theme in their lives. The accountants were obsessed with succeeding and they put other activities at a lower priority. They focused obsessively on their goals. They had reasons to justify their behavior, and had become de-sensitized to the world around them. Under these circumstances, being obsessive made sense and being insensitive to others was seen as a commitment to a goal—an obsessive way of justifying behavior that was uncaring and disconnected. Their obsessions had changed the rules. They were not concerned with the ethics of professional accounting, but obsessed with success and profits. They had eliminated other themes from their lives and became insensitive enough to believe their focus was valid. They became lost in obsession, and pursued their goals without regard for others around them (figure 9.1).

Anything Goes!

At this stage in a climate of greed, the people in the climate may become dangerous to themselves and others. They have justifications for their behavior, their behavior becomes devoid of sensitivity, and they are focusing obsessively on their goals. Under these circumstances, it does not seem difficult to do almost anything to succeed. In the case study, many of the accountants saw themselves as "good people," in their interviews with Samuel. Their behavior may have been illegal and unethical, but they seemed in denial. They were working in a climate that accepted aberrant behavior, and they were obsessed with achieving goals under the assumptions that "All bets are off" and "Anything goes." Those were the unspoken rules driving them. They had sold out to their obsessions, and were capable of doing almost anything to achieve success. In a climate of greed, terrible things can happen when the climate loses its boundaries, and people stop recognizing where the boundaries once stood. In the minds of the accountants, they were professional people who were doing what was necessary to succeed. They felt their behavior was justified and they were committed to succeeding under the terms established within the climate of greed (figure 9.1).

Hoard

Greedy people may become successful in obtaining their goals, especially when the climate condones their behavior. However, there may be the possibility looming in the background that others may be just as greedy, and are more than willing to use similar tactics to take success away. A climate of greed does not seem to generate high levels of trust, and success based on greed, may promote the notion that people will do anything to succeed, even steal another's success. Under these conditions, greedy people have a tendency to hoard what they have gained, an approach that falls in line with their insensitive and obsessive behavior. Unfortunately, hoarding behavior, by no means, guarantees happiness or self-satisfaction—more often it foreshadows the opposite. Greedy people may spend their lives looking over their shoulders, wondering when someone else will take away their success. Hoarding behavior can be just as insensitive and obsessive as chasing after goals, with the same disconnections and compulsions. A climate of greed can be a state of mind created to justify obtaining and hoarding goals, without serious emphasis put on the circumstances surrounding these goals. It can be a method for getting from point "A" to point "B" without considering important experiences along the way. Unfortunately, such methods for success may leave people missing important lessons that could make the journey to success more insightful, and obtaining success more rewarding (figure 9.1).

Conciliating Greed

Greed seems filled with justifications leading to insensitive behavior. One of the characteristics of greed might be to keep emotions at a minimum, so greedy people can remain insensitive and focus obsessively on their goals. This means greedy people may have decided beforehand on their goals, and have a plan of action that may not include flexibility or sensitivity. Conciliators, who respond to greed-oriented conflicts, need to realize that greedy people usually have a clear plan to solve their problems, and may be more inclined to focus obsessively on personal solutions, than to change them at the request of a conciliator.

Greed seems similar to egotism in that egotists defend their positions at all costs and greedy people do anything to achieve their goals. Both take an all-or-nothing attitude toward others and both find little wrong with their behavior. The problem for conciliators is how to help people, who act insensitive, obsessive and are capable of anything, actually listen to someone who is trying to help them. They seem to act in a similar fashion as egotists. They know what is good for them and have little trust in the help of others—making reconciling greed-oriented conflicts tricky propositions. The following are methods that approach these problems in an attempt at resolving greed–oriented conflicts:

Historical Implications for Greed

Conciliators might take into account that greed can be an acceptable part of any culture, and may dominate the emotional climate of that culture at specific periods in history. During these moments in history greed may have a dramatic influence on the people of that culture. For example, the story told about the famous General George Armstrong Custer, and the equally famous General Crazy Horse and the Battle of Little Big Horn may verify this point (Sandoz, 1966). Both were similar in many ways. They represented their cultures as generals and both were fearless warriors. However, at the Battle of Little Big Horn, General Custer perceived the battle differently than Crazy Horse. At that time, the culture of the United States viewed Native people differently than today, and accepted certain reasons for justifying Custer's behavior. His decision to charge into the Battle of Little Big Horn was based, partially, on making a name for himself—another acceptable premise of U.S. culture at that time in history. On the other hand, Crazy Horse was not following similar cultural premises as Custer, but was fulfilling his responsibilities in a culture where being a great leader meant protecting the people of the tribe. We know how the story ends with Custer charging into the Little Big Horn only to lose his life and the lives of his men, while Crazy Horse did not charge out to meet Custer. He had no intention of becoming different than the role he played within the Sioux Nation.

Both Custer and Crazy Horse found reasons for justifying their behavior, based on the unspoken rules found in their culture. For Custer, charging into battle can be seen in his desire to become someone within the opportunistic culture of the United States, at that time. With these justifications driving him, he desensitized himself to others, focused obsessively on his goal, and was prepared to do anything to succeed. On the other hand, Crazy Horse justified not charging into battle based on being sensitive to the needs of his people, a hallmark of his culture.

It may be important for conciliators to understand the power culture has on the behavior of people, at any given time in history. In our case study, the accountants may have been influenced by a culture similar to the one found in the late nineteenth century by Custer, and, like Custer, they too may have been influenced by an emotional climate that accepted justifications for desensitizing their behavior, and focusing obsessively on goals. In dealing with greed-oriented disputes, it may be important and timely for conciliators to point out the power and influence certain historical premises have on the justifications of people in the culture, and the importance of *talking through* these justifications.

This also is present in the case study. Samuel began the conciliation process by having the accountants discuss their personal justifications, and how they were enmeshed within the emotional climate of greed found at the accounting firm. He pointed out that "being professional accountants" may have been compromised by a culture where "obsessively becoming the most successful accountants" was superseding their professional integrity. He helped them look at the historical justifications found in the existing culture of their working environment, and then pointed out how to separate their justifications from the climate of greed that, he believed, had developed in parts of the accounting industry.

Connecting the Cognitive with the Emotional

Greed appears to be built on justifications with little consideration given to feelings. Greedy people seem to put their feelings aside and focus obsessively on their goals, and justify their behavior by declaring that the ends justify the means. This translates into the end result becoming valued more than the process of getting to the end. Feelings represent a part of the process that needs to be sacrificed for the final goal. For example, a son decides not to fulfill the wishes of his father, by following in his footsteps and becoming a medical doctor. However, the father disregards his son's point of view, based on the merits of being a productive member of the medical profession, and pushes him to enroll in medical school. The son reciprocates by being insensitive to his father's wishes. They remain insensitive to each other based on justifications that their point of view is best for the future. The results of their disagreement can range anywhere from the father winning the dispute, and the son thanking his father for pushing him to be a doctor, to the son disowning his family and running off to pursue a life of his own.

In this example, the problem for a conciliator is that both outcomes are resolved without either party considering the emotional side of the dispute. Somewhere in the emotional climate surrounding this dispute, personal beliefs and feelings become disconnected. From a conciliation point of view, greed oriented disputes may require a connection between people's cognitive and emotional perspectives, for the final solution to gain validity. From the above example, without the father emotionally connecting to his son's point of view, he may push him to be a doctor, but be perceived as an authoritarian personality to be avoided at all costs. Furthermore, without the son emotionally connecting to his father's point of view, he may run off and pursue a life of his own, but be perceived as an ungrateful child that never appreciated all that was given to him. In both cases, the lack of emotional reconciliation for each other's point of view has colored the final resolution of the dispute.

A similar phenomenon develops in the case study. The accountants were making the decision to practice illegal accounting procedures based on the beliefs that it was acceptable. Everyone else was doing it. Samuel tried to reconcile these beliefs by asking the accountants how they *felt* about such practices. If the accountants successfully re-connect their feelings to their justifications, there may be a higher probability that some of them will believe their accounting practices are unacceptable. The problem with greed-oriented disputes is that emotions are ignored, making the most outrageous behavior seem justifiable. It seems that the responsibility of conciliators might be to reconnect feelings with beliefs, so reconciling greed-oriented disputes is not perceived as an unbalanced exercise in logic.

Obsessed People Do Not Listen

Greed-oriented disputes are based on people who have found reasons to justify their behavior and have desensitized themselves from others, and are now in a position to focus obsessively on their goals. For conciliators, the notion of focusing obsessively on goals may raise important issues. First, greedy people may have a tendency to *pseudo-listen* to the suggestions of others. They may *fake* listening to other opinions and become obsessed with hearing only those issues that will help them achieve their goals. Secondly, when they listen to others, they may *selectively listen* to only those issues that will help them attain what, they believe should be the final outcome. The combination of pseudo-listening and selective listening can create a climate of obsession that puts greedy people out of sync with the dialogue of others. For example, a greedy small town administrator may change the climate of a town meeting by rationalizing what the end result should be when discussing certain topics with community members. By becoming insensitive to their points of view and focusing obsessively on goals, the discussion can create a greed-oriented dispute:

- The administrator may nod his head, indicating he is listening to the points of view made by the community, but actually he may be thinking of his next response to achieve his hidden agenda.
- The administrator may obsessively go over the points he is trying to make and only respond to community members who agree with his position.
- The administrator may listen to the points of view made by community members, only to ambush them with a lecture about the importance of his point of view.
- The administrator may reward only those community members who agree with him, changing the experience from a meeting to a tribunal.

By practicing these types of behaviors, a town meeting can become polarized into those community members who may tell the administrator what he wants to hear and others who may become frustrated in the process expected in town meetings, and discontinue participation in the business of the community. By obsessively focusing on his goals, the administrator misses an opportunity to engage community members in discussion, and successfully bring people together by using the fundamental tools found in a democracy.

Conciliators can neutralize the obsessions of greedy people, by helping them get back in sync through effective listening skills that show an understanding of their true feelings. In greed-oriented disputes, an obsession with goals seems justified while listening to others may seem less significant in achieving these goals. The value of listening can be replaced with an obsession to do things a certain way, making the idea that the shortest distance between two points is only a straight line, a common belief in greed-oriented disputes.

Anything Goes!

She made up her mind that seducing her best friend's husband was going to be her next important sexual accomplishment. She would spend countless hours making inquiries about his likes and dislikes and found ways of showing up at their apartment at opportune times, where the evening would end with the three of them talking over intimate matters that only friends would share. She would baby sit for their children and constantly send them notes or gifts, creating a sense of obligation on their part to reciprocate. Gradually, she would find ways to visit them separately, creating the unspoken rule that it was acceptable to spend time together as a couple. During moments alone with her friend's husband, she subtly criticized her friend's behavior and pointed out how, "Your wife is not being sensitive to your needs." Eventually, she was able to seduce him, followed by threats that her guilt over what they had done may force her to disclose the affair. Her threats were effective. He continued seeing her even though he truly was in love with his wife. However, she began to smother him with phone calls, demands, and requests for money, which he reluctantly agreed to, while increasingly feeling devastated by their behavior. Finally, he became overwhelmed with remorse and told his wife. She was shaken by their behavior and wanted to be left alone, which encouraged her so-called friend to covet her husband even more. She would say, "Look she does not care about you and it is time for you to leave her." Fortunately, a relative of the couple intervened and helped them survive the storm in their relationship. Reconciliation took place by an understanding that the incident was based on greed, and that such insensitive behavior seems more the product of obsession and not a legitimate commitment to loving another person.

In greed-oriented disputes, many times "anything goes!" The above example gives testament to this phenomenon. The friend of the couple had justified, in her mind, that it was acceptable to pursue her best friend's husband. She de-sensitized herself to the consequences of her behavior, focused obsessively on her goal and was willing to do anything to achieve seducing him. From a perspective of greed, a person does what is necessary to succeed and almost any behavior might be acceptable under these conditions.

Another example can be seen in the case study, where the accountants seduced each other into believing their behavior was acceptable and that under these conditions, "anything goes." Again, we see how justifications can influence greed-oriented disputes. Very little difference may exist between the accountants and the best friend, as far as justifications for greedy behavior, and in both examples, conciliators may need to point out how these justifications lead people to finally believe in their aberrant behavior. Success, love, happiness, security and many other themes in life seem legitimate aspirations to pursue. However, when these themes are influenced by insensitive behavior, obsessive focusing on goals, and believing anything goes, then the possibility of creating greed-oriented disputes can remain an ever present possibility.

Hoarding Behavior

Hoarding behavior seems closely aligned with other stages of greed. It becomes filled with insensitive behavior, obsession, and an attitude that others will behave in a similar fashion and must be kept at a distance. Historically, we have used words such as avarice and covetousness to define this stage of greed, but whatever word used, the end result is similar. Greedy people may not like to share what they have coveted (Young-Mason, 2001). Take for example, stories told in the legal community about the surviving children of parents who have passed away. The children experience a dramatic shift in attitude towards each other when dividing their parents' material possessions. There are stories where siblings stop talking to each other, and find themselves in the middle of an emotionally ugly dispute, based on disagreements over "who gets what!" We have heard stories of family members sneaking into the houses of deceased relatives and filling the trunks of their cars with possessions they feel rightfully belong to them. In examples such as these, we witness the rapid deployment of a greed-oriented dispute among surviving family members.

In the case study, the bosses at Technext and Ajax Accounting followed a similar pattern of greed, where hoarding the profits they had accumulated was a common practice. They created stock options and other gratuities as rewards for achieving their goals and they "cooked the books" to covet their gains. They remained insensitive to stockholders and did what was necessary to accumulate wealth. In the end, they hoarded their wealth, by subtly practicing deceptive practices, so that others would not find out.

The irony of this behavior is that Technext and Ajax hoarded profits as a means of accumulating wealth under this insensitive assumption. Profits were the ultimate achievable goal of their business. However, when they achieved their goals, they needed to hoard the profits and therefore practice similar activities as those methods used in obtaining their goals. They believed that the ends justified the means, only to find out that obtaining the ends and keeping them created similar greed-oriented disputes. Conciliators may be in a position to point out how hoarding can produce the same results as greedily pursuing these ends, and that guarding against others can be a full time job filled with obsession, insensitivity and aberrant behavior, whether, it is relatives hoarding the possessions of recently deceased parents or corporate bosses cooking the books to covet the profits of a company.

A Peacemaking Alternative: A Climate of Generosity

Donna was taking over from a professor who taught the graduate research course for the past twenty-five years, in the education department at a prominent southern university. The course was notoriously difficult and many students dreaded it as a part of their graduate study. The former syllabus, for the course, was daunting, and Donna wondered how any student could successfully complete the time-lines established for finishing the course. It required students to identify a research problem that would be used in a graduate thesis. It covered information on how to review the literature in researching this problem, and it surveyed methods of statistics that would help in creating a methodology for completing the research. The former professor approached the course as though it was the "union card" for successfully completing the graduate program, and numerous examples of students failing research circulated through the conversations of each new graduate class. Apparently, the course had become the focal point of who successfully graduated from the program and who did not. To make matters worse, for the graduate students, was the former professor's insensitive, mean-spirited approach to presenting the material.

Donna entered the classroom of the graduate research course with a similar trepidation as the graduate students glaring back at her. She would comment later that the students looked like deer caught in the headlights of an oncoming car—unblinking, frozen to the desks before them. She gazed around the room realizing she was facing fifteen people who probably were entering the research classroom with assumptions reflecting the course's infamous reputation. This was disturbing to her. She had access to former student research proposals, and even though they were technically correct, they lacked a curiosity for researching important problems within the field of education.

After handing out the syllabus for the course, which was much like the one given out by her predecessor, she asked the students to answer the following question, "How many in this classroom have a fear of research?" Slowly their hands were raised into the air until all but three people acknowledged their fears. Donna said, "I want you to know that research can be intimidating but we are going to create a climate, in this classroom, where we help each other become technically and personally involved with this subject matter."

For the next month, Donna discussed their fears of research. As students disclosed their fears, Donna would match students together who could help each other with technical problems, along with any emotional roadblocks to academic excellence. As it turned out, each student brought a specific expertise to the class and was asked to present their knowledge and opinions to the group. Initially, many topics had little to do with the technical side of research, but gradually a climate was established where students openly admitted their strengths and weaknesses. During this process, Donna would define specific research principles when they came up in conversation and, on occasions, she would express a need to cover certain materials by giving mini-lectures to the group.

The discussions lasted five weeks and were dissolved when everyone agreed they had experienced an increase in their levels of confidence. What followed were visits to the library, technology lab, mathematics, and statistics departments, where she created outside resources for her students to use in the development of their proposals. Each remaining class began with an open forum where students shared their successes and failures, what resources they used after visiting outside facilities, and their progress toward the final goal of creating a research thesis. The open forum was followed by breaking students into groups according to similar interests. Donna would move from one group to the next answering questions, giving directions and sharing encouragement when students began feeling overwhelmed or confused.

The final proposals, presented to her at the end of the course, were extraordinary. Not only did they reflect a fundamental understanding of graduate research, but they were filled with creativity and a sense of personal involvement. Through the shared generosity created in the emotional climate of the course, the students made research more than a union card for passing graduate school. It now stood as an example of what graduate school could be all about. In the years that followed, Donna made copies of former student proposals to hand out on the first day of class. Former students of research were pointing out to another new group of tentative researchers, what was possible when people work together.

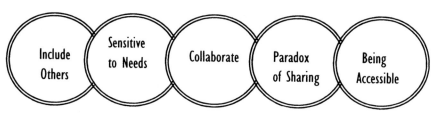

Climate of Generosity
Figure 9.2

Include Others [7]

A climate of generosity begins in a similar fashion as a climate of greed, where both are based on justifications about how people should conduct their behavior. The difference lies in the type of justifications made. Greedy people believe that self-serving behavior can be acceptable, and in many cases, preferable in achieving their goals. The opposite seems true in a climate of generosity. Generous people begin from a belief that including others in goals and aspirations may be a more desirable and productive enterprise (Wilson, 2013; Marts, 1996). In the case study, the college professor who taught the graduate research course prior to Donna was working from a justification that excluded student input. The course was rigidly structured, where the professor judged not only student performance, but also who would eventually graduate from the program. The intent was to justify one professor's blueprint for success in graduate research, where the activities in the course satisfied the needs of the professor not the students.

A different justification was made by Donna even though she fundamentally was teaching the same material after taking over the course. Donna's beliefs were based on the justification that including others would make the research course a richer experience for both the students and the teacher. A climate of generosity begins with a belief in the input of others and it grows with the help of others. Donna structured a course that considered student involvement in the research process and not research as a final goal. She believed excellence in teaching could be achieved by including others in that learning process (figure 9.2).

Sensitive to Needs

Donna understood that including students in the learning process was possible, by being sensitive to their needs. She formed a theme-centered group and had students talk about their fear of research. During that time, she matched students with similar goals and she made sure both cognitive and affective goals were considered. When she believed specific research topics should be covered. Mini-lectures were given to meet these needs. Donna believed that reaching out to her students would help her construct the material in a more meaningful way. She included their needs into the curriculum as a method for learning graduate research, and she strengthened the importance of research by being sensitive to these needs.

The practice of being sensitive to the needs of others may create an unspoken rule, that generosity can be a vital component within any group pursuing a common goal. Over time, such generosity may encourage group members to reach out and help others, when they need it. This becomes a different premise than performing activities only according to the needs of an authority. Being sensitive to the needs of others can create an awareness of rich new avenues for successfully pursuing any goal. In Donna's case, she not only strengthened the skills of her graduate students but she created a more accurate and dynamic graduate course, by sharing the issues found in research (figure 9.2).

Collaborate

By collaborating on each student's personal needs, Donna was in a position to have students effectively collaborate on the goals of the course. To some, this indirect method may seem a waste of time however it appears that few significant problems are created when students initially pursue their personal needs, before focusing on the goals of a course. In fact, many graduate courses may be strengthened by this procedure (Riveros, 2012; O'Shea, Williams & Sattler, 1999).

However, we see a clash between the previous professor's values and the values Donna maintained in her style of teaching. The previous professor's methods for teaching graduate research would have penalized students who wavered from the goals developed for the course. The professor's goals were the only acceptable focus for receiving passing grades. Student needs were seen as a distraction in achieving the rigor needed to achieve these grades. The focus of the course was in developing an acceptable product, completing assignments, and passing examinations. However, in Donna's course, student collaboration raised graduate research to a more involved level by filling the class with personal analysis and self-evaluation. Students were able to create an emotional involvement with the material, while simultaneously discovering their strengths and weaknesses. Assurances were made that personal weaknesses, in research, would be resolved through the collaborative efforts of the class (figure 9.2).

Paradox of Sharing

The genius in Donna's approach was in realizing that students helping each other to succeed, paradoxically, could help *her* to succeed. A climate of generosity may set the stage for helping all involved share an investment in the final outcome. Helping others in the pursuit of success may create valuable allies, who expand and enhance the nature of the goals that lead to success. Donna was unimpressed with prior thesis proposals emanating from her former colleague's graduate research classes. Technically, they were correct but they lacked the vitality of people having a curiosity for graduate research. The proposals demonstrated an understanding of the material but lacked an emotional connection to it.

In Donna's research class, students were developing proposals filled with the input of others, and through their shared commitment, research was crafted around each student's personal involvement with the materials of others. The goals of the professor, and the course, were transcended by richer and more meaningful goals that became working parts of all the proposals in the course. Donna seems to have disproved the adage that, the shortest distance between two points is a straight line. The research proposals, received at the end of the course, were richer and more meaningful than anything that came before them. She strengthened the research course and the students' abilities to perform research by sharing knowledge in the classroom setting. She helped others to succeed and they, paradoxically, helped her obtain the rigor required in courses found in graduate education (figure 9.2).

Being Accessible

To sustain a climate of generosity, Donna established a library of graduate student proposals that were handed out at the beginning of each new graduate research course. She believed that generosity was enhanced by accessibility and she wanted her new students to have access to successful proposals, and the level of expectations that could be achieved if everyone worked together on common goals. Donna's expertise was not based only on her ability as a graduate research teacher. Her ability was based on a more demanding formula —the expertise of the professor, combined with student/professor efforts, a willingness to share these efforts with others and a commitment to accessibility, so others can learn from these efforts.

Some would argue that true academic rigor only comes from a curriculum that is challenging and forces students to meet the strict demands of experts, who have the knowledge to evaluate the performance of their students (Braxton, 2002). For some, this form of rigor requires a structured syllabus that leaves little room for the needs of students and their differing points of view. It is a philosophy of education that holds validity in most circles of higher education and is practiced at many graduate schools (Gatz, 2000). It is based on students proving their abilities by demonstrating their understanding of the subject matter presented by the professor. In the right hands, this approach can be challenging, dynamic and highly competitive. In the wrong hands, it runs the risk of insensitivity, obsession with goals, rigidly upholding rules that inhibit learning, and hoarding knowledge, as though it was a treasure hidden by an expert. Donna created a climate of generosity that offered an alternative model for academic rigor in higher education. It was based on meeting student needs, collaboration between professor and students, sharing information with others, and accessibility—all of this justifying her reasons for including students as an integral part of graduate research (Olsen, 1999) (figure 9.2).

Cultural Implications

The culture of consumerism is creating a climate of greed and is usually defined by the pursuit and possession of things. The pleasure is not so much in the possession of things as in their pursuit. Once consumers obtain an item, it temporarily satisfies desire, and the item loses some of its appeal. That is why shopping, not buying, is the heart of consumerism. Greed keeps us focused on what we do not yet have, and blinds us to all that we already have. Greed guarantees that, no matter how much we acquire it will never be enough. Building a society or a life based on the culture of consumerism can create serious conflicts.

The culture of consumerism gathers momentum in disintegrating traditional cultures worldwide. Manufacturers in poor countries and in China are exploiting workers to keep up with the demands of consumers around the world, based on a climate of greed. For example, long working hours, inhumane working and living conditions, and a lack of safety features in many factories around the world are becoming the norm not the exception. In recent years, two factories in Pakistan and Bangladesh caught fire and hundreds of workers were killed because safety features were lacking. Both factories were making products for famous brands. Deep within a climate of greed lies the irony of exploiting workers and then having these workers pay for items that were made on the backs of other exploited workers. It may be that conciliators at the societal level need to understand the problem before they can intervene, whether they are politicians, leaders of nations, or CEOs of international companies. Beyond consumerism is the cultural battle taking place in countries faced with conflicting models of economic development.

The case study shows the management side of such greed. Not only is the culture of consumerism wrecking some cultures around the world, it is also having devastating effects on the middle class of some of the rich countries. It becomes increasingly difficult to balance wealth when a climate of greed is controlling the manufacture and sale of consumer goods. Greedy people find justifications for their actions through their obsession with wealth.

Notes

7. Information for including others can be found in the following book., Blanchfield, K. E., & Ladd, P. D. (2013). *Leadership, violence and school climate: Case studies in creating non-violent schools.* Lanham, MD: Rowman & Littlefield Education. 215–227.

Chapter 10

Anxiety, Fear, and Conciliation

Anxiety and fear historically have fallen into the realm of psychiatrists, psychologist, and mental health counselors. Many cases of anxiety and fear can be recognized as mental health disorders with general anxiety disorder, post-traumatic stress disorder, and attention deficit disorder, just to name a few. Fear also can be found in the realm of mental health professionals through forms of obsessive compulsive disorder, agoraphobia, and paranoia. In the field of conciliation, anxiety and fear are more about the emotional climate they create among people than any one person. It could be argued that being in a climate of anxiety or fear may eventually lead to possible mental disorders, or at least contribute to them.

In this chapter, we will see how a climate of anxiety and fear can develop into problems related to mental and physical problems. Even though, emotions are mostly found in the mental health professions, emotions have also entered the realm of conflict resolution. Conciliators are those professionals who intervene when the emotional climate of a conflict or a dispute needs a change in environment. Occasionally, people cannot continue resolving their conflicts or disputes without a conciliator. It is the process of stabilizing relationships between disputing people so parties can talk about their conflicts, move on to a more formal process such as mediation, or simply feel more comfortable around other people.

The chapter will also describe why anxiety may be more dangerous than fear in certain types of conflicts. At least with fear, people know what is threatening them. Whereas with anxiety there still is that uncertainty about where the threat is coming from. It may be that effective conciliators sometimes need to change a climate of anxiety into a climate of fear before a more stable climate such as climate of safety can be established among a people. Another term for conciliation is peacemaking. Sometimes making peace with others or making peace within one's self, requires feeling safe and secure within a climate that emotionally and physically offers protection from outside forces.

It may be that psychiatrists, psychologists and mental health counselors are trained to facilitate change with patients and their families, and conciliators are trained to change the emotional climate found within an environment based on how these people live. The following case study is directed toward such a situation where conciliators could have added a valuable asset if the people in charge had made arrangements for helping their employees make a successful transition to a future life.

Case Study

Times were hard for employees working for an automobile parts manufacturing company housed in rural Alabama. Jobs were going to places like Mexico, China and still to be announced locations. There was a climate of uncertainty among auto parts workers who lived in this rural area where the company was the major source of employment. Production was slowly decreasing. It seemed the major focus was not on manufacturing but on whether parts of their company were going to be outsourced to another location. Employees were worried and signs of their worry were becoming evident in their work. Auto parts were being manufactured at a lower quality than what was considered common practice at the plant, and the worry was spreading. The local newspaper ran editorials about the possibility of plant closure, and the community constantly talked about what would happen if this reality happened to their families.

What made things worse was this phenomenon was going on for the past five years with no real disclosures or information from company management. People who worked at the plant along with local store owners, and other community members seemed in crisis. The doctors and the hospital twenty miles away had remarked at the increase in mental and physical problems coming from the area surrounding the company. Though no one openly connected their mental health and medical symptoms to the possible plant closure, underneath there was an unspoken understanding as to where the uncertainty was coming from. With the increase in physical and mental symptoms came a decrease in productivity. People were in the dark, as they continued to do their jobs manufacturing auto parts.

Finally, after five years of uncertainty, management at the company announced there were going to be layoffs in anticipation of the company closing within the next year. For some employees this was devastating news; as for others the news brought an odd sigh of relief. Though they felt threatened, at least they knew clearly what the threat entailed for their future. When the pink slips of employment termination started to flow, some fell apart and decided to go on welfare, while others took a stand and risked moving to other locations. Even though, this uprooted families, communities and businesses, the threat was clear and they were now trying to resolve a conflict that was going on for five years. In the end, some employees felt ruined while others became more resilient and moved on. It was obvious these people needed help in understanding the threat to the future confronting them. Unfortunately, rural Alabama was not the only area facing this conflict where some form of conciliation could have helped. Things were changing and society was facing the overall anxiety of having to face the continuous shrinking of its middle class work force.

Climate of Anxiety and Fear
Figure 10.1

Understanding an Emotional Climate of Anxiety and Fear

Feeling Uncertain vs. Feeling Threatened [8]

An emotional climate of anxiety begins when people sense subtle uncertainties about their future. As much as guilt is an emotion focusing on the past, anxiety is an emotion signaling future uncertainties. It is a subtle sense of not knowing what will happen, and the lack of control connected to this uncertainty. An emotional climate of anxiety emerges when enough people focusing on a similar problem become uncertain about the future outcome of this problem, and create expectations that demand their attention. Usually, this phenomenon of uncertainty accumulates over time until it reaches a critical mass, and causes an impact on people's feelings and behaviors. We see this happening in the case study, where for five years a climate of anxiety is accumulating in a rural town in Alabama. Finally, the uncertainty is replaced with feeling threatened by the announcement that the plant is closing.

An emotional climate of fear does not begin with uncertainty, but starts with a knowable threat that people understand and that forces them to deal with their future. When it was clear to employees that the plant was closing, they were threatened but not uncertain at about where the threat was coming from. They had gone from uncertainty to experiencing a real threat to their livelihood. By clarifying the threat, they were in a position to make choices even though they were stressful choices (figure 10.1).

Focus Narrows vs. Clarifying the Threat

With the accumulation of uncertainty, an emotional climate of anxiety can force people to narrow their focus in order to make certainty out of uncertainty. This becomes evident in the case study, when employees of the company, family members, business owners, and community members kept thinking about what was going to happen to them.

When people have problems based on uncertainty, the tendency is to narrow the focus and try to solve the problem. Many conflicts and disputes are solved by continuously focusing on problems, until some certainty appears. For example, if it is Monday and a student has an English test on Friday, and he or she has lost confidence in passing it, then the student may not notice the beautiful blue sky on Tuesday. On Wednesday the student may not notice the compliment received from another student, or the trouble with a boyfriend or girlfriend might go un-noticed on Thursday. The student's focus may have narrowed to such a degree that he or she is primarily thinking about the test. The English exam narrowed their focus, and in doing so, cut out confidence needed to be a successful English exam test taker.

We see this happening in the case study where the employees of the plant are so focused on whether they will have a job that production quality drops adding more uncertainty to the problem. However, once they find out the plant is clos-ing, the climate shifts from a climate of anxiety to a climate of fear where the actual threat is clarified and employees are in the position to take or not to take a stand. In some respects, a climate of fear forces people to choose where they stand on a threat. It allows them a choice in the face of a clarified threat (figure 10.1).

Constant Worry vs. Taking a Stand

In a climate of anxiety, feelings of uncertainty can lead people to narrow their focus, in order to solve conflicts or disputes. However, if the focus narrows to an extreme and dominates peoples' thinking, then constant worry may develop, making the problem more difficult (Hinton & Earnest, 2010; Barlow, 1991).

People tend to narrow their focus when feeling uncertain about their prob-lems. It helps in bringing certainty to uncertainty. However, when people *over-focus* on a problem without any success in solving it, then constant worry has a high probability of entering the equation (Koerner & Dugas, 2008; Keinknecht, 1991). In the case study, a whole section of rural Alabama became caught in feelings of constant worry. Unfortunately, their worry was counter-productive, causing them to narrow their focus even further. Eventually, worry led to a narrower focus and a narrower focus led to increased worry. Over time, this reciprocal relationship produced mental health symptoms and physical health problems.

However, when the climate shifted from anxiety to fear, the people affected in rural Alabama at least had a choice to either fall apart emotionally and physically or to take a stand and try to protect themselves and their families. When looking at this experience from a mental health perspective, it may be more advantageous to be in a climate of fear rather than a climate of anxiety—even though most people would rather not be in either of them (figure 10.1).

Symptoms Develop vs. Go into Action

Developing symptoms from constantly worrying about a conflict or a dispute is a common next step in a climate of anxiety. All the ingredients are there to change peoples' emotions and behavior. Uncertainty, narrow focus and constant worry, may all contribute to people having psycho-somatic, behavioral, emotional, and possibly, cognitive changes in their everyday activities (Feero & Steadman, 2010; Keable, 1997). In the case study, people were experiencing all of the above symptoms. There was open agreement from hospitals and doctors that mental and physical problems were on the rise.

A climate of anxiety can cause constant worry, literally, to change subtle nuances in people's lives. When people narrow their focus and constantly worry about problems, with time, they may have a tendency to become highly vulnerable to a climate filled with anxiety. One of the problems with anxiety is the development of symptoms, when people are at their weakest moments. Constant worry may have a tendency to neutralize people's coping mechanisms, or at least suspend them from use. For example, highly competent professionals with a myriad of skills may find in a climate of anxiety, that their skills are overpowered by their constant worry. Newly developed symptoms of procrastination, lack of creativity or loss of energy may take their place, and this may eventually cause more worry.

In a climate of fear similar symptoms can develop as in a climate of anxiety, yet with one major difference. In a climate of fear, people are free to go into action by facing their fears. They can become more proactive than reactive. In the case study, there were people devastated by the plant closing, while others went into action, and tried to overcome the disaster by seeking other avenues of employment (figure 10.1).

Crisis Mode vs. Relief and Release

In a climate of anxiety, uncertainty can lead to narrowing one's focus. Focusing on a problem to an extreme, can create constant worry. Worrying over an extended period of time, can create the probability for the advent of debilitating symptoms. Debilitating symptoms eventually may lead people, to crisis mode and crisis mode can lead to physical and mental illness (Lowell, 2012; May, 1950).

Crisis mode is that point in anxiety when people no longer need to be thinking about the original uncertainty that caused their focus to narrow. People develop debilitating symptoms, no matter what they are thinking. In the case study, hospitals were filling up and doctors were being over-worked based on more people falling into crisis whether from the uncertainties at the plant or that problem combined with uncertainties at home or in the community. Crisis mode is when anxious people develop debilitating symptoms, even while performing activities that were formerly filled with confidence (LaTorre, 2001).

In the case study, with the advent of crisis mode, anxiety has evolved full circle: uncertainty leads to a narrow focus, a narrow focus to constant worry, constant worry leads to debilitating symptoms, debilitating symptoms to crisis mode and finally, crisis mode to more uncertainty. Such a vicious cycle, if not stopped, can create chronic psychological and physical disorders with anxiety as the overriding symptom or cause (Psik, 2015; Barber & Crits-Christoph, 1995).

However, with the announcement of the plant closing, employees and their families entered a new climate. Now they were afraid but knew exactly what was at the center of their fear. They were at that existential moment of giving in or going into action. Those that went into action had a stronger chance of eventually feeling some form of physical and psychological release, leading to some form of relief. (figure 10.1)

Conciliating Fear and Anxiety

The philosopher, Kierkegaard once said that, "Life was like trying to walk through the raindrops of anxiety" (Beabout, 1996). A conciliator (or anyone else for that matter) probably will not get through any dispute without anxiety being a part of their emotional experience. Conflicts can be filled with uncertainty and uncertainty can lead people in conflict to narrow their focus, with the hope of solving a problem. To a conciliator, it may be important the level of anxiety experienced by individuals involved in a conflict. At one end of the emotional spectrum is the normal anxiety a group experiences when conflicts appear in; schools, workplaces, families, communities and any other venue where people find themselves disagreeing with each other. Reconciliation of anxiety, in these circumstances, may be unnecessary. A group of people who narrow their focus to resolve a dispute may build confidence in their ability to survive anxiety and solve problems by periodically narrowing their focus.

At the other end of the spectrum are those who have suffered the tension of anxiety for too long a period of time, and have gone to the depths of pain not necessarily connected in any conflict. Psychologists, psychiatrists, counselors and others are more qualified to treat people who experience constant worry regardless of the circumstances. There are many pages of the *Diagnostic Statistical Manual 5* dedicated to the treatment of anxiety based disorders to help such people (Obiols, 2012; Tracy, et al. 1997).

However, conciliators can be crucial in reconciling conflicts where people have finally clarified the threat connected to their conflict. Under these circumstances, intervention by a conciliator may help change anxiety to fear where the people in conflict can take a stand. It may be the support and guidance of a conciliator that helps people in conflict become successful in dealing with their fears. It may be such an intervention helps people in conflict go into action in their search for relief and release. The following are methods a conciliator can use in helping people work through their anxiety in order to face their fears.

The Difference between Fear and Anxiety

Here are two similar stories to demonstrate the difference between fear and anxiety.

Fear

A man was digging a drainage ditch in the middle of large field. He was warned that a killer bull was in the field, but the bull was nowhere in sight. As he was digging, he looked up on the hill and saw a huge boulder, but when he looked again the boulder was gone. The man felt a sudden threat that the bull was near. When he looked up again, there was a 1,500 lb. bull about thirty yards away, staring at him. Immediately, he ran for the fence that was fifty yards away, and barely cleared it with the bull directly behind him. He jumped over the fence, and with a huge sigh of relief, let out a muffled grunt.

In this story a man is threatened by a bull. He clarifies where the bull is located. He takes a stand and risks running for the fence. He jumps over the fence and feels a sigh of relief. This story may seem threatening, but it is a conflict with a clear beginning, middle and end. Conciliators may help people with their fear, so they also can clarify a threat, in order to take a stand and get relief. Being afraid, can actually helps some people in conflict resolution. It focuses people on a specific threat and forces them to take a stand. In the example, the man may actually learn how to dig a better drainage ditch and avoid the bull by numerous successful confrontations with it.

Anxiety

A man was digging a drainage ditch in the middle of a large field. He was warned that a killer bull was in the field, but the bull was nowhere in sight. As he was digging he looked up on the hill and saw a huge boulder, and when he looked again, it still was a huge boulder on a hill. The man began to feel uncertainty about where the bull was located. Later that day, there was movement in bushes in a hollow nearby but a flock of partridges fluttered out of the bushes. Near the end of the day, he felt a vector of warm air on his neck. He quickly turned around and it was a vector of warm air on his neck. Over the next few days, he stopped thinking about his girlfriend, the dance on Friday night and the money he was making. One question kept entering his mind, "Where is the bull?" After a week, the man noticed that when he approached the field his hands started to sweat, and his heart began to beat rapidly, and the drainage ditch stopped being a straight line. A few weeks passed and he realized that the same symptoms he was experiencing when entering the field were now happening while in the safety of his apartment. Finally, he decided the job was not worth it and he quit.

In this story the man is uncertain about the location of a killer bull. His focus narrows to locate it. He cannot locate it and begins to constantly worry about its location. With time, he develops symptoms every time he enters the field. Finally, he has symptoms whether he enters the field or not. Unlike fear, anxiety does not clarify the threat, and without a clear threat, no stand can be taken, and without taking a stand, little relief appears in sight. Sometimes conciliators can help people change their anxiety to fear. Though fear can be threatening in anxiety-oriented conflicts, it can be far less damaging. Fear allows people to take a stand and find relief. Anxiety offers constant worry, debilitating symptoms, and crisis mode.

Surviving Expectations

People are different and what they expect out of any given set of circumstances may vary. This also applies to how people resolve conflicts. Some will expect resolution of a conflict to be 100 percent successful and will suffer with anxiety if the 100 percent is not achieved. Others will settle for a compromise and are content with 50 percent resolution and others are so uncertain, they have no idea what to expect. Conciliators are not in a position to dictate at what level people should resolve their conflicts, but they are in a position to help disputing parties clarify their expectations and live with the results. In the case study, plant employees suffered a debilitating climate of anxiety. However, when the announcement came that the plant was closing effective conciliators were made available to help employees with their fear of losing employment. There purpose was not to locate jobs, but they were available to relieve fears regardless of the outcome (Mareschal, 2002).

Expanding the Focus

At this moment *do not* think of the number seven!

If you are now continuing to read, please answer the following questions: "Did you find the number seven lurking in your mind, even after being told not to think about it?" or "Did you have to take a brief moment to remove it from your mind?" If the answer is "yes" to either of these questions, then you may have experienced the difficulty some people have in expanding their focus when solving a conflict. We have a natural tendency to narrow our focus when faced with conflicts, and in most circumstances, looking at conflicts more specifically may help us resolve these conflicts (Griffin & Griffin, 1997; Carrier et al. 1984). Yet, as seen in the above example, a person may have difficulty *not* thinking of the number "seven," even when asked to stop thinking about it. This simple trick gives an example of how we spontaneously narrow our focus when solving problems, and it indicates the difficulty we may have in expanding our focus, even after deciding not to resolve a problem.

However, our difficulty may not be in saying that conflicts usually cause an experience of acute anxiety. Actually, we may need a certain level of anxiety to help us clearly focus on effectively resolving our conflicts. It is our inability to *expand* our focus, when we fail to solve these conflicts that may cause acute anxiety to flourish. We may constantly focus on conflicts we find difficult to solve while ignoring other problems that accumulate over time. In the case study, it was five years of uncertainty of not knowing the future for plant employees that led to acute anxiety.

The announcement that the plant was closing created fear yet with the proper conciliation from a professional or within the minds of plant employees some form of taking a stand and developing an action plan was now possible. Ultimately for employees and their families, reconciliation of this conflict was in their ability to *expand their focus* to an acceptable level where they could face their fear of the future.

The Difference between Worry and Concern

Betty and John were parents of a teenage daughter, Julie, who enjoyed being with her friends, especially on weekends. The problem was that Julie seemed to have so much fun with her friends that she continuously came in late, causing her parents high levels of anxiety. The first step they made was to change their anxiety to fear. They took a stand by clarifying exactly what was the uncertainty. This changed when Betty and John bought their daughter a cell phone for her birthday. Even though they were still afraid, they took a stand on what threatened them. It was not the time spent with her friends nor was it fear over type of friends she was seeing. They had concluded their primary fear was for Julie's safety. Now that she had a cell phone either of them could call when they started feeling anxious. They had changed their uncertainty found in anxiety to taking a stand regarding their fear.

In the above example, Julie's parents were faced with an anxiety-oriented conflict that caused them to worry about her safety, constantly. The more they worried, the more anxious they became, leading them to trying curfews and other forms of punishment. The problem was their worry had not lessened their level of anxiety, but had increased it, especially when Julie was having fun and forgot to come home on time. They changed their anxiety to fear and then to a plan for safety.

In this case, reconciliation became possible when they changed their anxiety to fear and then a plan for safety. Anxiety is an indiscriminate sense that something bad is going to happen in the future. It does not need a base of facts nor does it require that people specifically think through their conflicts. Fear is the act of pinpointing the threat that is causing conflict and setting into operation some plan to relieve that conflict. Betty and John changed their anxiety to fear when they realized that it was Julie's safety that was of most concern. When they bought her a cell phone, they could check in anytime their anxiety reached higher levels. By changing anxiety to fear, they reconciled the constant feelings of worry they experienced, when Julie would come home late from seeing her friends. Conciliators are in the same position as Julie's parents. Many situations can be filled with anxiety and require someone to reconcile people's anxiety to fear. Fear may not, necessarily, solve conflicts, but it can specifically clarify them for successful reconciliation. It is easier to help someone with their fear than with their anxiety where clarifying a threat and taking a stand can lead to someone's ultimate safety.

The Art of Referral

For conciliators, referring anxious people to a mental health professional may be the most effective alternative when anxiety-oriented conflicts have reached crisis mode. Conflicts are phenomena that pertain to a specific set of circumstances such as anxiety in the workplace, or anxiety in schools. When anxiety reaches crisis mode, people go beyond specific conflict and suffer from, uncertainty, constant worry and debilitating symptoms, regardless of the circumstances. Also, there are anxiety based disorders such as general anxiety disorder, anxiety associated with depression, attention deficit disorder, and others that *do not only* originate from anxiety-oriented conflicts (Hedman, 2014; Griffiths, 1997).

Conciliators are individuals involved in conflict resolution, not life style disorders that originate from historical or biological sources. However, the art of referring a friend or co-worker to a mental health professional is within the rubric of reconciliation. It can be important that conciliators have resources available for referral.

For example, John was creating many anxiety-oriented conflicts with colleagues at work. Steve was asked by his superiors to reconcile the climate of anxiety present within the workplace environment. After conciliating numerous disputes between John and other employees, it became obvious that John was suffering from more than anxiety-oriented conflicts at work. Fortunately, for Steve, his place of employment had an effective "Employees Assistance Program." Steve referred John to a mental health professional, eventually isolating John's drug and alcohol problems. John's eventual problems had a mental health and addiction diagnosis. However, his problems did create a climate of anxiety in his workplace. By referring John to an E.A.P. counselor, the anxiety-oriented conflicts in the workplace stopped.

Many times, conciliation becomes the first step to counseling and psycho therapy, when anxiety reaches the level of crisis mode. At this point, anxiety has transcended the label of a conflict. It has become a disorder or a disease that needs long term care, not conflict resolution. Yet, conciliators can be crucial in helping colleagues, family members, neighbors, and troubled students find the appropriate treatment for their anxiety. This may also apply to the experience of fear. If there is little relief and release from clarifying a threat and taking a stand, it may call for a mental health professional to help develop a plan that helps create safety.

A Peacemaking Alternative: A Climate of Safety [9]

Lynn and Tony were on their way to making two negative experiences into one positive experience. They had been trying for years to have children but with little success. The day they decided to adopt was the first step in having a new outlook on life. Jenna was a ten-year-old adolescent who had bumped around from one foster home to another. She was pretty, bright, and completely filled with anxiety and insecurity about who was going to eventually care for her.

Lynn remembers the first time she saw Jenna. She was standing in a line of girls with her best clothing on—hoping some couple would pick her for their own. Jenna had been through this "sorting" procedure many times before, but most children picked were younger and less worldly. Beyond her forced smile, Lynn could see eyes filled with fear—waiting for one more disappointment to take place. Maybe it was Jenna's eyes, or maybe her effort to smile that drew Lynn into making conversation. "How many of these events have you been to?" asked Lynn. Jenna replied, "This is my eleventh one." Lynn said, "I want you to meet my husband, Tony, and decide whether this event will be your last." Jenna's face softened and a bright, effortless smile crossed her face. Lynn introduced them by saying, "Tony, this is Jenna. Jenna, this is Tony." It was a modest introduction for what turned out to be a long lasting relationship between three spontaneous people.

Jenna is now twenty-five years old and has been asked to give a speech at Lynn and Tony's twenty-fifth wedding anniversary. After sharing numerous humorous stories about the three of them, Jenna tells the guests the one gift from Lynn and Tony that she is most thankful for receiving over the years. Jenna says:

> My parents have given me many things over the years but there is one thing that means more to me than all the rest. When I was ten, they said we would be a family and they stuck to their word. Before that time, I felt uncertain about my future and had no idea what was going to happen to me. My parents have this remarkable ability of making me feel "ok" about myself even when things are not "ok." They tolerated all the uncertainty and insecurity that accompanies being a teenager and young adult. Now that I have finished college, it is

clear to me that having the feeling of safety that your family is behind
you and will protect you is one of the greatest gifts anyone can receive.

For Lynn and Tony, their daughter's remarks reflected their sentiments about
her. Lynn stood and said the following:

Thank you, Jenna, for remarks any parent would cherish, forever.
Before you entered our lives, we were two people looking for a family. We were uncertain about our chances of that ever happening and
insecure about our future. When you entered our lives, our uncertainty and insecurity vanished. For better or worse, we were determined to make our family work. You say that we were there for
you, but the opposite is also true. You were there for us.

Climate of Safety
Figure 10.2

Risk

In the case study, all three family members took a risk when Jenna was adopted.
Initially, no climate of safety existed for these three people. It was only after
Lynn and Tony decided to risk adopting Jenna, and Jenna accepted them as her
parents, that a climate of safety became feasible. In an anxious and uncertain
world, it may be hard to imagine a climate of safety being established without
some form of risk-taking generated out of facing one's fear. It may be equally
hard perceiving a climate of safety continuing without continued risk. It may
take courage to create a climate of safety. There may be little guarantees that
your efforts will be successful. In the case study, Jenna had attended ten different adoption parties before Lynn and Tony approached her. Each time, she was
willing to risk the fear of rejection to obtain her goal of being adopted. Lynn and
Tony, also, were willing to risk. Though an older child, they were relying on
their instincts that Jenna would fit within their family system. All of these people were willing to take risks, in order to feel more secure. A climate of safety
begins by initially taking a risk and unlike a climate of anxiety, it is not caught
in constant worry to avoid risk (figure 10.2).

Certainty

What people are risking, in establishing a climate of safety, may be a sense of certainty that others will be there when uncertainty enters their lives (Barlow, 1991). In many respects, certainty is the feeling many people seek when experiencing a climate of anxiety and certainty is the motivation for risk taking when attempting to face one' fear (Horn, 2013; Bar-Tar and Spitzer, 1999). In the case study, Jenna lived in a climate of anxiety, where she felt uncertain about her future. Lynn and Tony offered her many possibilities through adoption, but the possibility she most cherished was the sense of certainty that they would be there for her. A lack of certainty was at the base of her anxiety, and she believed that finding certainty was her pathway to the future. Lynn and Tony were working from a similar premise. They wanted a family and were looking for a child who could create that certainty in their lives. Together they overcame their fear by making a commitment to be there for each other, no matter how much uncertainty entered their worlds. A sense of certainty can become the underlying base that allows people to expand their focus. It can be the unconscious sense that someone will be there for you and will make things safe.

A sense of certainty can be an anchor in a sea of uncertainty. This does not mean that in a climate of safety, all experiences in life will be free of anxiety or fear. What it may mean is that a climate of safety may have elements that allow for some portion of peoples' experiences to feel safe, in spite of overwhelming anxiety or fear. This phenomenon was at the heart of Jenna's speech to her parents. She was saying "I knew you would be there for me, no matter what happens," and this was the gift she most cherished (figure 10.2).

Focus Expands

With a sense of safety established within a person's life, expanding one's focus to experience different possibilities can become a viable option. One of the tragedies of children who have little sense of safety in their lives can be the narrow focus they may choose, in search of changing their uncertainty to certainty. In the case study, it was only after Jenna lived with Lynn and Tony in a climate of safety that she began to expand her focus beyond looking for a family. What if Jenna is not adopted by Lynn and Tony, and becomes one of many children who continue to move from one foster parent situation to another. Never having experienced a climate of safety, she may spend the rest of her life, narrowly focusing on finding the right friends, or the right spouse, or the right job that will bring safety into her life. Instead of feeling safe enough to expand her focus on her blessings she may narrow her focus in search of relieving her ongoing fear about life, in general. Not having experienced a climate of safety, Jenna may have a difficult time being satisfied with others in her life. She may have narrowed her focus to constantly worry about her future, instead of expanding her focus and having a future. Worrying about living, and actually living, seem to be two different phenomena, where one narrows your focus to counter act the un-certainty and threats in life, and the other expands your focus where anxiety and fear become one of many different life experiences (figure 10.2).

Tolerance

The philosopher Gabriel Marcel once said that the secret to life was in becoming "comfortable with ambiguity" (Gallagher, 1962). In a climate of safety, devel-oping a high tolerance for uncertainty may be one gift that the climate offers. Having grown comfortable with certainty and expanding one's focus to a diver-sity of experiences, people in a climate of safety may be in a position to tolerate uncertainty, better than anxious people living in uncertainty or fearful people unable to take a stand. It seems easier to feel comfortable with the ambiguities life has to offer when you have someone or some thing to fall back on. In the case study, Jenna, Lynn and Tony were able to tolerate higher levels of uncer-tainty. They knew they had each other. They felt safe that no matter what hap-pened, the family would be there for them. They were in a better position to tol-erate ambiguity. They had the safety found in supporting each other. People in a climate of safety seem better equipped to tolerate anxious and fearful moments in their lives, when they have the help of others. A climate of safety can become the "safety net" that people count on to break their fall. Jenna, Lynn and Tony could tolerate the ambiguity found in life. They could always count on their family to be there for them (figure 10.2).

In Control

If you ask an anxious person what is the one most disturbing feeling when going through anxiety, they may say their sense of being out of control (Elliot et al. 2011; Baum & Singer, 1980). A climate of safety can counteract a sense of be-ing out of control by established practices of confronting one's fears by risk tak-ing, creating a sense of relief and release and developing a high tolerance for uncertainty. It appears that the more people practice these behaviors, the less likely a climate of anxiety will develop, and where a climate of fear can be over-come by taking risks. A climate of safety requires risk, courage, open minded-ness, and a tolerance for ambiguity. The reward for such a climate can be the sense that, to a certain extent, you have life under control. In the case study, Jenna, Lynn and Tony shared that sense of having their family under control, when they honored each other at the twenty-fifth wedding anniversary party. They made a point of acknowledging how each family member contributed to keeping their climate of safety alive. Anxiety was a part of their family system, as much as fear, much like any family system. The difference was their com-mitment to "being there" for each other, despite the uncertainty and threats. They had created a safe climate in the family that counteracted their anxiety and fear. They were safe within themselves and within their family. Their goal of taking two negative experiences and producing a positive one had prevailed. (figure 10.2).

Cultural Implications

Some people believe that we live in a culture of fear which has created a climate of anxiety in our everyday lives. We live in a globally connected world and with the help of mass media we are aware of the tragedies going on in the world. The reality is that we as a nation are safer, healthier, living longer and more secure in our environments than any population in history, yet there is this widespread perception among many people that; the risk of danger is everywhere, that we are not safe, and that the future is bleak. For instance, some television shows seem almost single-handedly intent on triggering our anxieties, while fear of crime makes us hyper vigilant in urban settings. The media dwells on deadly diseases, drug abusers, online pedophiles, bird flu, mad cows, anthrax, immigrants, environmental collapse, mass shooting and of course the fear of terrorism. Hence, mass media is contributing to the culture of fear and creating a climate of anxiety. The negativity in the news penetrates the way we think and act without us being fully aware.

In the case study, the employees of the automobile manufacturing plant had no idea what their futures held for them. They were in constant awareness that their lives could dramatically change overnight. For five years they waited in a climate of anxiety. When the plant finally closed the climate dramatically changed from a climate of anxiety to a climate of fear. However, at least now some of them took a stand to face their fear. Unfortunately, for some people a climate of fear has turned into a culture of fear where feeling threatened has been normalized into the culture. Iraq and Syrian refugees flee their countries but more importantly they are fleeing the culture of fear that has taken over from the historical culture that is left behind. One of the great dangers facing us as a society is not necessarily any one person's aberrant behavior. More importantly may be the emotional climate in which our behavior takes place. In our contemporary world we risk emotional climates of fear, anxiety, hatred and others, turning into unspoken rules that begin to define changes in our culture where violence and mental illness seem more the norm than the exception to the norm.

Notes

8. Information about feeling threatened can be found in the following book. Blanchfield, K. E., Blanchfield, T. A., & Ladd, P. D. (2008). *Conflict resolution for law enforcement: Street smart negotiating*. Flushing, NY: Looseleaf Law. 17–26.

9. Information about creating a climate of safety can be found in the following book. Blanchfield, K. E., & Ladd, P. D. (2013). *Leadership, violence and school climate: Case studies in creating non-violent schools.* Lanham, MD: Rowman & Little field Education. 15–39.

Part III
Emotions and Mediation

Chapter 11

The Phenomenon of Mediation

In the following chapter, we give an example of a typical mediation. The case study we present was an actual mediation session that took place between a mother and a daughter, and reflects some of the most important points in doing mediation. Themes such as empowerment, critical thinking, and assertiveness come to mind when doing these types of mediations. In the mediation session, the mother and daughter are empowered to create their own solutions to their problems. They critically think through their points of view, and with the help of the mediator they assertively state their issues that are in conflict. Without the help of a mediator this conflict may turn out differently. Empowerment could be replaced with "power plays" Critical thinking may not exist where people are talking "at" each other, not "to" each other. This may cause a communication style not based on assertiveness but aggression. Mediation is a process where people have the opportunity to solve problems within a structured format. The mediator's responsibility is to keep the format working, in order to create a fair and balanced agreement.

The case study is followed with methods and techniques for successful mediation. The past chapters have talked about different emotional climates, and how they affect successful conciliations. In this chapter, we point out the importance of a climate of neutrality as the beginning point of any mediation. Without a neutral climate to start, mediations go out of balance and usually fail. Successful mediators then look for common ground. Finding common ground helps bring people together while making what is in disagreement less complicated. Common ground helps in bringing people in dispute together through common agreement. With common ground being established, issues are isolated for a negotiation based on the thoughts and beliefs of the disputants, not the mediator. Finally, a fair and balanced agreement is reached where both parties feel they have gained from the mediation experience. The chapter ends with exercises and charts to help practice the art of mediation along with three different types of mediation being used in today's society. Also added to this are cultural implications of mediation down through history.

Case Study

Jane and her mother, Suzanne, battled through many disputes ever since Suzanne's and Jim's divorce a year ago. At sixteen Jane was changing. She wanted more independence from her mother. Her relationship with boys was beginning to blossom and she found her mother's "old fashion ways" a burden to her social life. Suzanne was also in the process of change. After Jim's departure her relationship with Jane deteriorated and anxiety was developing over Jane's rebellious attitude toward just about anything.

Exasperated, Suzanne turned to a friend who recommended they contact a local mediation center in their area. The next day she called and a receptionist explained the mediation process and agreed to set up a mediation session if Jane also agreed to participate. That night Suzanne described the process to Jane who immediately wanted to know whether someone would listen to her point of view. Suzanne said, "I was told that both of us will be given equal time to discuss our problems." Reluctantly, Jane agreed to a mediation session scheduled for early next week.

Suzanne and Jane arrived at the mediation center on Tuesday of the following week and were greeted by a mediator who asked them to please come in. The room was modestly decorated with a rectangular table with four chairs situated in the middle of a well-lighted room. In front of each chair were paper, pencils and drinking water. The mediator instructed them to sit opposite each other and the mediator sat directly between them. "Thank you for coming to the mediation session this evening. My name is Tish and I will be your mediator. I am a volunteer from the community and I am professionally trained to mediate disputes between people with opposing points of view." The mediator looked at both of them to see if they had any questions. Both Suzanne and Jane nodded their heads in affirmation and then Tish continued by saying, "How shall I address you during the mediation session?" Jane replied, "You can call me Jane. That would be fine." Suzanne said, "You can call me Suzanne but I would prefer if Jane called me 'mom.' Tish looked at Jane and asked, "Your mother would like you to call her mom. Can you agree to that?" Jane looked at her mother and said, "Yeah. I agree."

Tish said, "Thank you both for agreeing to that matter. Let me explain the mediation process. First, I will ask for your agreement on a list of ground rules that you see before you. After everyone has agreed I will ask both of you to give an opening statement describing what brought you to the mediation session. An open dialogue will follow where finding mutual common ground is our goal. If we find enough common ground, it will put us in a position to isolate issues that are important to both of you. Having isolated issues, you both will have an opportunity to create options for changing those problems causing the dispute. Finally, we will work together and draw up a final agreement, in your words, that includes your chosen options. Do you have any questions on the mediation process?"

Jane and Suzanne agreed they did not have questions, so Tish went through a list of ground rules such as: no name calling, agree to equal time, each speak one at a time, agreement on length of time for the mediation, agreement on confidentiality and agreement on taking breaks during the mediation. The mediator guided them through the ground rules and agreements were reached on all of them. Agreeing on the ground rules allowed Suzanne to ask the next question, "Who would like to start?" Jane said she wanted to start but before she began Tish looked at Suzanne and said, "Jane would like to start. Do you agree?" Suzanne said, "Well, she always starts at home!" Tish looked at Suzanne again and said, "If you want to start that is also fine but we have to agree on who will go first. Jane would like to go first. Do you agree?" Suzanne said, "Yes, I agree."

Jane began, "My life is a living hell since Dad left. Mom has turned into this bitch and won't let up on me!" Tish stopped her and said, "Remember our ground rule about no name calling. Could you try that statement in a different way?" Jane replied acerbically, "Ok! My life has been very difficult ever since my father left. My mother constantly gives me a hard time and that is why I am here tonight." At that point Jane looked at her mother for a reply. Tish looked at Jane and said, "Is that all you want to say for now?" Jane replied, "Yes!" Tish turned to Suzanne and said, "It is your turn to give an opening statement. Please go ahead." Suzanne looked at Jane and said, "Do you have any idea how difficult the last year has been for me. You act like nothing around the house matters and you would rather be with your friends. I am sick of staying up nights worrying about where you are, and who are these mysterious friends? You could at least call me."

After her statement Jane and Suzanne looked to the mediator for direction. Tish said, "Does anyone choose to add more to their opening statement?" Neither of them wanted to add more so Tish continued by saying, "Thank you for opening the mediation process with your statements. Our next step is to continue this discussion only this time I would like you to look directly at each other when you say something. To refresh your memories here are some talking points you might want to consider. Jane you said that life has become difficult since your father left and in the last year difficulties between you and your mother have surfaced. Suzanne, you have stated it also has been difficult for you in the last year especially regarding Jane's friends and where she spends her time. Are these statements accurate?" Tish looked at Jane and she said, "Yeah! That is pretty much it." Tish then looked at Suzanne and she said, "Yes! They are accurate." Then Tish made this statement, "Do you agree it has been difficult for both of you in the last year?" Tish turned to Jane and she said, "Yes!" Then turned to Suzanne and she said, "Yes!" Tish then said, "So you both agree that life was not as difficult before this last year." Jane and Suzanne both said, "Yes!" Tish then said, "You both agree that you got along before last year and that problems between you have been going on for about a year." Tish looked at both of them and they nodded in agreement and then asked, "Who would like to continue and let's try to focus on the last year?"

The next half hour was spent with Jane and Suzanne describing how difficult each found their relationship in the last year. When they made statements about how they resented the other's behavior, Tish would point out common ground that both agreed they resented each other. When they both explained how much had changed in their relationship, Tish again pointed out that both were in agreement about the dramatic changes that took place. When Jane would tell her mother, "You don't understand me!" and Suzanne quickly retorted, "No! You don't understand me!" Tish would calmly get an agreement on how communications had broken down.

Jane and Suzanne went back and forth defending their points of view and venting their feelings, while Tish continued pointing out common ground. Somewhere in all the venting, Tish noticed the emotional climate had shifted and both were discussing a more logical defense of their main issues. At this point, Tish reviewed what had happened so far. "It seems both of you have had an opportunity to truly let the other know what is on your mind. First let me review what you have in common and then maybe we can isolate some important issues. Can you both agree to this?" Jane and Suzanne both agreed. Tish continued by reviewing the common ground:

> You both have agreed that you got along with each other until last year, and you are in agreement that difficulties began over this one-year period. You also are in agreement that the difficulties of the last year have caused dramatic changes in your relationship, and you have agreed that a breakdown in communication is one of the more dramatic changes. Jane you have agreed with your mother that she has been suffering and Suzanne you are in agreement that sixteen is a difficult age to experience such changes. Where you still have disagreements are: Jane, you would like more independence in the following areas; how you spend your free time and who are you with, when you have free time, and Suzanne, you still have issues surrounding anxiety with Jane's behavior with her friends, and Jane's general attitude when at home. Does my description sound like the issues?

Both agreed, but Suzanne added "communication breakdown" as another issue up for discussion. Jane agreed.

At this point in the mediation, Tish pointed out how much they had in common and encouraged them to continue by developing options based on the issues that were still in dispute. Tish reminded them of the issues isolated so far and of the one issue brought up by Suzanne as a reminder, "communication breakdown." Tish continued by saying, "As your mediator, I want to inform you that negotiating options on these issues is your responsibility because the results will affect both of you. So, you are now empowered to come up with options that cover all the issues. Where would you like to start?" It was Suzanne who went first when she asked Jane, "Why don't you bring your friends to our house so I can meet them. Maybe that would help relieve some tension." Jane replied, "They are afraid to come over because they think you are angry with them, for some reason." Suzanne said, "It is not that I am angry with them but the hour they call is after eleven thirty at night and that is too late." Jane finally said, "I have an idea. Why don't I bring them over so you can see they are normal and I will not use the phone after 10 p.m. Suzanne made a counter offer, "How about nine thirty?" Jane said, "Ok! But maybe you could make one of your famous barbecues and meet them during a cookout at our house." Suzanne said, "Do they like barbecue?" Jane replied, "Sure they do. How about asking them?" Suzanne said, "Well . . . ok." Tish interrupted their negotiations by paraphrasing what had been accomplished:

> Suzanne, you have made an offer regarding use of the phone by asking Jane to hold any calls after nine thirty, and Jane has agreed. Jane, you have put an option on the table to have your mother meet your friends at a barbecue that she will prepare and Suzanne has agreed. We still have Jane's issue of free time and Suzanne's issues of Jane's attitude and anxiety over her behavior; and finally there is an issue for negotiation regarding communication breakdown. Let us take one issue at a time and work through them.

They both looked at Tish and nodded in agreement. From that point on, they bargained for Jane's free time, Suzanne's concern with Jane's attitude, and the issue of communication breakdown.

After negotiations had ended, Suzanne and Jane turned to the mediator for the next step. Tish responded by saying, "I want to congratulate you on the hard work you demonstrated in the options phase of your mediation. At this point, I am going to review the common ground you have established, and then help draw up an agreement that includes the options you negotiated. First, let me review the common ground:

> You both agreed that life has become difficult in the last year and it was not as difficult before the divorce. You also have agreed that a great deal of resentment about each other's behavior has been building up over the last year. You are in agreement over how much both of you have changed, and how these changes have caused a breakdown in communication. Jane you have agreed that your mother has suffered and Suzanne you have acknowledged that sixteen is a difficult age to experience such changes. Keeping this common ground in mind, let us draw up an agreement.

The following is the agreement drawn up by the mediator with Jane and Suzanne's input:

- Jane has agreed to stop all telephone calls by friends at nine thirty each evening.

- Suzanne has agreed to have a barbecue to meet Jane's friends on Saturday June 25 at 2 p.m.
- Jane has agreed to be home by nine thirty on school nights except school events and twelve o'clock on weekends
- Suzanne has agreed to allow Jane use of the car for school events and will agree to other free time, as long as Jane calls and informs Suzanne of any changes.
- Jane has agreed to work on her attitude, especially her manners when she comes home from school.
- Suzanne has agreed that Jane, at sixteen, is older and should be treated more as an adult. She will discuss problems with her and stop lecturing.
- Both Jane and Suzanne agreed that when these changes become overwhelming, they will discuss them before communication breaks down.

Tish gave both of them an opportunity to review the points in the agreement, and asked if they had any questions. Both said it was fair and balanced. Tish reminded them it was their agreement and living up to it was also their responsibility. Finally, Tish congratulated them on having the courage to face each other and discuss their problems. After everyone shook hands, Jane and Suzanne left the office both saying to Tish, "thank you" for helping them get through a difficult period in their lives.

Understanding a Climate of Mediation

The previous example is typical of mediations found in community oriented mediation centers, and the story is not unique to parents and children falling into conflicts after a divorce. Conflict concerning single-parent families are one of many examples in the myriad of disputes mediated every day. The case study shows the underlying structure of mediation through the eyes of a mediator, who demonstrates its effectiveness when peoples' issues and emotions are taken seriously.

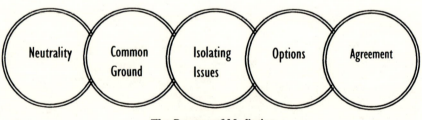

The Process of Mediation
Figure 11.1

Creating Neutrality

The first step in creating a climate for mediation is to assure that equality and neutrality are intricately connected to the mediation process. A mediation climate may fail if equality and neutrality are not established from the beginning. In the case study, a neutral third party from the mediation center treats Suzanne and Jane equally, long before they enter the actual mediation. The coordinator at the center told Suzanne that Jane also must agree to the process so both were equally invested in the mediation. The office at the mediation center had a rectangular table, so both Suzanne and Jane had equal distance from Tish. They had paper for writing, were provided pens, pencils, and drinking water. They were given copies of the ground rules and both were given an opportunity to make an opening statement. All of these geographic and social preparations had a specific purpose in the mediation. They created a climate where the mediator was viewed as a neutral third party, and the opposing parties would be treated equally without imposing judgments or taking sides (Mayer, 2003).

Balance is another main concern facing a competent mediator. When Tish addressed Suzanne, addressing Jane immediately would follow. After Tish stated the ground rules of mediation; each ground rule was balanced by agreements from both Suzanne and Jane. Starting the mediation was presented to both parties so equal opportunity existed for going first, giving the initial protocol a sense of balance. In more formal mediations, procedures may be more intricate such as found in custody and visitation mediations, where court procedures are included in the ground rules; however, the initial intentions found in all mediations are the same (Lippke et al. 2009; Slaikue et al. 1985). Creating a climate for mediation requires the mediator to remain neutral, so opposing parties have equal opportunities to express balanced points of view (Garcia, Vise & Whitaker, 2002). In successful mediations, equality, neutrality and balance must be upheld or people in conflict may not openly express their thoughts and feelings. Suzanne and Jane were treated equally, and Tish remained neutral and the climate remained balanced. Together they created a workable climate where thoughts and feelings were expressed and the mediation process continued in a fair and equitable manner (figure 11.1).

Finding Common Ground

Finding common ground seems an un-natural next step in the mediation process. From early childhood, many of us were raised to solve problems by analyzing peoples' differences, but in mediation, looking for what people have in common becomes a mediator's next step. If mediators were given the task of rendering a final judgment in the mediation process, then analyzing differences would be a valid enterprise, but mediators do not render final judgments—they guide others to that end (Moore, 2003). Whatever is most effective in making the process a success becomes more important than an analysis of peoples' problems. Finding common ground is probably the strongest tool a mediator possesses in guiding people to successful resolution of their conflicts. For example, Suzanne and Jane did not need a mediator who analyzed their communication problem and then demonstrated how to fix it. They directly or indirectly experienced this problem for the last year, and it was their problem. However, all their thoughts and feelings connected to the communication problem made it seem impossible to solve on their own. They required someone, other than themselves, to actually "shrink" the communication breakdown problem to a size that was workable and less overwhelming (Ladd, 1989). Tish pointed out common ground and mentioned that the communication breakdown was recent and occurred within the last year due to several changes. Agreements from Suzanne and Jane on all aspects of common ground made the issue of communication breakdown reasonable and manageable.

Finding common ground changed how both of them perceived the problem. Without common ground, the problems in dispute seemed overwhelming and insurmountable but with common ground, they agreed it has been a rough year with many changes, causing expected levels of resentment, and maybe it is time to change the way we communicate. The mediator's responsibility after creating a climate of neutrality is to allow people an opportunity to vent their thoughts and feelings; while, the mediator constantly looks for common ground. The more established common ground, the less overwhelming are peoples' perceptions of the conflict, and the closer people come to solving their problems (figure 11.1).

Isolating Issues

Isolating issues in mediation can be a different process than found in other problem solving techniques, such as isolating issues in a court of law (Bennett & Herman, 1997). In the case study, isolating Jane and Suzanne's issues might have happened much earlier if Tish disregarded mediation skills and became a fact finder after their opening statements and could have; systematically analyzed these facts, by isolating facts into issues and then developed options around these issues. Such procedures follow logical methods for problem solving but are less effective in mediation. The reason lies in their inability to let emotions surface in the mediation process. Mediations are a blend of issues and emotions and both may need consideration for mediations to be effective.

Remember, Suzanne and Jane spent the last year having difficulties in communication, resenting each other and going through stressful changes. Rushing directly into issues even if known, may not give equal opportunity to discover the emotional baggage attached to these issues. The dramatic issues in a conflict can be only part of the story. Some conflicts carry unforgettable emotional experiences that carry as much importance as the issues (Jones & Bodtker, 2008; Sautter, 1995). This was the case in Jane and Suzanne's dispute. Tish could have isolated issues after their opening statements, because enough facts were available to achieve that goal. However, Tish waited until both shared their thoughts and vented their feelings, and common ground was established before isolating any issues. Isolating issues too early in the mediation process can be a common mistake made by mediators with superior analytical abilities but little awareness of the emotions connected to the conflict. People may need time to work through these emotional roadblocks affecting their lives before issues seem relevant.

Another reality, especially in everyday mediations, is that emotions may be *the issues*. For example, Suzanne and Jane's resentment of each other might have been more important to them, than a need for a time schedule for phone calls or issues surrounding meeting certain friends. If resentment became their main issue, the conversation in the mediation, may shift to discussions of resentful feelings and not factual issues. Resentment could eventually emerge as the isolated issue presented to both parties by the mediator. Sometimes actual issues are stated early in mediations as a cover for more sensitive emotional issues, and will remain undercover if the mediator prematurely isolates issues before emotions emerge in the conversation (Mayer, 2000).

Finally, two major shifts in the emotional climate of disputants take place in effective mediations. The first is in the initial stage, when the mediator creates a climate filled with equality, neutrality and balance. The second shift in the climate is when people have finished venting their feelings. After people have conveyed their thoughts and feelings clearly, and when emotions have become calmer and more business-like. It is at this point mediators are in a position to isolate issues. When people, in mediation, stop venting and start repeating their important issue a mediator realizes that the main issues of those in conflict have reached the point of negotiation and need to be isolated. After Jane and Suzanne worked through their anger and resentment; the mediator noticed a shift in the climate, because both started discussing resolvable issues. Tish took this opportunity to isolate issues for the eventual negotiations, that were about to take place (figure 11.1).

Choosing Options

Choosing options can be the creative "empowerment" stage in mediation. People are encouraged, at this point, to develop options for resolving their disputes. For the most part, mediators keep their role to a minimum in this stage of the mediation process; whatever is negotiated will affect the disputing parties, not the mediator. However, having people empowered to negotiate options is what mediation is all about. Mediators set the stage for negotiations by creating a climate of neutrality, finding common ground and isolating issues. It is now the role of the parties, in conflict, to seek viable options to these problems. Mediators help in the negotiation in a minor way by reminding people of previously isolated issues, pointing out any new issues that may need discussion and presenting one party's option to the other party in an understandable, reasonable manner.

At this stage in the mediation process, mediators act as referees in the bargaining taking place between people in conflict. They do not suggest what options either person should choose nor do they give advice on what options are best suited for their needs. However, mediations have their limitations. If there are any guidelines connected to the mediation such as found in more formal and legally oriented mediations, the mediator reminds both parties of these restrictions (Despotovic-Stanarevic, 2010; Goodman, 1996). Also, certain mediating parties, taking part in negotiations, may need the help of the mediator, especially when the participating parties in conflict are having difficulty getting started in the negotiation process. The mediator may remind them of isolated issues or give them general categories for consideration, but does not direct them in negotiating any specific item in any specific way. Sometimes, staying out of the negotiations becomes difficult for mediators who have competently held positions of authority, where giving direction may be a large part of their jobs. However, mediation is a democratic process based on free choice and it adheres to the principle that people have the ability to solve their problems. Without empowering people in the negotiation stage of mediation, all previous stages may seem irrelevant. Creating a climate of neutrality, finding common ground and isolating issues are activities that empower people to find acceptable answers to their conflicts. Effective mediators know that timing remains a more effective skill in the negotiation stage of mediation than over-involvement. Knowing when to remind people of issues or when to move on to the next round of negotiations on a new issue becomes the responsibility of the mediator (Hammond, 2003) (figure 11.1).

Making an Agreement

After options are negotiated, mediators encourage disputants to make an agreement that is fair and reasonable. Reaching agreement is the responsibility of the people in dispute; however, formatting the agreement is the responsibility of the mediator (Sarabando, Dias, L. and Vetschera, 2013; Folberg & Taylor, 1984). In the final step of a successful mediation, the mediator helps in the development of a plan based on the wishes of both people in dispute. Tish presented Jane and Suzanne with a plan that included agreements on seven points where all points were developed with everyone's input. If the language confused either party or the mediator found discrepancies that were overlooked, then the rough draft of the agreement would be rephrased until agreeable to everyone. For example, in the final agreement, Jane agreed to be home at nine thirty on school nights and twelve on weekends. If they only negotiated a time limit for school nights the mediator might pose the question, "Would you like a time limit for weekends?" By making these small logistical interventions, the mediator helps strengthen agreements by including commonly overlooked specific issues connected to the main agreement. Finally, agreements can be written or verbal, depending on the needs of the people in conflict. More formal mediations are usually written because details hold considerable weight in final agreements. Less formal mediations do not need a written agreement and may sustain an informal process, possibly concluding with a review of the agreed issues and a "hand shake." Tish went over the agreement between Jane and Suzanne and specifically asked if the agreement was acceptable and if any changes should be made before they finally agreed. The agreement was acceptable and everyone shook hands. This ended a successful mediation where both parties where satisfied with the results (figure 11.1).

Basic Mediation Skills

Creating Neutrality

Staying neutral, usually is not described as a skill, but for mediators, it becomes a fundamental indicator of success or failure in the beginning stages of mediation.

Spatial Balance

This is when the mediator adjusts the room, the furniture and other parts of the setting so that people enter a mediation feeling they have an equal opportunity to resolve their dispute. One of the most effective ways to accomplish spatial balance is by having a room with a rectangular table and at least three chairs. The mediator sits between the mediating parties and communicates the same verbal and non-verbal gestures to both of them. If the mediator makes a gesture to one, then a reciprocal gesture is made to the other. For example, if you look at one party while discussing ground rules, then it may be important to look equally at the other or if one party wants writing paper, the other also may need paper.

Temporal Balance

Here is the ability of the mediator to listen equally to both parties in dispute. If one party talks for five minutes, then the other party should have an opportunity to talk for an equal amount of time. Balancing time between both people in dispute can be upheld with a ground rule requesting equal time when discussing mediation issues. This may be especially important in the beginning of mediation when rules are tested and behavior is established for discussions. If people balance their time in the beginning portion of mediation, then, balance has more probability of following through the rest of the mediation process.

Moral Balance

This is making sure that both parties have an opportunity to speak their minds, and are not judged by the mediator or by each other. Balancing the opening portion of mediation by not making judgments sends a message that the mediator's purpose is to facilitate communication, not judge right or wrong. Moral balance demonstrates to the parties, that mediation is a different process than other more evaluation-oriented settings. Keeping this in mind, mediators should be careful not to make any verbal or non-verbal gestures that may be misinterpreted as a judgment, either positively or negatively.

Developing Ground Rules

Confusion and miscommunication are reduced if a mediator successfully describes certain ground rules to the parties before the mediation begins. Ground rules are the foundation of any mediation and remain the most important element in a climate of neutrality. The following are a typical set of ground rules in an everyday mediation (Rubin, 2014; Mosten, 1997):

- There are times during mediation when emotions may run high but can we agree to treat each other with common courtesy?
- Sometimes in the heat of emotions we may call each other names that stop the mediation process. If this happens, can we agree to re-group and use different language when talking to each other?
- Everything said here is confidential and should be kept in this room. You have the right to take notes but let us agree to destroy them at the end of the mediation.
- Can we agree to give each party an equal chance to discuss their point of view?

Making an Opening Statement

Most often, the conversation between disputing parties begins with an opening statement from both parties. The mediator may say to the disputants, "Who would like to start?" Once this agreement is established, a mediator may say to the first disputant, "Can you share what brought you to mediation?" After the first disputant's opening statement is made, then, the other disputant gives an opening statement or responds to the first disputant's statement. When both opening statements are completed, the mediator encourages the disputants to engage in open dialogue.

Roadblocks to Neutrality

On occasions mediating parties use the opening minutes of mediation to "power play" each other. The following are examples of power plays used during the creation of a climate of neutrality.

Co-Mediator

When one mediating party assumes the mediator's task is to help the other party accept his or her position, the mediation faces the roadblock of co-mediation. If the "power play" becomes successful, communication breaks down and the person acting as co-mediator assumes a superior position. The mediator is tricked into co-mediating against the other party in dispute.

Story Telling

When one party gives a long discussion of the problem, the mediation can lose effectiveness, because lengthy stories give the story tellers an upper hand in the mediation. The mediation now focuses on the story not the dialogue between disputants. Parties in dispute may have a story to share but it should not be told under the time constraints established by the mediator.

Over-Involvement

When the mediator constantly focuses on one disputant over the other. The geography in the mediation shifts, where the mediator seems to be over-involved with one disputing party. The other party may misinterpret this as favoring the other side. Over-involvement can be caused by the mediator feeling more comfortable with one disputant over another. If continued, the mediation may eventually go out of balance.

Finding Common Ground

Common ground can be at the heart of successful mediations. A mediator may enter mediation only to find disputants polarized against each other, where, mediating an agreement may appear unlikely. Common ground brings disputing parties closer together and demonstrates that people in conflict are not that different from each other, and may have certain fundamental common beliefs. Some of these common beliefs are based on *issues* such as, both parties agreeing they were friends before the dispute began. Other beliefs are based on commonly held *emotions* such as both parties agreeing they have been frustrated with each other for quite some time.

Issue-Oriented Common Ground

During a mediation session both parties might say they agree to a particular issue discussed in the conversation. For example, a teacher and a parent during mediation may both believe the best interest of the student is an important factor in resolving a school-related conflict. The common ground stated by the mediator may sound like this, "So you agree that the student's best interests are important to both of you." If both parties agree, you have found *issue-oriented common ground*—focusing on the best interest of the student.

Emotion-Oriented Common Ground

Sometimes, mediators help people in conflict, by showing how their conflict has emotionally affected both of them. When this happens, the mediator is pointing out *emotion-oriented common ground*. An example of this could be, "So you agree that the dispute has angered both of you and that you both are becoming frustrated and 'stuck.'" Again if they both agree, you have found emotion-oriented common ground, focusing on anger leading to frustration.

The more common ground found in mediation, the less confusion over isolating issues in a conflict. Common ground limits conflict by creating agreement (Cheng, 2015; Freedman, 1998). It gives people in conflict an opportunity to perceive important issues that still need discussion. It focuses peoples' thoughts and feelings while eliminating extraneous information from the mediation process.

Roadblocks to Common Ground

Sometimes mediators rush to isolating issues and skip common ground, because issues are factual and require less risk emotionally. A mediator, fearing emotional conflict, may rush to issues and avoid the experience of refereeing peoples' emotional outbursts. Without giving mediating parties an opportunity to emotionally express their feelings, the mediator eliminates essential elements of their conflict and thereby changes the dynamics of the mediation process. (Bailey & McCarty, 2009; Gray, 1989).

By avoiding emotions, the mediator also can lead disputing parties into issues that are safer for discussion. Leading disputants to discuss specific issues works well in a court of law but can fail in mediation. Disputing parties arrive at issues for negotiation that were indirectly chosen by a mediator, who was unable to let disputants vent their feelings. When this happens, the mediator does not referee the discussion but controls it.

Isolating Issues [10]

Isolating issues requires mediators to make mediations specific and clear. Here may be where having a linguistic understanding of the dispute becomes a valuable asset. Three important skills needed by mediators when disputing parties are venting their feelings or telling their stories are paraphrasing, re-framing, and reviewing, especially when a conversation is not working and intervention is needed to put the discussion back on track.

Paraphrasing

Here is the ability of the mediator to stop mediation and briefly describe the essence of both party's agreements and disagreements, at any point in the mediation. Another way to say this is, "Paraphrasing is the mediator's ability to "map out" the essential points taking place during the mediation process in a brief and understandable manner." Paraphrasing becomes useful when emotions run high or when communication bogs down. Mapping out peoples' conversations can put their discussions into perspective while allowing emotions to be expressed freely. These "maps" or paraphrases can become benchmarks in successful mediations. They can convey what has been accomplished and how far they must go before reaching an agreement.

Reframing

This is another important skill that "softens the blow" when people shock each other with their inappropriate remarks during a mediation. This can happen; when language becomes too harsh, the message too overpowering or when the other party cannot understand what is being said. When an inappropriate remark is delivered, the mediator re-frames these remarks to the party who is having difficulty receiving the other's message (Marcum, 2012; Bandler & Grinder, 1982). Reframing is literally what the word implies. A mediator takes the unreceivable message of one party and puts it another way or re-frames it until it is clearly received by the other party. For example, if a student says to another student in mediation, "You have been a liar and a cheat when you said you would stay away from my girlfriend. You lied to me!" When reframed by a mediator, it may sound something like this, "What John is trying to say is that you agreed to stay away from his girlfriend but you haven't done that yet." Reframing avoids potential breakdowns in peoples' discussions and makes what is said to others more acceptable, allowing both parties to continue in the mediation process.

Reviewing

Here is a technique for filling in those silent moments during mediation, when disputants have bogged down and have difficulty talking to each other. At these moments, a review of the themes previously mentioned gives the mediation a renewed focus that places the mediation back on track. Usually when a silent moment occurs, one or both disputing parties may turn to the mediator for direction. At moments like these, reviewing what has been accomplished, may give new direction to the conversation.

Roadblocks to Isolating Issues

Not Letting Issues Emerge

Issues that are stated in the opening moments of mediation may not remain the only issues of importance throughout the mediation process. For example, this happens in highly emotional mediations, where strongly held feelings cloud the issues in conflict. Sometimes the issues that seemed important in the "opening statement" phase of mediation become secondary or forgotten after parties have vented their feelings. Successful dialogue that includes a thorough venting of issues and emotions unfold naturally and limit over-analysis through the whole mediation process.

Choosing Options

The negotiation stage in mediation empowers people in conflict to create options that reflect their thoughts and feelings in the mediation process. During this stage of mediation, democratic principles are given an opportunity to be employed through negotiation. The following are three common types of options found in everyday mediations.

Options Based on Consensus

One form of option people in dispute consider are options based on consensus. Common sense tells us why consensus based options are popular in mediation. These options are more likely to succeed, because they benefit both parties in dispute. Options that are mutually beneficial to both parties also add to the mediation's common ground. This style of options creates consensus, much in the manner that finding common ground helps in isolating issues (Finkelstein et al. 2009; Fisher & Ury, 1991). For example, a parent and teacher having a communication problem over a child's performance in school agree that written feedback between them will benefit the student's success. By finding consensus on *feedback*, the teacher and parent are led to other issues specific to finding creative options leading toward the student's success.

Point/Counter Point Options

Another type of option found in mediations is concerned with balancing one option against another. Point/counter point options are the "quid pro quo" formula in negotiating options in mediation (Williams, 1998). For example, in our case study, Jane wanted better privileges based on free time and Suzanne wanted Jane's attitude to change at home. If Jane is willing to do something for Suzanne, then Suzanne is willing to reciprocate and do something for Jane. Mediaations are filled with options that negotiate the needs of the people in dispute by balancing the wants and needs of others. However, balance is the key word in point/counter point options. If one party is willing to do ten things for the other but the other has not reciprocated by an offer in return, then the negotiation becomes out of balanced and probably will fail.

Caucusing

This is a technique for meeting individually with one party for negotiation purposes while the other party remains outside the mediation room. Caucusing may be useful when hidden agendas are breaking down negotiations and begin to stonewall effective options. By having the other party wait outside, the mediator is able to talk candidly and avoid awkward moments for both parties (Hoffman, 2011; Susskind et al. 1999). However, caucusing seems a method of last resort and not as a general practice in creating options in mediation. Over use of caucusing may limit shared participation needed for both parties in creating mutually acceptable agreements. One method for avoiding over use of caucusing can be to find a substantial amount of mutually agreed on common ground. The more common ground, the more people are willing to face each other and negotiate viable options for successful agreements.

Roadblocks to Choosing Options

Difficulty Being Empowered

Some people have difficulty being empowered, and developing a creative list of options. This can be based on inexperience, or sometimes on people's fear of the negotiation process. In either case, this roadblock may develop in the option stage of mediation. Mediators may have to empower disputants by giving general categories of what has been discussed, in order for the negotiations to continue. However, this is different than telling disputants what they should discuss or what they should decide. Some mediators, with the best intentions, begin to "micro-manage" the options stage by directing disputants to what they believe are the effective options. What is lost in this process is eventual ownership of the agreement by those in conflict. Facilitating disputants in developing personal options can be one of the true art-forms in effective negotiations.

Making Successful Agreements

A mediator's responsibility is to draw up agreements that do not judge either party in dispute. By describing options acceptable to both parties for inclusion into the final agreement, mediators create a descriptive framework that is free of generalizations or judgments.

The Importance of Being Specific

The more specific the language, the higher probability people will honor their agreements. As previously stated in analyzing the case study between Suzanne and Jane, it was important to include all specifics that allowed both of them a better understanding of how to behave differently after the mediation was concluded. If the language in the agreement does not specifically describe, step by step, each point, then the agreement may lose its ability to give specific direction to those in dispute (Moore, 2003). Being specific also helps mediators avoid writing an agreement that is judgmental. Judgments are more concerned with themes such as; guilty vs. not guilty. Mediated agreements are not looking for winners and losers. They should be written so both parties specifically understand what they believe is an acceptable agreement.

Using the Language of the Disputants

Not all mediated agreements are written in the language of the disputants. An example of this can be found in custody and visitation mediations where the court requires a specific language to be included in the final documents. However, it is important for mediators within the limits placed on them to come as close to the language discussed during the mediation process. It is most important that the mediated agreement reflect the words used during the options stage of the mediation. Agreements are stronger when disputants recognize their points of view being acknowledged, both in their negotiations and in the final agreement.

Keeping the Agreement Balanced

Balance is an issue resonating all through mediation and balance also should be reflected in the final agreement. Agreements that favor one party over the other either reflect a mediation that was out of balance from the beginning, or became weighted to favor one party during final negotiations. Agreements that favor one side over another rarely work. Balance is a term that should be in the mediator's mind all through the mediation, and especially in drawing up the final agreement. In mediation, balance reflects fairness, and creating a fair and balanced process is one of mediation's major goals.

Roadblocks to Successful Agreements

Incomplete Agreements

One of the major roadblocks in reaching a successful agreement is when mediators fail to include isolated issues emerging earlier in the mediation. All isolated issues should be negotiated and options developed before reaching a final agreement. If this does not happen, agreements are viewed as incomplete and lose legitimacy in resolution of the dispute. It is important that mediators make sure isolated issues are represented in the final agreement in some form, either written or verbal.

Contingency Agreements

Another difficult roadblock to successful mediations is when an agreement is contingent on additional information or future performance by one or more parties in the dispute. Mediation runs into difficulties when one or both parties back out of the agreement by using excuses that additional information was not provided or agreeing only after observing if someone's behavior changes in the future. For example, a person in conflict may say, at a future date, "Additional information has changed my mind," or "your behavior has changed my mind."

Agreements in Principle

When both parties agree in principle but the details are not worked through, the agreement is weakened because the only agreement made is the *intent* to agree. Such agreements are usually vague and give little information for any specific behavioral or emotional changes. Agreements in principle are sometimes not legitimate agreements but a method for avoiding change. This happens especially when agreements are unbalanced and seem to favor one side. In this case, a person will agree in principle to end the mediation but with no intentions of living up to the agreement.

Three Styles of Mediation [11]

Mediation as a phenomenon has evolved over the last forty years and is becoming one of the fastest growing professions in the area of human services (Wood, 2004; Brett at al. 1986). However, in spite of the growth, people still ask questions such as, "What is the difference between mediation and arbitration? Or, are there different styles of mediation?" Answering these questions helps us realize the dramatic changes taking place in our legal system and society in general. For example, Alternative dispute resolution, or ADR, continues to make its mark on the legal arena and schools of law, graduate schools, bar associations, and state and local courts, continue a process of transformation from litigation to alternatives that recognize differing points of view (Brown, 2013; Riskin, 1994). Arbitration stands at the foundation of this movement and some would argue that mediation found its roots in arbitration (Murray, 1996).

However, arbitration and mediation are based on different principles. As stated in the Introduction of this book, arbitrators act as informal judges, hearing both sides of a conflict, drawing conclusions based on pre-determined guidelines, and rendering final decisions. As we have seen in this chapter, mediators act as neutral third parties that facilitate and referee mediating parties to resolve conflicts on their own (Mostern, 1997).

Beyond differences between mediation and arbitration are those schools of mediation advocating different professional styles for being neutral third parties. We live in a complicated society filled with different forms of conflict and, as stated above, different factions in our society embrace mediation as a viable alternative for resolving conflicts. However, these different factions have put their personal "spin" on the mediation process. Old rules and guidelines may continue to be perceived as desirable when resolving disputes. The following are three styles of mediation that are emerging in the alternative dispute resolution movement reflecting these differences.

An Evaluative Style of Mediation

An evaluative style of mediation can be confusing to people who see mediators only as neutral third parties, because somewhere in the mediation process a mediator may make a "neutral evaluation" (Donohue, 2011; Rifkin, Millen & Cobb, 1991). Let us take an example from the court system to unravel this somewhat paradoxical statement. Mediators, practicing divorce mediation, may have certain stipulations from the courts that guide the mediation process and limit the scope of the divorce mediation agreement (Jessani, 2011; Kressel et al. 1994). For example, the court may have standards for an acceptable custody and visitation agreement or it may have a formula for distributing a couple's assets.

Both of these stipulations will have an influence on the divorce mediation, and the mediators' behavior through the entire process. First, the mediator will have to inform the mediating parties of these guidelines and include them in any agreement on ground rules. Secondly, in the negotiation stage of mediation, the mediator may have to make a neutral evaluation when people in conflict develop options that will not be acceptable to a judge or a court (Ross, 1997). In some ways, this style of mediation is a three-way process. Once an agreement is made between the disputing parties, it sent back to a judge who also may negotiate terms that he or she wants included in the agreement that fit the guidelines of the law. In this way the law is upheld while both disputing parties have an opportunity to resolve the dispute between them.

A Bargaining Style of Mediation

Mediators practicing a bargaining style of mediation do not adhere to the tight restrictions needed in an evaluative mediation style but the nature of the conflict does subtly direct discussions to possibly replacing the broken toaster in a consumer/merchant dispute or finally receiving a security deposit after restoration for damages in a landlord/tenant dispute. Mediators, in this style of mediation, empower mediating parties to air their differences and talk through the dispute, but they keep in mind that bargaining certain key issues will render successful agreements. Bargaining-oriented mediators can become more assertive bargainers in the options stage of mediations. Settling the dispute is favorable to the litigation that might ensue if the dispute stays unsettled (Honeyman, 1990). Bargaining skills are emphasized in this approach. Discussing options dominates peoples' intentions for being in this type of mediation. A bargaining style of mediation moves disputing parties through the mediation process with certain identified issues always present in the mind of the mediator (Winslade & Monk, 2000). For example, in a consumer/merchant mediation both parties successfully shared their thoughts and emotions, but no agreement was reached on the defective purchased item, then the parties may need yet another mediation to resolve the dispute. A bargaining style of mediating works effectively when certain issues in the mediation are clearly defined from the beginning and the mediator has an opportunity to help people bargain back and forth on these issues. One of the reasons for emphasizing bargaining is the connections between some business or professional relationship where a contract has been broken, and are not deeply rooted in emotional experiences between disputing parties. However, these conflicts still are a mixture of issues and emotions where the process of mediation and the product found in the final agreement hold equal weight.

A Transformative Style of Mediation

The case study in this chapter adheres to a transformative style of mediation. It most closely exemplifies a mediator as neutral third party. Outside guidelines or rules are not dictating the mediation's eventual outcome nor are pre-determined categories found in bargaining mediations. A transformative style of mediation believes that people have the power to resolve their conflicts and the responsibility of the mediator is in creating a process that allows people, in conflict, an opportunity to access that power (Nelson, Zarankin & Ben-Ari, 2010; Bush, 1994). For transformative mediators, the mediation process may be as important as the final agreement (Umbreit, 1995). They believe face-to-face discussion can change the issues in a conflict, and being empowered to develop options around these issues can transform peoples' relationships. They also believe that any final agreement may be only one of many transformations taking place in the mediation process (Winslade, Monk, & Cotter, 1998). An example of this can be seen in our case study where Jane and Suzanne had numerous issues covered in their mediation, yet the most important issue did not appear in their final agreement namely, Suzanne and Jane made peace with each other.

They transformed a stressful year of resentment and communication breakdowns into a chance for a new beginning. They now had a chance to live as a successful single-parent family. To further make this point, if Suzanne and Jane did not agree on stipulations in the agreement, yet left the mediation having gained respect for each other's differing points of view, then the primary assumptions made in a transformative mediation style, would still view it as a success, even though no agreement was reached. In mediations using a transformative style, numerous disputes ending without agreements may settle at a later date when the relationship makes further transformations, allowing for eventual acceptance of differing points of view (Hoskins & Stoltz, 2003). This style of mediation has relevance when people, in conflict, have a history of experiences with each other. The deeper the history between people in conflict, the greater chance layers of thoughts and emotions may influence the conflict's outcome. This makes a transformative style of mediation a popular alternative for family, school, workplace and community disputes where people are guided, in mediation, by their feelings and behavior, not by outside rules or regulations or any specific issues such as, payment for services rendered. In a transformative mediation, the process has as much or more importance than the final mediated agreement. Mediators, practicing this style of mediation, are constantly in tune with the mediation process, looking for occasions when they can continue empowering people to resolve their conflicts.

Emotions and Three Styles of Mediation

Emotions enter into all three mediation styles and it would be difficult to evaluate whether one style favors emotions over another. At first glance, one may assume that an evaluative style of mediation is controlled by certain guidelines and procedures; therefore, emotions are also controlled. Yet, mediations requiring an evaluative style may be highly emotional. This can be seen in some special education mediations where parents' emotions may run high, or mediations centered on obtaining custody and visitation agreements decreed from family

court, where "fighting over the kids" can be a highly emotional experience.

A bargaining style of mediation focuses on issues, where a contract has been broken or someone has not lived up to a previously agreed upon gesture of intentions. Again, it would appear that issues should dominate the mediation process. However, when a person feels that others are not acting with the truest definition of "good will" then emotions can be thrust into the center of the mediating process. Although emotions rarely are defined in the final agreements, they can dominate the discussion, especially in the beginning stages of the mediation process.

A transformative style of mediation accepts emotional change as one of its premises in successfully completing the mediation process. It is not only peoples' behavior that is transformed in this style. Working through emotional roadblocks to successful mediation agreements is a corner stone of this process. Everyday disputes found in families, schools, workplaces and communities come with emotional baggage connected to issues in dispute, and sometimes, the emotional baggage turns out to be the *real* issues. This style of mediation assumes that feelings, connected to peoples' disputes, need successful transformations, as much as, their behavior. Mediators, using this approach, recognize emotions in both the mediation process and the final agreements.

Cultural Implications

Mediators have historical roots dating back to early Christianity. It is said that Jesus was one of our first mediators in his efforts to resolve disputes between his disciples and Jewish religious leaders. However, mediation is not only Christian. Both Chinese and Japanese cultures have an established tradition of consensus building through mediated agreements performed by elders in the community. In the Western Hemisphere mediation also has cultural tradition in the community as illustrated in long standing Native American rituals. An example is the Iroquois confederacy where a form of mediation accounts for the discussions and agreements reached among Native American people on issues affecting family, culture and national pride.

Also, an informal justice system is widespread throughout the Indian sub-continent, especially in the rural and remote regions. The system is called "Jirga" or "Punchayat" depending on the language of that region. In the Indian sub-continent mediation is an old, active and diplomatic form of institution for centuries comprising of a body including respectable elders of the village. This body is responsible for settling all conflicts and maintenance of law and order in the community. Mediation is still preferred in some parts of the Indian sub-continent due to their remoteness from the city court system and also because people believe in the power of conflict resolution at the community level with minimum expenditure.

In the very beginning of the United States of America, Benjamin Franklin pioneered democracy by bringing disputants together under a climate of humility in order to resolve disputes. He believed that humility was at the heart of a democracy and he modeled this by listening to both sides of a conflict as a neutral third party. In many respects, Franklin believed that liberty and democracy are best served through humility. His form of mediation was based on the assumption that people in dispute have a far better understanding of their problems and should be given the liberty to resolve them. He also believed that many disputes were better off being handled through mediation than through litigation.

Though the methods and styles of these early mediators may be slightly different than the techniques found in this chapter, the basic concept of mediation is the same as our early ancestors. The idea of empowerment, assertiveness, critical thinking and neutrality are found in this history of conflict resolution. Mediation has a strong cultural base for those interested in finding its roots.

Notes

10. More information on isolating issues from a mediation perspective can be found in the following book. Fisher, R., & Ury, D. (1983). *Getting to yes: Negotiating agreements without giving in.* New York: Penguin Books. 34–46.

11. More information on styles of mediation can be found in the book by. Whatling, T. (2012). *Mediation skills and strategies: A practical guide.* London, UK: Jessica Kingsley Publishers. 153–158.

A Mediation Exercise

The following is a mediation checklist for evaluating your performance after completing mediation. Check off activities that took place and discuss with others high points in the mediation and potential changes for making the next mediation more successful.

	Yes	No
Creating Neutrality:		
Did I present the ground rules in an effective manner?	☐	☐
Did I keep balance both temporally and spatially?		
Did I allow an ample opportunity for opening statements?	☐	☐
Did I remain in control during this stage of mediation?		
Did I receive agreement on all ground rules before continuing?	☐	☐
Finding Common Ground:		
Did I find issues that both parties had in common?	☐	☐
Did I successfully review common ground?		
Did I look for *factual* and *emotional* common ground?	☐	☐
Did the common ground make the dispute more reasonable?		
Did mediating parties have an opportunity to vent their feelings?	☐	☐
Isolating Issues:		
Did the parties discuss issues when the venting slowed down?	☐	☐
Did the parties repeat important issues over and over again?		
Did I remind people what issues were still in dispute?	☐	☐
Did I reframe issues that were emotionally charged?		
Did I isolate issues for both parties in dispute?	☐	☐
Choosing Options:		
Did I empower mediating parties to solve their dispute?	☐	☐
Were consensus and point/counterpoint options discussed?		
Did I suggest categories for discussion during negotiations?	☐	☐
Did I paraphrase peoples' offers, making them more negotiable?		
Did I review the options accepted by both parties?	☐	☐
Making an Agreement:		
Did I write the agreement in the mediating parties own words?	☐	☐
Was the agreement balanced between both parties?		
Did I avoid contingency agreements?	☐	☐
Did I make the agreement specific?		
Did I review the mediation agreement and thank both parties?	☐	☐

Text Box 11.1

Chapter 12

Emotions and Mediation

The following chapter shows how the emotions discussed in this book affect the mediation process. It will demonstrate some of the difficulties found with emotions when mediating between disputing parties. It also will give guidelines for overcoming these emotional experiences during a mediation. It is hoped these guidelines will be useful in the practice of mediation where emotions run high and where a conflict is more than issue–oriented. It may be that dealing successfully with emotions makes the difference between a successful or unsuccessful mediation process.

Mediating Anger

It is safe to say that many beginning mediators eventually are faced with mediations where emotions are running high and disputing parties find the other party being unreasonable. This can be especially true in mediations where opposing parties previously have tried to discuss their conflicts and have failed. In these mediations, anger is a phenomenon that must be addressed or obtaining a final agreement may be wishful thinking on everyone's part. Keeping this in mind, mediation can be an ideal forum for resolving disputes between angry people, if specific issues are understood.

Anger-oriented conflicts begin with someone acting unreasonably, causing another to become angry. This frequently happens in emotionally charged mediations and if mediators make accurate assumptions and follow specific guidelines, anger can be reconciled effectively. First of all, the purpose of mediation is to create a reasonable format for people to discuss their conflicts (Malin, 2009; Barsky, 1983). Mediators should not assume that anger is an emotion they are going to keep out of mediation. The assumption should be that mediation creates a climate where people are allowed to express their anger but must follow certain ground rules. The intent is not to stop anger but to reconcile it skillfully.

215

From the beginning of mediation, the ground rules should reflect the senti- ment that anger is acceptable, but only if specific ground rules are followed such as, no name calling or use of foul language. Clear ground rules regarding anger, helps mediators sustain stability and establishes the next stage of mediation, where finding common ground becomes important. Angry people need a forum for venting their anger and before any issues are discussed, the venting of anger may be crucial. A common mistake some mediators make when people are vent- ing their anger is to rush ahead and isolate issues, as an attempt at calming angry outbursts. A better strategy may be to allow the anger to flow while the mediator looks for common ground. As long as, the opposing parties are following the ground rules, anger is probably an emotion that needs to be expressed by both sides. By finding common ground, mediators slow down the exchange of anger, demonstrating that both parties are not as polarized as they may believe. Also, finding common ground slows the pace of the mediation, allowing reason to return.

Many mediators ask the question, "So how do you isolate issues when op- posing parties are expressing anger?" When both parties have vented their anger and are conducting their conversation in a more business-like manner, isolating issues becomes more appropriate. It may be at this point that explosions have taken place and both sides have obtained distance for their conversation to be- come reasonable. Negotiations need reasonable conversation formed by reason- able issues. Isolating issues of angry people can be issues affected by unreason- able explosions rather than reasonable thinking.

Another question frequently asked is, "What can you do when opposing par- ties have isolated the issues and are starting to put options on the table for nego- tiation, and someone again becomes angry?" The temptation is to continue with negotiations because both parties have come so far in the mediation process, and on occasions, continuing mediation does work. However, when anger flairs up during negotiations it may also indicate that more venting of anger is needed before the negotiations can continue. When this happens, here are items to con- sider:

- Was anger created because the mediation was not balanced?
- Was anger established as common ground, with both parties agreeing that anger is affecting a successful mediation?
- Has the mediator referred to the ground rules on anger, as a way of defusing explosions?
- Has the mediator properly used the skills of re-framing and paraphrasing to slow down the anger?

Any one of the above approaches can be successful in defusing angry explo- sions, but another method is commonly used, especially when opposing parties have reached the negotiation stage, in mediation, but still have problems with anger. Caucusing is a method where both sides have an opportunity to speak privately with the mediator to negotiate an agreement (Moore, 2003). Caucusing can be effective in mediation, as a last resort, where anger is involved. It gives opposing parties an opportunity to get spatial and temporal distance in order for reason to return. Where caucusing seems to create problems are in mediations where timid mediators use caucusing too early, as a method for avoiding angry explosions, or when disputants use caucusing to manipulate the process and avoid speaking directly to each other. In these cases, disputing parties may need to vent their feelings and the overuse of caucusing may curtail their opportunity to emotionally express themselves. Caucusing too early, may not help people express their anger, but may help bury it for a future moment. Using caucusing to manipulate the mediation process rarely makes for lasting agreements. Unfortunately, the moment may come, at the end of mediation, where people may sabotage the agreement because they never had the chance to express their anger.

Mediating Resentment

For some, mediation may be a welcome choice for those feeling oppressed by the frustrating fallout felt by disputants from resentment-oriented conflicts. Employer/employee, parent/child, landlord/tenant, and other mediations formed around possible perceptions of oppression, may have one or both parties feeling frustrated, stuck, and victimized. Many mediators have commented that mediation empowers resentful people to discuss their points of view in the presence of a neutral third party, and that alone can be empowering to disputants experiencing resentment. One of the more important assumptions mediators need to consider when mediating with resentful people is that mediation offers a forum for direct, candid communication to take place, and that indirect methods of gossip and innuendo are not the only methods for resolving conflicts.

This assumption can begin in the mediator's opening statement. It is not uncommon for successful mediators to point out that mediation is a process that survives on direct communication, and the more opposing sides talk directly to each other, the more successful the mediation process. Also, empowerment in mediations can be most effective when the mediator establishes a balance of power from the beginning. Emphasis should be put on the ground rules that both parties have equal opportunity to speak, equal time to state their feelings, and a fair and equal exchange of issues to be discussed.

For disputants who feel resentful, establishing equal rights and a sense of empowerment might be mandatory for a successful mediation (Schermuly, Meyer, & Dämmer, 2013; Neumann, 1992). Why might these elements be mandatory in mediations filled with resentment? The answer is "At least one of these people may be in a power imbalance with the other, where it has not been possible to speak equally." If this is the case, it may require the resentful party to speak through the mediator until empowered to speak directly to the other party. However, the goal is to have both parties speak directly to each other, and resentful people may have a better chance if they eventually speak directly. With this in mind, too much paraphrasing and re-framing can give indirect discussion an opportunity for remaining indirect. This could be one of the main reasons resentment-oriented conflicts have a tendency to bog down. Without direct communication the mediation could go in circles.

Going in circles is a concern that mediators must address in resentment-oriented mediations, where disputing parties have difficulty expressing the important issues in conflict. Resentment during mediation is unlike mediations with anger, where a frightened mediator may move too quickly in order to avoid angry outbursts. In resentment-oriented mediations, the opposite seems more common. Opposing parties may flounder to the point where their thoughts and feelings are hidden by indirect communication. Mediators may have to remind disputants of what has been said and accomplished, with the goal of moving opposing sides toward negotiations. In resentment-oriented mediations, empowering disputants to be assertive and specific, may be one of the mediator's goals. The more mediators help opposing parties talk directly to each other, find common ground, and isolate issues, the more accurate and successful may be the mediation.

In resentment-oriented mediations, if opposing sides get angry, it could be viewed as a success—at least they are talking directly to each other. They are now venting their feelings without the use of gossip, sarcasm or other forms of indirect communication. Sometimes inexperienced mediators will view expressions of anger as an indication that the mediation is getting out of hand. In resentment-oriented mediations, getting angry may be necessary for resolving disputes that pertain to an imbalance of power. Mediators should encourage the anger under the guidelines established in the ground rules, and keep balance by empowering the oppressed party to conduct the mediation on equal terms with the opposing party. Here are further points to consider:

- Emphasize the mediation process is their opportunity to make individual choices in a clear and direct manner.
- Direct the conversation away from the mediator and have disputants directly talk to each other.
- When disputants use indirect communication, reframe their language into more direct, digestible statements.

Finally, a crucial stage in resentment-oriented mediations occurs when resentful people are in mediation's options stage for resolving conflicts. Often the opposing side, holding the most power, may try to dictate what options are acceptable. Mediators have an opportunity to allow parent and child, employer and employee, landlord and tenant and other possible power imbalances, to participate in creative problem solving. Here is where options are based on consensus and both sides have equal input into the final agreement. Challenge both disputants, when negotiating options, to work together on developing balanced alternatives.

Mediating Revenge

Revenge-oriented conflicts may be suitable for mediation. They give disputing parties an opportunity for changing their revenge into an agreement based on justice. Many people come to mediation feeling violated, in some way. Some of these people are seeking ways to emotionally get back in balance. Mediation can be an opportunity for disputing parties to specifically face their emotions. The biggest concern for mediators, in mediating revenge-oriented conflicts, is discovering whether the parties are agreeing to end violations or are using the process as a means of retaliation. On-going relationship conflicts, family feuds and disputes over property are but a few of the revenge-oriented conflicts that find their way to mediation. One of most important assumptions a mediator can make in these conflicts is, "Are both parties entering the mediation in the spirit of good-will?" (NOAA, 2004).

However, revenge can be viewed by many, as a solution to conflicts. If mediation is being used as a form of retaliation, then frequently these intentions show themselves when asking for agreement on the ground rules in the beginning of mediation. In these cases, revenge-oriented conflicts should not continue until both sides agree to ground rules based on ending retaliation, not creating more of it. Agreeing to fair and balanced ground rules sets the stage for developing options based on justice not revenge.

The key to mediating revenge-oriented conflicts may be in creating options that both sides believe are fair. Being violated and thrown out of balance seems a major portion of revenge-oriented conflict, and options may need to appear as non-threatening and balanced. That is why the use of caucusing when disputants have been retaliating against each other, seems counter-productive. Privately talking to the other side may be all that is needed for someone to perceive the mediation as out of balance. Revenge is based on plans for retaliation against others. These plans are private affairs where people bide their time for retaliation. Caucusing gives the appearance of encouraging plans based on revenge more than justice. Plans are developed without the presence of the other party. Revenge-oriented disputes may require opposing sides to develop agreements in each other's presence, so a fair and balanced climate prevails.

One of the main signs that revenge-oriented mediations are not fair and balanced may be during the agreement stage, if one side agrees but contingent on the other side accomplishing their part of the agreement first. These are called contingency agreements and can be another way of retaliation. For mediators, contingency agreements mean the vengeful parties still do not trust each other, and the mediation process probably needs to go back to discuss the dispute until violations are neutralized, and disputants feel emotionally in balance. Here are further points to consider:

- It is important to keep balance in mediations filled with revenger. Usually, violated disputants are out of balance emotionally and need balance to successfully complete mediation.

- Violated disputants need to discuss emotional issues, as well as logistical issues. Look for emotional common ground to bring them together.
- Remember that revenge can be viewed by some as a solution to a problem. Present mediation as an alternative solution to problems.

Finally, revenge-oriented mediations may be highly emotional based on the degree that opposing parties have bided their time and have waited to retaliate. Keeping this in mind, the mediator's main responsibility may be making sure both parties are emotionally in balance by the close of the mediation. If emotional balance is reached, disputants have a higher probability of seeing the mediation as fair.

Mediating Apathy

It is hard to picture apathetic people in mediation. It is a voluntary process that requires self-directed participation on both sides. However, apathy-oriented mediations do exist. People who are mandated to mediation through a court referral may be apathetic and view the process as offering little hope in resolving conflicts. Mediation may appear as one more agency attempt at micro-managing their lives, where little seems resolved or changed (Nowell & Salem, 2004). Another example, are certain divorce mediations, where both parties experience constant conflict and may enter mediation as numb participants who are mediating emotionally charged issues affecting children and other family members. In both examples and others, one reality may hold true for the mediator. Apathy-oriented mediations can be difficult. Apathetic people may be numb and may find little meaning or hope in the mediation process.

In apathy-oriented mediations, the opening statement by the mediator becomes crucial. It may be important for mediators to work from the assumption that people are numb and have lost a certain amount of hope. They need encouragement from the mediator that mediation is worth their while. In the mediator's opening statement, it could be vital that correct semantics be used as encouragement. For example, mediators could speak in terms of "when we reach an agreement" as opposed to "if we reach an agreement." Other pre-suppositions such as, "we will write the final agreement in your language, or when we isolate your issues, or we will all look for the best options to resolve this conflict," are all statements offering hope.

Beyond talking in a more positive manner, mediators may find themselves injecting feelings into the mediation process. This is accomplished through finding emotional common ground. This becomes an important step for apathetic people in mediation. Agreeing the dispute has caused similar feelings, goes a long way to finding meaning in the mediation process. For example, a divorcing couple having difficulty establishing a visitation schedule, may be motivated by the mediator who points out, "So you both agree that you will miss your children and want a schedule where you are emotionally connected to their lives." Such common ground has a reasonable probability in bringing feelings of positive regard to the surface, and sometimes mediators need to assist opposing parties with such emotions.

However, the ability of the mediator to help apathetic people reach feelings of emotion walks the line between counseling and mediation. The question is, "How do mediators draw disputing parties out emotionally without losing a sense of neutrality?" The answer may be by finding emotional common ground. Sometimes even a neutral third party has to risk saying, "So you both agree you feel devastated by this dispute."

Another problem in apathy-oriented conflicts may be the possibility that cynical behavior of the disputing parties will affect the mediation process. Cynicism, sometimes, is the language of apathetic people and when this happens in mediations, it may require mediators to re-frame the cynical language out of peoples' responses. For example, a mediator might have to reframe this statement, "How can I trust someone *like her* in solving this problem?" to "How can I trust her so we can solve this problem?" The first example is typical of an apathetic person being cynical. The second demonstrates the same statement after it was subtly reframed by a mediator. Here are further points to consider:

- Be patient with apathetic disputants. They may be late bloomers in the mediation process. Be careful not to move too quickly in isolating issues or crating agreements.
- Let disputants develop alternatives that are personal and meaningful. Apathetic disputants may follow the mediator to resolve the mediation. Resist the temptation, even when disputants bog down and lack energy to proceed.

Finally, agreements in mediations with apathetic people may require the mediator to be specific in drawing up agreements. Many mediators will tell you, vague agreements do not work when people are apathetic. The more specific and descriptive the agreement in apathy-oriented mediations, the higher chance it may have for success. Apathetic people may need all the support they can get and a clear and specific written mediation agreement may appear stronger than any verbal gesture of support.

Mediating Guilt

Balance becomes a key issue in guilt-oriented conflicts. Power imbalances are usually found with guilty parties *giving in* to stronger and more verbal opposing parties. Guilty people may feel they have done something wrong, have regrets, experience self-blame and feelings of worthlessness. Mediators involved in mediations with high levels of guilt, may need to keep a balance of power from the ground rules through to the agreement. This becomes no more evident than in family mediations, where a dominant figure blames others for the family's problems. Guilt can be a powerful tool for controlling conflicts, and dominant family figures have been known to avoid family mediations for fear of losing their power. However, if a dominant figure does agree to mediation, then mediators may have to put special emphasis on keeping the mediation balanced.

Mediators observing clear power imbalances may discover that a dominant opposing party will make the other party feel guilty through numerous methods. On occasions, the dominant party may try to become co-mediator by lecturing to the other party about ways he or she can change their behavior. An inexperienced mediator may fall victim to these lectures and shift the balance of power toward the dominant party. Another tactic used by dominant parties to create guilt, is story telling. Here a long story is told to monopolize the conversation, where the other party is to blame for ongoing disputes. In both of these examples, mediators may need to have ground rules for equal time and an agreement that the mediator remains a neutral third party—with no helpers.

It also may be important in conflicts with high levels of guilt, to be a spokesperson for guilty disputants when they feel unable to speak for themselves. People who feel guilty may have regrets, blame themselves and, many times, feel worthless. Their ability to stand up for their principles may be in jeopardy because of low self-esteem. As neutral third parties, mediators are not in a position to advocate for any disputant, but they can paraphrase what a guilty person is trying to say to a dominant opposing party. This helps in keeping balance in the mediation. For example, a guilty woman married to a domineering man enters mediation, and the man begins speaking to her in a condescending tone. The mediator realizing an imbalance of power, draws on the intent of what the woman is trying to say, and paraphrases it to equal the responses of the dominant husband. With the mediator's help, the guilty woman is able to specifically discuss issues that were previously impossible.

Also, in conflicts where guilt is used, a bigger problem may be in getting the dominant disputant to attend mediation. For example, in an employer/employee mediation, employers may be reluctant to attend because of their fear of losing authority if they act as equals with employees. They may believe their power lies in making judgments and keeping others in lower positions of power. Ironically, experience shows that, if an employer agrees to attend a mediation session, then most of the conflict may be resolved by the act of showing up. Actually, employers who attend mediations with their employees, many times, gain power not lose it. Sometimes the process of mediation becomes as important as reaching an agreement. Employers, who reach out to solve problems through mediation, can be perceived as more than an authority. Employees may see them as effective problem solvers who will do what is necessary to resolve a conflict. Here are further points to consider:

- Talk in a highly descriptive manner without sounding judgmental. Guilty disputants may look for reasons to blame themselves. The more self-blame they express during the mediation, the more difficulty in isolating issues.
- Be specific with guilty disputants. They have a tendency to talk in vague and general terms. Constantly paraphrase their vague language into language that is specific and concise.

- Be careful not to ask too many questions during the mediation. Guilty disputants may feel on trial and blame themselves instead of developing options during the mediation.
- Watch out for others "guilt tripping" disputants into feelings of worthlessness and shame. In the ground rules, make a stipulation that both side will not blame each other but will work toward a reasonable agreement.

Using guilt to control others has been a popular method of conflict resolution, over the years, for many people perceived to have authoritarian personalities (Saulnier & Sivasubramaniam, 2015; Dunbar, 1995). However, in an Information Age, using guilt may be less effective in a society that allows many diverse points of view to enter the conflict resolution process. Mediation can help guilty people, and the dominant people who make them feel that way, by offering an alternative to judgments and control. Through mediation, guilt-oriented conflicts can be resolved through a democratic process that values opposing points of view.

Mediating Egotism

Outside of mediating conflicts filled with anger. Conflicts filled with egotism can cause serious trepidation for inexperienced mediators. It is the egotist's need to be right that poses difficulty in mediation, where both sides of a conflict are given equal consideration. In some cases, mediations filled with egotism are the other side of mediations filled with guilt or resentment. An egotist's need to be right may generate these feeling in opposing parties, and create the same power imbalances as discussed earlier in mediations filled with either resentment or guilt. Furthermore, getting egotists to mediate can be an accomplishment in its own right. The process of mediation assumes that both parties have the right to express a legitimate point of view. Egotists work from the assumption, that their point of view is the right point of view. Any time an egotistical person agrees to mediation, it could be viewed as a minor success. Experience shows, egotistical people appear more comfortable when they have power and control over others. It may be their way of coping with their insecurity.

Let us assume that egotistical people do agree to mediation. What strategies should a mediator consider, so egotists do not take over mediation sessions? First, experience shows us that egotistical people, in some manner, may make a play for power. The term used in mediation circles is "posturing" (Wade, 2004). Egotists may posture for control of the session by making demands, questioning the process, or challenging ground rules. It may be important for mediators to remain in control, especially in the beginning of mediations when an egotist is one of the disputants. Here are methods for achieving this:

- Do not continue in the mediation process until egotists have agreed with all the ground rules.

- Do not explain mediation to egotists with the hope of convincing them to participate. Describe the process and ask if they agree to participate.
- Watch for answering countless questions posed by egotists. It may throw the balance of power in their favor, early in the mediation.
- Remain in control of the session. There is ample time to empower both sides later in mediation to resolve disputes.
- Remember, if egotists agree to all the ground rules, they are closer to giving up their need to be right and being in control.

Many egotists who agree to the ground rules in mediation have little reason not to cooperate. When egotists finally decide to participate in the mediation process, they have relinquished their most prized assumption, namely, a need to be right. That does not mean they will not try to be right during the mediation session. Their egotism may not have completely dissolved. What it may mean is that they have decided to participate in mediation with a sense of good–will, leaving their power plays behind. Experienced mediators will tell you that mediations involving egotists can be filled with tension until everyone agrees to cooperate. After that, they may be similar to other balanced mediations. One reason may be that egotistical people run the risk of being isolated and alone, because of their condescending behavior. Mediation can be viewed as a compromise where they partially give up their need to be right, and, in return, are more accepted by others. Ultimately, egotists may feel alone and mediation may be a safe way to reconnect with a disputing party.

Mediating Greed

One of the problems with greed-oriented mediations is that greedy people may believe they have the right to win the mediation, at all costs. Of course, such an assumption works contrary to the mediation process. However, certain consumer/merchant, labor/management, and other negotiating style mediations have to confront the historical fact that other dispute resolution methods have justified all kinds of adversarial behavior for resolving conflicts. Fortunately, people who agree to mediation usually are not thinking about underhanded methods but are more focused on resolving conflicts democratically (Fiester, 2014; Shailor, 1994).

What greedy people may bring to the mediation process are hidden agendas. Usually greedy people, with hidden agendas, are more than willing to agree to ground rules. It is after this point where the trouble begins. Finding common ground may not be the type of activity that interests a greedy disputant. Usually, they want to go directly to the issues and focus primarily on their hidden agendas.

Mediators can counteract greedy behavior by spending extra time finding common ground. It may be important for greedy disputants to re-sensitize themselves by agreeing to what they have in common. The creation of common ground may make it difficult for greedy disputants to maintain hidden agendas or to focus obsessively on just their goals. Establishing common ground early in greed-oriented mediations can make it easier to keep final agreements balanced. Neither party will be perceived as obtaining a goal at all costs.

Sometimes it may be important for mediators to thoroughly describe the mediation process to greedy people in mediations. Opposing parties, who are greedy, can still find common ground if they understand mediation is not designed for someone to win and another to lose. Its philosophy is based on creative problem solving where people get what they want by talking to each other. Aggressive people, who agree to mediation, may need to understand the difference between getting what you want and helping everyone get what they want, out of a conflict. Litigation has created a mind set in our society; there are winners and losers that answer to an independent judge to determine who is right and wrong. Though this philosophy is popular, it is changing, and mediation continues developing as an alternative method for conflict resolution (Barsky, 2000).

Many times, greed-oriented conflicts come to mediation expecting a judge or arbitrator to render a decision. Under this format, aggressive, sometimes greedy, people present facts that will win a conflict. Mediation is more than facts; it encompasses human emotions and human dialogue. It is designed as an alternative to winning or losing a conflict. Mediators might want to take the time by informing opposing parties of the difference between having a hidden agenda for winning and being open to discussing the issues and emotions in a conflict— no matter where the path may lead the mediation. Let us summarize what has been said:

- It is important for greedy disputants to re-sensitize themselves by talking about both facts and feelings.
- The options stage in mediation can be important when dealing with a greedy disputant. The more alternatives generated, the more difficult it becomes is using obsessive behavior toward a single goal.
- The creation of common ground makes it more difficult to hoard possessions or other people, for that matter. Establishing common ground early makes it easier to keep the final agreement balanced.
- If greedy people continuously try obtaining their goals at all costs, the mediator may choose to stop the mediation session until parties are willing to negotiate in good faith.

Mediating Jealousy

Many jealousy-oriented conflicts between neighbors, siblings, co-workers and lovers find their way to mediation. It offers a fair and balanced forum for negotiating people's fear of losing something. In jealousy-oriented conflicts, mediators may want to consider working from the assumption that opposing parties may be afraid of losing power, control, time, "face," or any other person or thing they feel needs protecting. Keeping this in mind, mediators may want to consider the high probability that jealous people have already decided what they are protecting, before entering the mediation process. This assumption seems similar to the assumption made in greed-oriented conflicts, only greedy people may have already decided what they want, compared to jealous people who may have decided what they are going to protect.

Jealousy-oriented mediations can be emotional events, because such issues as saving "face" or protecting one's honor usually carry strong emotional investments. However, these issues may be the very reasons jealous people seek mediation as a method for conflict resolution. Jealous people may be afraid of losing something, send out warning signals, put in claims, and use force when necessary. Jealousy-oriented conflicts that have reached the level of using force can make the dispute more overwhelming than people expected. Mediation seems a viable option in jealousy-oriented disputes after force has failed to resolve the conflict to anyone's satisfaction. Under these circumstances, mediation becomes a moderate alternative. Many court referrals, dealing with some form of jealousy-oriented conflicts such as divorce and pre-divorce, harassment, sibling rivalries and others, are amenable to mediation for people afraid of losing something (Stoner, 1999):

- Have a ground rule that both parties agree not to threaten each other. Threatening statements are power plays to gain advantage, especially when discussing issues surrounding losing face, "turf," or jealousy between two lovers. Without agreeing to a ground rule for stopping threats, many jealousy-oriented mediations fall into claiming and counter-claiming, either people or things, through the rest of the mediation session.
- Find common ground as soon as possible. Claiming and counter-claiming behavior is reduced with the establishment of common ground The more common ground, the less there is to claim.

Watch for jealous disputants trying to resolve conflicts pre-maturely. Similar to the phenomenon found in greed-oriented conflicts, jealous disputants have a tendency to arrive at solutions before problems have been thoroughly discussed. Experienced mediators find that pre-mature solutions in jealousy-oriented mediations, lead to claiming and counter-claiming and not a fair and balanced negotiation of options.

Mediating Anxiety

Mediation can be a more reasonable forum for anxious people in conflict. Especially when anxiety may be the actual cause of conflicts found in family court, small claims court, and other more formal venues where problems develop between people who know each other (Gale et al. 2002). Many of these conflicts, are based on people having lost confidence in others they once trusted with their marriages, children, or their friendships. In place of trust emerges anxiety and doubt about continuing these relationships. In these cases, mediating anxiety may be as crucial as negotiating specific issues in conflict. Keeping this in mind, the more emotional common ground found in anxiety-oriented mediations, the less anxiety experienced by opposing parties during the mediation process. Finding emotional common ground can create certainty that disputants, involved in mediation, are experiencing similar feelings. Keeping this in mind, anxious disputants probably need to feel secure with the mediation process, and finding emotional common ground could be a major consideration for mediators faced with anxiety-oriented conflicts.

It is understood that any mediation takes place with a certain level of anxiety, and that mediators can address it even before disputants arrive at mediation (Genevieve, Chornenki & Hart, 2001). For example, here are some security oriented procedures for reducing anxiety:

- Have as many safety-oriented items available before disputants arrive. Many mediators provide tissues, writing paper, pens or pencils, drinking water, and directions to the restrooms.
- Understand the value of "small talk" before mediations begin. Small talk creates a certain comfort with opposing parties before mediation without having the mediator lose any neutrality. Talking about the weather or sporting events, or any other relevant topic, takes the edge off the emotional climate surrounding mediation. However, small talk should be used with both parties so neutrality is maintained and people do not perceive any favoritism on the mediator's part.
- Mediators should take their time in mediations showing high levels of anxiety. Anxious disputants may need extra time to formulate their issues, and may need to feel emotionally secure before they are willing to isolate them.
- The mediator's tone of voice has bearing on different mediations. For example, anger and egotism oriented mediations may require the mediator to use an assertive tone with disputants, in order to create adequate boundaries for successful discussion. Mediations involving apathy, guilt and anxiety may require the opposite. In anxiety-oriented mediations, speaking in a soft, low tone of voice makes more sense than assertive language.
- When getting an agreement on ground rules, include a ground rule that addresses interruptions. For example, if one disputant interrupts another, have a ground rule to stop the interruptions and allow a disputant time to finish their point of discussion.

Mediating Hatred

The first question that needs to be asked in hatred-oriented mediations, "Is it possible to mediate hatred-oriented conflicts?" The answer is a cautious, "Yes." Hatred is a phenomenon based on rejection, alienation, condemnation, violence and destruction. When hatred-oriented conflicts reach their later stages, they increasingly become more difficult to mediate. That is why many mediation centers are hesitant to mediate any conflict that includes violence. First of all, the violence involved in some conflicts may be a felony or misdemeanor that requires traditional court action such as found in physical abuse, battering, assault, and other disputes involving acts of violence.

The problem with hatred-oriented conflicts is that violence may be perceived differently by those in conflict. It is not that hateful people get angry and explode through a violent act, or want to use violence as a form of retaliation, or use violence as a response by a jealous lover against a loved one. In hatred-oriented conflicts violence, usually, is not used as a reaction to unreasonable behavior, feelings of violation or even a fear of losing someone. In hatred-oriented conflicts, violence, many times, is a part of an ideology and can be a deliberate act based on a philosophy of rejection, alienation and condemnation of others. Under these circumstances, mediation may appear, to some, as trying to change an established ideology and may be asking too much, even of mediation.

Mediations are possible in resolving conflicts with hateful people but success usually is determined by the degree of good will expressed by the disputants during the mediation process. However, it is difficult to say when hateful people stop being moderately hateful and become fully immersed in their hatred. The key still may lie in the mediator determining whether the disputing parties are serious about mediation, or see it as another vehicle for their personal brand of violent ideology. Mediation may only be possible when opposing parties both agree to act with good–will, when mediating conflicts. For example, mediations based on prejudice, may have a chance for success. Ignorance and fear are conflicts that can be overcome in a mediation session. However, when mediators consider disputes based on racism or terrorism, it is anyone's guess whether there will be enough good will to go around, and as far as terrorism is concerned—recent events have demonstrated the implausibility of negotiating with people who have an ideology based on violence and destruction (Constantine, 2002).

Mediating Fear

In a mediation, one of the main concerns for everyone involved is safety. This becomes a paramount issue when disputants are afraid. In mediations where people in dispute are afraid of the process of mediation, it becomes important to take disputants step by step through what are the phases that they can expect during the mediation process. This may take a little longer than disputants who are eager to deal with their problems. However, mediation is a process where emotions play a large role in whether they succeed or fail. Taking the time to make the disputants feel safe, adds to the mediation success rate.

Another fear oriented issue in mediation is when one disputant seems to be overpowering the other. Here is where a mediator may want to use skills of reframing and common ground to slow down the mediation, while making it less fearful for the afraid disputant. This may mean that the mediator needs to spend more time finding common ground. The more the disputants agree, the less fear factor enters into the mediation process. Fear, many times, is caused by disputants being too polarized where the distance between them on issues seems unsafe to risk both issues and emotions. The more common ground created, the more amenable disputants are to resolving the conflict.

People who enter a mediation experiencing fear do have an opportunity to clarify what is threatening them, and take a stand on their fears with the help of a mediator. In some respects, mediation changes a person's anxiety to fear under a controlled environment. It may be scary to face another person in a mediation, but it may be far more detrimental to spend days or weeks worrying about what to do while feeling the grips of anxiety. Working through one's fear during a mediation may be one way to relieve the stress of constant worry while creating an agreement where both parties benefit.

Bibliography

Aberill, J. R. (1980). A constructivist view of emotion. In *Emotion: Theory, Research and Experience*. Edited by R. Plutchik, and H. Kellerman. New York: Academic Press.

Adamczyk, A., Gruenewald, J., Chermak, J., & Freilich, J. D. (2014). The relationship between hate groups and far- right ideological violence. *Journal of Contemporary Criminal Justice. 30*(3), 310–32.

Adler, R. S., Rosen, B. & Silverstein, E. M. (1998). Emotions in negotiations: How to manage fear and anxiety. *Negotiation Journal. 14*, 161–79.

Adorno, T. W. (1969) *Authoritarian personality*. New York: Norton Press.

Agibalova, T. V., Petrosyan, T. R., Kuznetsov, A. G., Gurevich, G. L., & Shuvalov, S. A. (2014). Features of the formation, course, and treatment of alcohol dependence in patients with post-traumatic stress disorder. *Neuroscience and Behavioral Physiology, 44*(9), 1068–72.

Aledort, S. L. (2014). Excitement in shame: The price we pay. *International Journal of Group Psychotherapy, 64*(1), 90–103.

Allred, K., Mallozzi, F. Matsui, F., & Raia, C. (1997). The influence of anger and compassion on negotiation performance. *Organizational Behavior and Human Decision Processes. 70*(3), 175–87.

Armstrong, M. A., & Rose, P. (1997). The group therapy for partners of combat veterans with post-traumatic stress. *Perspectives in Psychiatric Care. 33*(4), 14.

Ashanasy, H. W., Hartel, C. J., & Zerbe, W. (2000). *Emotions in the workplace: Research, theory and practice.* Westport, CT.: Quorum Books.

Augsburger, D. W. (1992). Conflict: the power of honor, dignity, and face. In David W. Augsburger, *Conflict Mediation across Cultures: Pathways and Patterns.* Chapter 3, 74–112. Louisville, Kentucky: Westminster/John Knox Press.

Bader, E. J., & Baird-Windle P. (2001). *Targets of hatred: Antiabortion terrorism.* New York: St. Martin's Press.

Bailey, J. D., & McCarty, D. (2009). Assessing empowerment in divorce mediation. *Negotiation Journal, 25*(3), 327–36.

Bandler, R., & Grinder, J. (1982). *Reframing: Neuro-linguistic programming and the transformation of meaning.* Moab, UT: Real People.

Barber, J. P., & Crits-Christoph, P. (1995). *Dynamic therapies for psychiatric disorders: Axis I.* New York: Basic Books.

Barlow, D. H. (1991). Disorders of emotions. *Psychological Inquiry. 2*(1), 58 –72.

Barsky, A. (1983). Emotional needs and dysfunctional communication as blocks to mediation. *Mediation Quarterly. 2*, 55–66.

———. (2000). *Conflict resolution for the helping professions.* Stamford Ct.: Brooks/Cole.

Bar-Tar, Y., & Spitzer, A. (1999). The effect on coping of monitoring, blunting and the ability to achieve cognitive structure. *Journal of Psychology. 3*(4), 395–413.

Bauer-Wu, S. (2010). Mindfulness meditation. *Oncology, 24*(10), 36–40.

Baum, A., & Singer, J. E. (1980). *Applications of personal control.* Hillsdale, NJ: Lawrence Erlbaum Associates.

Bazemore, G., & Griffiths, C. (1997). Conferences, circles, boards, and mediations: The new wave of community justice and decision making. *Federal Probation. 67*, 25–40.

Bazerman, M. H., Curhan, J. R., Moore, D. A., & Valley, K L., (2000). Negotiation. *Annual Review of Psychology.*

Beabout, G. A. (1996). *Freedom and its misuses: Kierkegaard on anxiety and despair.* Milwaukee, WI: Marquette University Press.

Becvar, D. S. (1997). *Soul healing: A spiritual orientation in counseling and therapy.* New York, NY: Basic Books.

Bell, R. A., Roloff, M. E., Camp, K. V., & Karol, S. H. (1990). Is it lonely at the top: Career success and personal relationships? *Journal of Communication. 40*, 24–45.

Bennet, T. (2012). The role of mediation: A critical analysis of the changing nature of dispute resolution in the workplace. *Industrial Law Journal. 41*(4), 479 – 80.

Bennett, M., & Herman, M. (1997). *The art of mediation.* New York, NY: NITA.

Betz, E. (2015). "Des is halt so": Explaining, justifying, and convincing with halt. *Die Unterrichtspraxis, 48*(1), 114–18.

Bishai, D., Ghaffar, A., Kelley, E., & Kieny, M. (2015). Honoring the value of people in public health: A different kind of value. *World Health Organization. Bulletin of the World Health Organization, 93*(9), 661–62.

Block, J. (1957). Studies in the phenomenology of the emotions. *Journal of Social Psychology.* LIV, No. *19*.

Bransen, J. (2006). Selfless self-love. *Ethical Theory and Moral Practice, 9*(1), 3 25.

Braxton, J. M. (2002). Selectivity and rigor in research universities. *The Journal of Higher Education: Gale Group. 64*(6), 657–68.

Brett, J. M., Drieghe, R and Shapiro, D. L. (1986) Mediator style and mediation effectiveness. *Negotiation Journal. 2*, 277–85.

Brinkman, R., & Kirchner, R., (1994). *Dealing with people you can't stand: How to bring out the best of people at their worst.* Toronto, CA: McGraw Hill.

Brockington, I. (2011). Maternal rejection of the young child: Present status of the clinical syndrome. *Psychopathology. 44*(5) 329.

Brown, D. (1982). Divorce and family mediation: History, review, future direction. *Conciliation Courts Review. 20*(2), 1–37.

Brown, E. (1992). A gathering for peace at Ganondaga. Ganondaga, NY: The
Friends of Ganondaga Newsletter.

Brown, S. K. (2013). Seeing the light: From litigation to mediation. *American Bankruptcy Institute Journal, 32*(5), 58–59.

Bush, B., & Folger, J. (1994). *The promise of mediation: Responding to conflict through empowerment and recognition.* San Francisco: Jossey Bass.

Butler, J. K. (1999). Trust expectations, information sharing, climate of trust, and negotiation effectiveness and efficiency. *Group & Organization Management, 24*(2), 217–38

Carol, J. A., Diesel, C. A., & Weber D (1994). Conversational dilemmas. In W.R. Cupach, B.Spitzberg (Eds.) *the dark side of interpersonal communications.* Hillsdale N.J.: Lawrence Erlbaum Associates.

Carrier, C., Hiqson, V., Limoski, V., & Peterson, E. (1984). The effects of facilitative and debilitative anxiety on note taking. *Journal of Educational Research. 77*(3), 133–40.

Chalmers, E., & Cormick, G. (1971). *Racial conflict and negotiation.* Ann Arbor, MI: Institute of Labor and Industrial Relations.

Cheng, F. K. (2015), Mediation skills for conflict resolution in nursing. *Nurse Education in Practice. 15*(4), 310–13.

Choi, J. J., Gilbert, M. J., & Green, D. L. (2013). Patterns of victim marginalization in victim-offender mediation: Some lessons learned. *Crime, Law and Social Change, 59*(1), 113–32.

Christian, T. (1981). *New York State Community Dispute Resolution Program.* Albany, N.Y.: Chapter 847 Laws of New York State.

———, (1988). Victim/Offender Mediation Program. *Office of Court Administration.* Albany New York: Unified Court System of the State of New York.

Cole, B.V. (2001). Nursing care at the end of life. *Perspective in Psychiatric Care. 33*(3), 77.

Constantine, M. G. (2002). Racism attitudes, white racial identity attitudes, and multicultural counseling competence in school counselor trainees. *Counselor Education and Supervision. 42*, 18–28.

Cook-Sather, A. (2003). Listening to students about learning differences *Teaching Exceptional Children. 35*(4), 22–26.

Corn, D. (2001). Brains not bombs: Fighting terrorism where it begins, in the mind. *Working for Change. 1*, 23–34.

Coughlin, E. (1993). When people make up their minds, psychologist says, they often do not really make up their mind. *Chronicle of Higher Education. 40*, 9–11.

Cummins, D. (1996). Person centered psychology and Taoism: The reception of Lao-tzu by Cal Rogers. *International Journal of Psychology and Religion. 6*(2), 107–28.

Cunningham, M (2003). Impact of traumatic work on social work clinicians: Empirical findings. *Social Work. 48*, 28–39.

Curtis, D. L. (1998). Reconciliation and the role of empathy. In *ADR Personalities and Practice Tips.* Edited by J.J. Alfini and E.R. Galton, 53, 63. Washington D.C.: American Bar Association Section on Dispute Resolution.

Damer, L. K. (2001). Inclusion and the law. *Music Educators Journal. 87*(4), 19 –22.

DeCarvahlo, R. J. (1991). *The founders of humanistic psychology.* New York: Praeger Publishing.

Despotovic-Stanarevic, T. (2010). Possibilities and restrictions of the implementation of mediation in domestic violence cases. *Temida, 13*(3), 25–40.

Deutsch, M. (1973). *Resolution of conflict.* New Haven, CT: Yale University Press.

Donohue, W. A. (2011). Transformative linguistic styles in divorce mediation. *Negotiation and Conflict Management Research. 4*(3), 200 –218.

Dunbar, E. (1995). The prejudiced personality, racism, and antisemitism. *Journal of Personality Assessment. 65*(2), 270–78.

Egerton, F. (2011). Nation and its discontents. *European Journal of International Relations. 17*(3), 453–74.

Elbogen, E. & Johnson, S. (2009). The intricate link between violence and mental disorder: Results from the National Epidemiologic Survey on alcohol and related conditions. *Archives of General Psychiatry, 66(2):152-161.*

Elliott, D. M.S., Polman, R., & McGregor, R. (2011). Relaxing music for anxiety control. *Journal of Music Therapy, 48*(3), 264-88.

Fang, B. (2003). An eye for an eye. *US News and World Report. 135,* 24–26.

Farrugia, D. (2002). Selfishness, greed and, counseling. *Counseling and Values. 46,* 35-47.

Fedrickson, G.M. (2002) *Racism: A short history.* Princeton, N.J.: Princeton University Press.

Feero, S. A. M., & Steadman, L. (2010). An exploration of the relationship between self-esteem, health knowledge, chronic dieting and body shape accuracy. *Perspectives in Public Health, 130*(4), 186–90.

Fiester, A. (2014). Using mediation skills in working with the "difficult" family in rehabilitation. *Topics in Stroke Rehabilitation. 21*(1), 1 – 6.

Finkelstein, A., Harman, M., Mansouri, S. A., Ren, J., & Zhang, Y. (2009). A search based approach to fairness analysis in negotiation, mediation and decision making. *Requirements Engineering, 14*(4), 231–45.

Fisher, R., Ury, D. (1991). *Getting to yes: Negotiating agreement w*ithout giving in. In Bruce Patton, 2nd ed. New York: Penguin Books.

Fitzpatrick, D. (1994). Striking a balance between creative and logical sites of the brain. *Westchester County Business Journal. 33,* 31–33.

Folberg, J. (1982). Divorce mediation: A workable alternative. H. Davidson et al. (Eds.) *Alternative Means of Family Dispute Resolution.* Washington, D.C.: American Bar Association.

Folberg, J., & Taylor, A. (1984). *Mediation: A comprehensive guide to resolving conflicts without litigation.* San Francisco: Jossey-Bass.

Freedman, S. (1998). Forgiveness and conciliation: The importance of under-standing how they differ. *Counseling and Values. 42,* 200–16.

Freely, M. (2001). The ignorance of islamophobes. *New Statesman. 130,* 18–20. Freeman, L. (1999). *Common ground: Letters to a world community of Mediators.* New York: Continuum International Publishing Group.

Fuller, L. (1971). Mediation – its forms and functions. *Southern California Law Review. 44*, 305–39.

Gale, J., Mowery, R. Herrman, M., & Hollett, N. (2002). Considering effective divorce mediation: Three potential factors. *Conflict Resolution Quarterly 19*(4), 389–420.

Gallagher, K. T. (1962). *The philosophy of Gabriel Marcel.* New York: Fordham University Press.

Garcia, A. C., Vise, K., & Whitaker, S. P. (2002). Disputing neutrality: A case of a bias complaint during mediation. *Conflict Resolution Quarterly. 20*(2), 205–30.

Gatz, D. B. (2000). High standards for whom? *Phi Delta Kappan. 81*(9), 681–94.

Gaylin, W. (1989). *Feelings: Our vital signs.* New York: Harper Pub.

———. (2003). *Hatred: The psychological descent into violence.* New York: Public Affairs.

———. (2009). *Hatred: The psychological descent into violence.* New York: Public Affairs.

Genevieve, A., Chornenki, A., & Hart, C.A. (2001). *Bypass court: A dispute resolution handbook.* Markham, Ont.: Butterworths Publishing.

Gibson, R. (2000). Post-traumatic stress disorder and the thalamic/cortical pause. *Etc.: A Review of General Semantics. 57*, 26–38.

Giorgi, Amedeo (1970). *Psychology as a human science.* New York, NY: Harper Row.

Goldberg, S. B., Green, E. D. & Sander, F.E.A. (1989). Litigation, arbitration, mediation. *American Bar Association Journal. 75*, 70–72.

Goleman, D. (1995). *Emotional intelligence: Why it can matter more than IQ.* New York: Bantam Books.

Goodman, A. H. (1996). *Basic skills for the new mediator.* Rockville, Maryland: Soloman Publications.

Goodwin, J. & R. Attias (1999) *Splintered reflections: Images of the body in trauma.* New York, NY: Basic Books.

Govier, T. (1998). *Dilemmas of trust.* Montreal, CA: McGill-Queens University Press.

Gray, B. (1989). *Finding common ground for multipart problems.* San Francisco, CA: Jossey-Bass.

Green, J. E. (2004). Apathy: The democratic disease. *Philosophy and Social Criticism. 30*(6), 745–68.

Griffiths, P. E. (1997). *What emotions really are: The problem with psychological categories.* Chicago, IL: University of Chicago Press.

Griffin, B. W., & Griffin, M. M., (1997). The effects of reciprocal peer tutoring on graduate student's achievement, test anxiety, and academic self-efficacy. *Journal of Experimental Education. 65*(3), 19–210.

Gulliver, P. H. (1979). *Disputes and negotiations.* New York: Academic Press.

Hallevy, G. (2011). Therapeutic victim-offender mediation within the criminal justice process - sharpening the evaluation of personal potential for rehabilitation while righting wrongs under the ADR philosophy. *Harvard Negotiation Journal. 16,* 65.

Halperin, E. (2014). Emotion, emotion regulation, and conflict resolution. *Emotion Review. 6*(1), 68–76.

Halsley, V. (1994). Disciplining for character. *Thrust for Educational Leadeship.24,* 30–33.

Hamburg, D. A., & Hamburg, Beatrix A (2004) *Learning to live together: Prevailing hatred and violence in child and adolescent development.* New York, NY; Oxford University Press.

Hammond, A. (2003). How do you write "yes?": A study on the effectiveness of online dispute resolution. *Conflict Resolution Quarterly. 20*(3), 261–86.

Hankins, G., & Hankins C. (1998). *Prescription for anger: Coping with angry feelings and angry people.* New York: Warner Books.

Hansen, J. M. (1998). Teaching for consequences. *Kappa Delta Pi Record. 35* (1) 18–20.

Harmon, J., & Sigelman, J. (2001). State anger and prefrontal brain activity: Evidence that insult-related relative left-prefrontal activation is associate with experienced anger and aggression. *Journal of Personality and Social Psychology. 80,* 797–804.

Hedman, A. S. (2014). Perceptions of depression, counseling and referral practices, and self-efficacy reported by Minnesota clergy. *Pastoral Psychology, 63*(3), 291–306.

Hendon, D. W., Hendon, R. A., & Herbig, P. (1997). *Cross Cultural Business Negotiations*. New York, NY: Praeger.

Henwood, K. S. (2015). A systematic review and meta-analysis on the effectiveness of CBT informed anger. *Aggression and Violent Behavior.* 1359–1789.

Herman, J. L. (1997). *Trauma and recovery.* New York, NY: Basic Books.

Herman, M. S. (ed.) (1994). *Resolving conflict: Strategies for local government* Washington, D.C.: International, City/County Managem.

Heyes, C. (2010). Mesmerizing mirror neurons. *NeuroImage, 51*(2), 789–91.

Hinton, R., & Earnest, J. (2010). 'I worry so much I think it will kill me': Psychosocial health and the links to the conditions of women's lives in Papua New Guinea. *Health Sociology Review, 19*(1), 5–19.

Hirschkind, C. (2010). Media, mediation, religion. *Social Anthropology.* *19*(1), 90–97.

Hoffman, D. A. (2011). Mediation and the art of shuttle diplomacy. *Negotiation Journal, 27*(3), 263-309.

Holtz-Munroe, A., Stuart, G. L., & Hutchinson, G. (1997). Violent versus nonviolent husbands: Differences in attachment patterns, dependency, and jealousy. *Journal of Family Psychology. 11*(3), 314–42.

Honeyman, C. (1990). On evaluating mediators. *Negotiation Journal. 6,* 8–47.

Horn, T. (2013). Facing fear and change. *International Journal of mental Health. 42*(2), 99–114.

Hoskins, M. L., & Stoltz, J. M. (2003). Balancing words: Human change processes in mediation. *Conflict Resolution Quarterly. 20*(3), 331–50.

Howse, R. (2003). *Pride and resentment.* Unpublished Policy Review.

Hubbard, A. S. E., Hendrickson, K, Dehrenbach, K., & Sur, J. (2013). Effects of timing and security of an apology on satisfaction and changes in negative feelings during conflicts. *Wester Journal of Communication. 77*(3), 305.

Jabbour, E. J. (1996). *Sulha: Palestinian traditional peacemaking process.* House of Hope, Palestinian Authority: Wi'am Palestinian Conflict Resolution Center.

Jenkins, R. L. (1950). Guilt feelings: Their function and dysfunction. In M. L. Reymert (ed.) *Feelings and Emotions.* New York: McGraw-Hill, 353–61.

Jessani, A. (2011). Representing your client during the divorce mediation process. *American Journal of Family Law, 24*(4), 189–93.

Johnston, P. D. (1995). Humility: A survival tool. *Etc.: A Review of General Semantics.* 51.

Jones, J. M., Dovidio, J. F., & Vietz, D. (2013). *The psychology of diversity: Beyond prejudice and racism.* New York, NY: Wiley-Blackwell.

Jones, T. S., & Bodtker, A. (2008). Mediating with heart in mind: Addressing emotion in mediation practice. *Negotiation Journal. 17*(3), 217–44.

Jorisch, A. (2004). *Beacon of hatred: Inside Hizballah's al-Manar Television* Washington, D.C.: Brookings Institute.

Kapur, V., & Rai, S. (2013). The experience of shame in social phobia. *Journal of Psychosocial Research, 8*(2), 299–311.

Keable, D. (1997). *The management of anxiety.* New York, NY: Churchill Livingstone.

Keinknecht, R. (1991). *Mastering anxiety: The nature and treatment of anxious conditions.* New York, NY: Persus Books.

Kitayama, S. & Markus, H. eds. (1993). *Emotions and culture.* New York, NY: American Psychological Association

Koerner, N., & Dugas, M. J. (2008). An investigation of appraisals in individuals vulnerable to excessive worry: The role of intolerance of uncertainty. *Cognitive Therapy and Research, 32*(5), 619–38.

Konstan, V., Chernoff, M., & Deveney, S. (2001). Toward forgiveness: The role of shame, guilt, anger, and empathy. *Counseling and Values. 46,* 26–35.

Kornelsen, L. (2013). The role of storytelling at the intersection of transformative conflict resolution and peace education. *Storytelling, Self, Society, 9*(2), 237–60.

Kressel, K., Frontera, E. A. Forlenza, S., Butler, F., & Fish, L., (1994). The settlement-orientation vs. the problem-solving style in custody mediation. *Journal of Social Issues. 50*(1), 67–84.

Kristeva, J., & Herman, J. (2011). Hatred and forgiveness. *European Perspectives: A Series in Social Thought and Culture. 14,* 369.

Kutinsky, J. K. (2004). *Mastering mediation: Using the psychology of conflict, risky choice and bias to improve alternative dispute resolution.* New York, NY: VDM Verlag.

Kwartler, R. (1980). This land is our land: Mohawk Indians vs. the State of New York. In R. Goldmann (Ed.) *Roundtable justice: Case studies in conflict resolution.* Boulder, CO: Westview Press.

Ladd, P. (1989). Appropriate dispute resolution: Methods for different types of disputes. *Expanding Horizons: Theory and Research in Dispute Resolution.* Washington D.C.: American Bar Association Press.

———. (1992). Family/School partnerships in resolving conflict with at-risk youth. *Solving the Problems of Youth At-Risk: Involving Parents and Community Resources.* Ed. Robert Morris, Lancaster, PA.: Technomics Publishing.

———. (2007). *Relationships and patterns of conflict resolution: A reference book for couple's counselors.* Lanham, MD: University Press of America.

Lakritz, N. (2007). Fear and ignorance are behind this new prejudice against minorities. *The Province. 26,* 24.

Lanceley, F. J., (2002). *On scene guide for crisis negotiators.* New York, NY: CRC Press.

Lande J. (1987). Speaking for mediation. *Mediation Quarterly.17,* 23–33. Lang, M. D., & Taylor, A. (2000). *The making of a mediator.* San Francisco, Ca: Jossey-Bass.

LaTorre, M. (2001). Therapeutic approaches to anxiety: A holistic view. *Perspectives in Psychiatry. 37*(1), 28–34.

LeVasseur, J. (2003). The problem of bracketing in phenomenology. *Qualitative Health Research. 13,* 408–21.

Lindsey, H. (2002). *The Everlasting hatred: The roots of Jihad.* New York, NY: Oracle Publishing.

Lippke, S., Wiedemann, A. U., Ziegelmann, J. P., Reuter, T., & Schwarzer, R. (2009). Self-efficacy moderates the mediation of intentions into behavior via plans. *American Journal of Health Behavior, 33*(5), 521–29.

Lowell, K. K. (2012). Bias and mental illness. *The American Journal of Nursing. 112*(8), 20.

MacFarlane, J. (1999). *Dispute resolution: Readings and cases.* Toronto, CA: Emond Montgomery.

MADD, (2002). Still MADD, still demanding. *Report/Newsmagazine. 29*, 37–40.

Madonna, J. (2011). Till death do us part: Hatred, love, and emotional communication. *Modern Psychoanalysis. 36*(1), 95.

Malin, B. J. (2009). Mediating emotion. *Technology and Culture, 50*(2), 366-90.

Marcum, T. M. (2012). Reframing the mediation lens: the call for a situational style of mediation. *Southern Illinois University Law Journal. 36*(2), 317.

Mareschal, P. M. (2002). Mastering the art of dispute resolution from the FMCS. *International Journal of Public Administration. 25*(11), 1351–78.

Marts, A. C. (1996). *The generosity of Americans: Its source – Its achievements.* Upper Saddle River, NJ: Prentice Hall.

Maryhen, M. C., Kreider, C., & Zupancic, M. K. (2000). Trauma and dissociation: Treatment perspectives. *Perspectives in Psychiatric Care. 36*, 49–56.

Maslach, C. (1982). *Burnout, the cost of caring.* Englewood Cliffs, N.J.: Prentice Hall.

May, R. (1950). *The meaning of anxiety.* New York, NY: Ronald Press Co.

———. (1972). *Power and innocence.* New York: W. W. Norton and Company.

May, R., Angel, E., & Ellenberger, H. F. (Eds.) (1958). *Existence: A new dimension in psychiatry and psychology.* New York, NY: Basic Books.

Mayer, B. (2003). *The dynamics of conflict resolution: A practitioner's guide.* San Francisco, CA: Jossey-Bass.

McGuire, R. (2001). Active listening. *British Medical Journal, 322*(7302), 7302.

Menkel-Meadow, C. (2009). Are there systemic issues in dispute system's design? *Harvard negotiation Law Review. 14,* 196

Merleau-Ponty, M. (1970). *Phenomenology of perception.* New York, NY: Routledge and Kagan Paul.

Meyerhoff, M. (2001). Self-fulfilling prophecy. *Pediatrics for Parenting. 19,* 8–10.

Mnookin, R. H., Susskind, L. E. & Foster, P. C. (Eds.) (1999). *Negotiations on the behalf of others: Advice to lawyers, business executives, diplomats, politicians and everyone else.* Thousand Oaks, CA: Sage.

Moehn, H. (2001). *Coping with social anxiety.* 1st Ed. New York, NY: Rosen.

Moore, D. B. (2003) *The mediation process: Practical strategies for resolving conflict.* San Francisco, CA: Jossey-Bass.

———. (1996). Shame: Human universal or cultural construct? In, *Shame and the Modern Self.* Edited by R. Dalzeill, D. Parker and I. Wright. Melbourne: Australian Scholarly Publishers.

Moore, R. S. (Ed.) (2002). *Terrorism: Concepts, causes, and conflict resolution.* Fort Belvior, VA.: U.S. Defense Threat Reduction Agency.

Moss, D. (1999). Carl Rogers, the person-centered approach, and experiential therapy. In the book by ed. Donald Moss, *Humanistic and Transpersonal Psychology: A Historical and Bibliographical Source Book.* Westport CT.: Greenwood Press.

Mosten, F. S. (1997). *The complete guide to mediation.* Chicago, IL: American Barr Association.

Murray, J. S., Rau, A. S., & Sherman, E. F. (1996). *Arbitration.* New York, NY: Foundation Press.

Nancy, J. (2014). Hatred, a solidification of meaning. *Law and Critique. 25*(1) 15–24.

Nash, J. (1966). *Authority and freedom in education.* New York, NY: John Wiley and Sons.

Nelson, N., Zarankin, A., & Ben-Ari, R. (2010). Transformative women, problem-solving men, not quite: Gender and mediators' perceptions of mediation. *Negotiation Journal, 26*(3), 287-308.

Neu, J. (2008). Rehabilitating resentment and choosing what we feel. *Criminal Justice Ethics, 27*(2), 31–37.

Neumann, D. (1992). How mediation can effectively address the male-female power imbalance in divorce. *Mediation Quarterly. 9* (3), 227–39.

Newman, J. (1986). *Fanatics & hypocrites.* Buffalo, N.Y.: Prometheus Books.

Newman, R. (1998). *African American quotations.* Phoenix, AZ.: Oryx Press.

Nicholson, N. (2001). The new word gossip. *Psychology Today. 34,* 40–46.

Nietzche, F. (1967). *The will to power.* New York, NY: Vintage Books.

NOAA (2004). *Guidelines for mediation.* Seattle, WA: NOAA Alternative Dispute Resolution Program.

Nowell, B. L., & Salem, D., (2004). State-Level associations: An emerging trend in community mediation. *Conflict Resolution Quarterly. 21*(4), 399– 419.

Nwagbara, U. (2013). Leadership Nelson Mandela. *Leadership. 9*(1), 141–44.

Obiols, J. E. (2012). DSM 5: Precedents, present and pro-spects. *International Journal of Clinical and Health Psychology, 12*(2), 281–90.

Olsen, D. G. (1999). Constructivist's principles of learning and teaching. *Education. 120,* (2), 347–59.

O'Shea, D. J., Williams, A. L., & Sattler, R. O. (1999). Collaboration across special education and general education: Pre-service teacher's views. *Journal of Teacher Education. 50* (2), 147–61.

Petersen, R. D. (2002). *Understanding ethnic violence: Fear, hatred and resentment in Twentieth Century Eastern Europe.* Cambridge, Ma: Cambridge University Press.

Pilluta, M. M., & J. K. Murnighan. (1996). Unfairness, anger, and spite: Emotional rejections of ultimatum offers. *Organizational Behavior and Human Decision Processes. 68,* 208–24.

Polanyi, M. (1964). *Personal knowledge.* New York, NY: Harper and Row.

Poster, E. (2003). Anger management 101. *Fortworth Business Press. 16*, 30-32.

Prater, T., & Kiser, S. B. (2002). Lies, lies, and more lies. SAM *Advanced Management Journal. 67*(2), 9–22.

Psik Adviye, E. Y. (2015). The role of worry and rumination in the symptoms of anxiety and depression. *Turk Psikiyatri Dergisi, 26*(2), 107.

Rahim, A. (2014). *Canadian Immigration and South Asian Immigrants*. www.Xlibris.com

Raines, S. S. (2013). Conflict management for managers: Resolving workplace   client, and policy disputes. *Jossey-Bass Business and Management Series.1*, 498.

Regel, S. (2009). A guide to psychological debriefing – managing emotional decompression and post- traumatic stress disorder. *Counseling and Psychotherapy Research. 9*(2) 129–30.

Retzinger, S. (1991). *Violent emotions: Shame and rage in marital quarrels*. Newbury Park: Sage.

Retzinger, S., & Scheff. T. (1996). Strategies for community conferences: Emotions and social bonds. In *Restorative Justice: International Perspectives*. Edited by B. Galaway, and J. Hudson, 315–36. Monsey, NY, NY: Criminal Justice Press.

———. (2001). Emotion, alienation, and narratives: Resolving intractable conflict. *Mediation Quarterly. 18*(12), 45–67.

Reyes, M. R., Brackett, M. A., Rivers, S. E., White, M., & Salovey, P. (2012). Classroom emotional climate, student engagement, and academic achievement. *Journal of Educational Psychology. 104*(3), 700.

Rifkin, J., Millen, J., & Cobb, S. (1991). Toward a new discourse for mediation: A critique of neutrality. *Mediation Quarterly. 9* (2), 151–64.

Riskin, L. L. (1994). Mediator orientations, strategies, and techniques. *Alternatives to the High Cost of Litigation. 12*(9), 111–15.

Riveros, A. (2012). Beyond collaboration: Embodied teacher learning and the discourse of collaboration in education reform. *Studies in Philosophy and Education, 31*(6), 603–12.

Rogers, C. (1956). *Client centered therapy*. New York, NY: Charles Merrill.

Ross, N. A. (1997) *You be the judge: The complete Canadian guide to resolving legal disputes out of court*. Toronto, Canada: John Wiley.

Rothchild, D. (2006) The logic of a soft intervention strategy: The United States and conflict conciliation in Africa. *International Negotiation.* *11*(2), 317 –39.

Rubin, P. A. (2014). 10 tips for a successful mediation. *American Bankruptcy Institute Journal, 33*(11), 40-41, 66.

Ryan, E. (2006). Building emotionally learned negotiators. *Harvard Negotiation Journal. 21*(2), 196.

SADD, (2004). Students against drunk driving. MADD website July, 2004.

Salzano, R. (2003). Taming stress. *Scientific American. 289*, 88−98.

Sampson, A. (2000). *Mandela: The authorized biography.* New York, NY: First Vintage Books.

Sandage, S. J. & Wiens, T. W. (2001). Conceptualizing models of humility and forgiveness: A reply to Gassin. *Journal of Psychology and Theology 29* (3), 201–211.

Sandberg, J. (2003). Ruthless rumors and the managers who enable them. *Wall Street Journal-Eastern Edition. 242*, B1-2.

Sandoz, M. (1966). *The Battle of Little Bighorn.* New York, NY: J.B. Lippincott.

Sang-Hun, C. (2014). Korean air faces flight suspensions over executive's snack tantrum. *New York Times.* http://www.nytimes.com.

Sarabando, P., Dias, L. C., & Vetschera, R. (2013). Mediation with incomplete information: Approaches to suggest potential agreements. *Group Decision and Negotiation, 22*(3), 561−97.

Saulnier, A., & Sivasubramaniam, D. (2015). Effects of victim presence and coercion in restorative justice: An experimental paradigm. *Law and Human Behavior, 39*(4), 378-87.

Sautter, R. C. (1995). Standing up to violence. *Phi Delta Kappan. 76*(5), 1−8.

Schaeffer, R. (1988). *Resentment against achievement: Understanding the assault on ability.* New York, NY: Prometheus Books.

———, (2001). Relieve your anxiety with yoga. *Natural Health. 32*, 42−44.

Scharff, J. S. (2001). *Self-Hatred in psychoanalysis: Detoxifying the persecutory object.* New York, NY: Cygnus Books.

Scheff, T. J. (1994). *Bloody revenge: Emotions, nationalism, and war.* Boulder, CO: Westview Press.

Scheff, T. J., & Retzinger S. M. (1991) *Emotions and violence; Shame and rage in destructive conflicts.* Lexington, MA: Lexington Books.

Scheler, M. (1961). *Resentiment.* New York, NY: Schoken Books.

Schermuly, C. C., Meyer, B., & Dämmer, L. (2013). Leader-member exchange and innovative behavior: The mediating role of psychological empowerment. *Journal of Personnel Psychology, 12*(3), 55.

Schultz, A. (1987). *The phenomenology of the social world.* Evanston, IL: Northwestern University Press.

Schumaker, J. F. (2004). In greed we trust. *New Internationalist. 369*, 34-35

Schweigert, F. J. (1999). Moral education in victim offender conferencing. *Criminal Justice Ethics. 18*, 213–22.

Settle, N. D. (2014). Mediation tips and techniques: Helping parties move ahead and overcome roadblocks. *The Brief, 43*(2), 16–24, 26–27.

Shah, S. R. (2003). *The Impact of Acculturation and Religion on Intergenerational Family Conflict for Second Generation Hindu Asian Indian Americans.* Ann Arbor MI: ProQuest Information and Learning Company.

Shailor, J. G. (1994). *Empowerment in dispute resolution: A critical analysis of communication.* Westport, CT: Praeger Publishers.

Shapiro, D. L. (2002). Negotiating emotions. *Conflict Resolution Quarterly. 20*(1) 67–82.

Shea, G. F. (1984). *Building trust in the workplace.* American Management Association's Membership Publications Division.

Simkin, W. (1971). *Mediation and the dynamics of collective bargaining.* Washington, DC: Bureau of National Affairs.

Singh, D., Aspy, & C. B. (1997). *Counseling for prejudice prevention and reduction.* Washington, D.C.: American Counseling Association.

Skinner, B. F. (1953). *Science and human behavior.* New York, NY: The Free Press.

Slaikue, K. A., Pearson, J., Luckett, J., & Myers, F. C. (1985). Process and outcome in divorce mediation. *Mediation Quarterly. 19*, 55–74.

Smedes, L. (1985). *Forgive and forget: Healing the hurts we don't deserve.* San Francisco, CA: HarperCollins.

————. (1993). *Shame and grace: Healing the shame we don't deserve.* San Francisco, CA: HarperCollins.

Stack, G. (1993). Nietzsche's earliest essays. *Philosophy Today. 37,* 153–70.

Stevick, E. (1971) An empirical investigation of the experience of anger. *Duquesne Studies in Phenomenological Psychology.* Vol. I. Eds. Amedeo Giorgi, Rolf Von Eckartsberg, William Fischer. Pittsburgh, PA: Duquesne University Press.

Stoner, K. E. (1999). *Using divorce mediation: Save your money & your sanity.* Berkeley, CA: Nolo Press.

Susskind, L. E., MnKearney, S. & Thomas-Larmer, J. (Eds.) (1999*). The Consensus building handbook: A comprehensive guide to reaching an agreement* Thousand Oaks, CA: Sage.

Symonds, P. M. (1968). The ego and the self. New York, NY: Greenwood Press.

Tannen, D. (1998) The Argument culture: Moving from debate to dialogue. New York, NY: Random House.

Terr, L. (1990). *Too scared to cry: Psychic trauma in childhood.* New York, NY: Basic Books.

Terry, S. (1987). Conciliation: Responses to the emotional content of disputes. *Mediation Quarterly. 16,* 45–52.

Theresa, M. and Lovett, S. (1993). *The best gift is love: Meditations by Mother Theresa.* New York, NY: Servant Publications.

Thomas, E., McGarty, C., & Mayor, K. I. (2013) Transforming "Apathy into Movement": The Role of Prosocial Emotions in Motivating Action for Social Change. *Personality and Social Psychology Review. 38*(1), 73–87.

Toros, H. (2008). We don't negotiate with terrorists. *Security Dialogue. 39*(4), 407–26.

Tracy, S. A., Chorpita, B.F., Douban, J., & Barlow, D.H. (1997). Empirical evaluation of DSM IV generalized anxiety disorder criteria in children and adolescents. *Journal of Clinical Psychology. 26*(4), 404–16.

Troester, R. (1996). *Jimmy Carter as peacemaker: A post presidential bibliography.* West Port, Ct.: Praeger Pub.

Trussler, M. M. (2009). Domestic violence. *The American Journal of Nursing. 109*(9), 12.

Umbreit, M. (1997). Victim-offender mediation in criminal conflict: Toward restorative justice. In E. Kruk (Ed.) *Mediation and Conflict Resolution in Social Work and the Human Services.* Chicago, IL: Nelson-Hall.

———. (1995). Humanistic mediation: A transformative journey of peace-making. *Mediation Quarterly. 14,* 201–13.

Van Epps, D. (2013). Public funding of community dispute resolution centers. *Dispute Resolution Magazine. 19*(2), 7.

Volkan, V. (1990). Psychoanalytic aspects of ethnic conflicts. In *Conflict and Peacemaking in Multiethnic Societies.* edited by J. Montville. Lexington, MA, and Toronto: Lexington Books.

———. (1997). *Blood lines: From ethnic pride to ethnic terrorism.* New York, NY: Farrar, Strauss & Giroux.

———. (1998). Ethnicity and nationalism: A psychoanalytical perspective. *Applied Psychology: An International Review. 47,* 45–57.

———. (1998). Psychoanalytic perspective on inter-group hatred. *Journal for Psychoanalysis of Culture and Society. 3*(1) 78–80.

Von Eckartsberg, R. (1970). On experiential methodology. *Duquesne Studies in Phenomenological Psychology: Volume 1.* Eds. Amedeo Giorgi, Rolf Von Eckartsberg, and William F. Fischer. Pittsburgh, PA: Duquesne University Press.

Wade, J. H. (2001). Don't waste my time on negotiation and mediation: This dispute needs a judge. *Mediation Quarterly. 18,* 259–80.

Wade, J. (2004). Dueling experts in mediation and negotiation: How to respond when eager expensive entrenched expert egos escalate enmity. *Conflict Resolution Quarterly. 21*(4), 419–36.

Wentzel, D., & Brysiewicz, P. (2014). The consequence of caring too much: Compassion fatigue and the trauma nurse. *Journal of Emergency Nursing, 40*(1), 95–97.

Whitehead, J. & Whitehead, E. (1994). Shadows of the heart: A spirituality of *negative emotions.* New York, NY: Crossroads Publishing.

Williams, B. (1993). *Shame and necessity.* Los Angeles, CA: University of California Press.

Williams, M. (1998). *Mediation: Why people fight and how to help them stop* Dublin, Ireland: Poolbeg Press.

Williams, M. B., & Sommer, J. F. (1994). *Handbook of post traumatic therapy.* New York, NY: Greenwood Press.

Wilson, I. (2013). Overwhelming generosity. *British Dental Journal, 214*(11) 541.

Winslade, J., & Monk, G. (2000). *Narrative mediation: A new approach to conflict resolution.* San Francisco, CA: Jossey-Bass.

Winslade, J., Monk, G., & Cotter, A. (1998). A narrative approach to the practice of mediation. *Negotiation Journal. 4,* 21–39.

Wood, J. (2004). Mediation styles: Subjective description of mediators. *Conflict Resolution Quarterly. 21*(4), 437–50.

Yanay, N. (2012). *Ideology of hatred: The psychic power of discourse.* New York, NY: Fordham University Press.

Yau-Fai Ho, D., Fu, W. & Ng, S. M. (2004). Guilt, shame and embarrassment: Revelations of face and self. *Culture and Psychology. 10* (1), 64–85.

Young, P. T. (1948). *Emotions in man and animal.* New York, NY: Wiley & Sons.

Young-Mason, J. (2001). Understanding suffering and compassion. *Crosscurrent. 51*(3), 347–58.

Zanna, M. P., Olson, J. M., (1994). *The psychology of prejudice vol. 7.* Hillsdale, N.J.: Lawrence Eribaum Associates.

Zartman, T. W., (2003). Negotiating with terrorists. *International Negotiation. 8*(3), 443–50.

Index

Young-Mason, J., 163

Zanna, M. P., 91
Zartman, T. W., 93

About the Authors

Peter D. Ladd, PhD, has been a tenured faculty member at St. Lawrence University in the Graduate School of Education for over forty years. He coordinates the Mental Health Counseling Program, and has worked for thirty-five years in St. Lawrence University's satellite graduate school program on the Akwesasne Mohawk Reservation. Over his career, he has written ten books, one of them winning a national book award. He has written numerous articles in the areas of addictions counseling, mental health counseling, relationship counseling, and conflict resolution. He was president of the Augsbury Institute for Youth and Families, and also established a Liberty Partnership Program, along with forming the St. Lawrence Valley Teacher Learning Center Dr. Ladd worked on the Akwesasne Mohawk Reservation for twenty five years where he established two mental health counseling centers and was the licensed clinical supervisor for the Tekanikonrahwakon Holistic Health and Wellness Program. He is a strong environmentalist and was president of Save the River (St. Lawrence River) in Clayton, NY.

Kyle Elizabeth Blanchfield, JD, is the executive director and founder of the Northern New York Centers for Conflict Resolution, which covers the entire northern region of New York State. She served as the former president of the New York State Dispute Resolution Association, and also a former justice court judge. She is an adjunct assistant professor of education in St. Lawrence University's Graduate Leadership Program. She teaches education law, conflict resolution, leadership and school violence, and leadership and school climate. Her talents also include being a liaison and mediator between government agencies, especially government agencies in Canada and First Nations Tribes. During 2007–2008, she was helping the Honorable Timothy Rowley, Pennsylvania Court of Common Pleas, establish a fully functioning, revised Family Court and Juvenile Court for the Pennsylvania Court System. Her scholarly activities have included three books and numerous articles in leadership, conflict resolution, and the law. She is a strong advocate for preventing violence in schools.